Palgrave Macmillan Studies in Banking and Financial Institutions

Series Editor: **Professor Philip Molyneux**

The Palgrave Macmillan Studies in Banking and Financial Institutions will be international in orientation and include studies of banking within particular countries or regions, and studies of particular themes such as Corporate Banking, Risk Management, Mergers and Acquisitions, etc. The books will be focused upon research and practice, and include up-to-date and innovative studies on contemporary topics in banking that will have global impact and influence.

Titles include:

Yener Altunbas, Blaise Gadanecz and Alper Kara
SYNDICATED LOANS
A Hybrid of Relationship Lending and Publicly Traded Debt

Yener Altunbaş, Alper Kara and Öslem Olgu
TURKISH BANKING
Banking under Political Instability and Chronic High Inflation

Elena Beccalli
IT AND EUROPEAN BANK PERFORMANCE

Santiago Carbó, Edward P.M. Gardener and Philip Molyneux
FINANCIAL EXCLUSION

Allessandro Carretta, Franco Fiordelisi and Gianluca Mattarocci *(editors)*
NEW DRIVERS OF PERFORMANCE IN A CHANGING FINANCIAL WORLD

Violaine Cousin
BANKING IN CHINA

Franco Fiordelisi and Philip Molyneux
SHAREHOLDER VALUE IN BANKING

Hans Genberg and Cho-Hoi Hui
THE BANKING CENTRE IN HONG KONG
Competition, Efficiency, Performance and Risk

Carlo Gola and Alessandro Roselli
THE UK BANKING SYSTEM AND ITS REGULATORY AND SUPERVISORY FRAMEWORK

Elisabetta Gualandri and Valeria Venturelli *(editors)*
BRIDGING THE EQUITY GAP FOR INNOVATIVE SMEs

Munawar Iqbal and Philip Molyneux
THIRTY YEARS OF ISLAMIC BANKING
History, Performance and Prospects

Kimio Kase and Tanguy Jacopin
CEOs AS LEADERS AND STRATEGY DESIGNERS
Explaining the Success of Spanish Banks

M. Mansoor Khan and M. Ishaq Bhatti
DEVELOPMENTS IN ISLAMIC BANKING
The Case of Pakistan

Mario La Torre and Gianfranco A. Vento
MICROFINANCE

Philip Molyneux and Munawar Iqbal
BANKING AND FINANCIAL SYSTEMS IN THE ARAB WORLD

Philip Molyneux and Eleuterio Vallelado (*editors*)
FRONTIERS OF BANKS IN A GLOBAL WORLD

Anastasia Nesvetailova
FRAGILE FINANCE
Debt, Speculation and Crisis in the Age of Global Credit

Dominique Rambure and Alec Nacamuli
PAYMENT SYSTEMS
From the Salt Mines to the Board Room

Andrea Schertler
THE VENTURE CAPITAL INDUSTRY IN EUROPE

Alfred Slager
THE INTERNATIONALIZATION OF BANKS

Noel K. Tshiani
BUILDING CREDIBLE CENTRAL BANKS
Policy Lessons for Emerging Economies

Palgrave Macmillan Studies in Banking and Financial Institutions

Series Standing Order ISBN 978–1–4039–4872–4

You can receive future titles in this series as they are published by placing a standing order. Please contact your bookseller or, in case of difficulty, write to us at the address below with your name and address, the title of the series and the ISBN quoted above.

Customer Services Department, Macmillan Distribution Ltd, Houndmills, Basingstoke, Hampshire RG21 6XS, England

The UK Banking System and Its Regulatory and Supervisory Framework

Carlo Gola and Alessandro Roselli

palgrave
macmillan

First published 2009 by
PALGRAVE MACMILLAN
Houndmills, Basingstoke, Hampshire RG21 6XS and
175 Fifth Avenue, New York, N.Y. 10010
Companies and representatives throughout the world

PALGRAVE MACMILLAN is the global academic imprint of the Palgrave Macmillan division of St. Martin's Press, LLC and of Palgrave Macmillan Ltd. Macmillan® is a registered trademark in the United States, United Kingdom and other countries. Palgrave is a registered trademark in the European Union and other countries.

ISBN-13: 978–0–230–54282–2 hardback
ISBN-10: 0–230–54282–4 hardback

This book is printed on paper suitable for recycling and made from fully managed and sustained forest sources. Logging, pulping and manufacturing processes are expected to conform to the environmental regulations of the country of origin.

A catalogue record for this book is available from the British Library.

Library of Congress Cataloging-in-Publication Data

Gola, Carlo.
The UK banking system and its regulatory and supervisory framework / Carlo Gola, Alessandro Roselli.
p. cm. — (Palgrave Macmillan studies in banking and financial institutions)
Includes bibliographical references and index.
ISBN 978–0–230–54282–2 (alk. paper)
1. Banks and banking–Great Britain. 2. Banking law–Great Britain. 3. Bank management–Great Britain. I. Roselli, Alessandro. II. Title.
HG2988.G526 2008
332.10941–dc22 2008029994

10 9 8 7 6 5 4 3 2 1
18 17 16 15 14 13 12 11 10 09

Printed and bound in Great Britain by
CPI Antony Rowe, Chippenham and Eastbourne

To Marta, Anita and Caterina
C. G.

To my dearest, little 'Lorenzaccio'
A. R.

Contents

List of Tables and Figures

Tables

Figures

Preface

It is sometimes better to define the contents of a book by what it is not intended to be. This book is not a theoretical research about the economics of banking and finance; there is no pretention to construct any coherent model lying behind the idea of systemic stability in the banking and financial area of the economy (as recently observed by Charles Goodhart, the very idea of financial stability lacks a convincing definition). Nor the book tries to identify the regulatory framework that better suits that model (a labour of Sisiphus, to quote again Goodhart). Even an explanation in general terms of what characterizes the role of the financial system in a developed economy is out of the boundaries of the book.

Also, the book does not make any attempt to enter the very debated issues arising from the dramatic development of 'new' financial institutions, instruments and markets, even less to express opinions on the benefits and costs of these developments, for the parties involved, the financial markets, the economy.

Another aspect that will be found missing is the European dimension of the themes discussed, even if we are fully aware of the increasing pervasiveness of Europe, in terms of interactions between financial institutions of different countries, of financial regulation and authorities' cooperation and coordination, that are particularly strong in banking, financial and, even more, in competition regulations. But we remain convinced of the specialness of the British financial system, which – we hope – will be explained in the various sections of this book. It is a specialness derived from several factors: from history, from the financial structure of the different sectors of the economy and its financial deepening, from the peculiarity of the City – its operators and markets – even from the supervisionary style of the financial authorities.

We are now approaching, by exclusion, what the book aims to be. In the last decades, much of the market and institutional scenery has disappeared into economic history. The affirmation of the global over the local, of finance over industry and commerce, of traders over traditional commercial bankers happened in many countries, not necessarily confined to the 'western' world, but probably the UK has seen the most of it. Britain has seen, is seeing, not only an increase in the economy's financial deepening (perhaps less strong then in other countries, but this also depends on the starting point, that was in the UK much higher), but a more transaction-oriented finance; a change in managing risks through financial products 'derived' from well established instruments; the emergence of new players like hedge funds and private equity funds; an increased international dimension, in terms of foreign banking presence, cross-border transactions, inward and outward investments, and an expansion of its foreign position as a result.

Liberalization, deregulation and technological advance, and a benign view of the regulators, are the prime movers and the common denominator of these trends, all the more striking when we know that, still in the late 1980s, a Nobel laureate, Lawrence Klein, stressing that 'the provision of financial services has become one of the fastest changing, rapidly growing sectors of our [US] economy', concluded that, anyway, 'we should preserve the existing safeguards in our banking legislation by keeping banks in banking activities and not in activities of financial conglomerates'. The single factors of change just mentioned have been at work in Britain as well as in other countries, but the financial landscape as a whole has probably changed more broadly in the UK then elsewhere. Our attempt is, in fact, to describe and, where necessary, analyse those changes.

This is done, first, by trying to give a historical perspective of those developments, going back to post-war years (Chapter 1) and then focussing more in detail on the more recent period, relying mostly on a database referred to the years 1990–2005, but giving more updated information and valuations on specific trends. Within this framework, we assess the sustainability of the balance sheets of the economic sectors: households, non-financial corporations and the foreign sector (Chapter 2). The features of the households balance sheet are also dealt in connection with the development of private pension schemes (Chapter 3). The banking and financial system, looking at institutions, markets, market infrastructures from a micro and macro-prudential perspective is considered (Chapters 4 and 5).

It should be stressed that the book was written largely before the financial turbulence of 2007, but we felt we could not ignore this crisis – still unfolding – even if any attempt of interpretation that goes beyond the descriptive, almost annalistic stage must be looked at with a great deal of caution. We therefore preferred not to proceed further and to stick strictly to the facts, without drawing any firm conclusion. We could not, however, dispense ourselves from providing an overview of some important aspects of recent development in financial engineering, which deeply affected the banking industry, such as the credit risk transfer, producing both opportunities but also new and very serious forms of market failures (Chapters 6 and 7).

The second section of the book moves from the structural/operational to the institutional/regulatory side. This part is very much devoted to the creation and working of the Financial Services Authority (FSA), and more generally to the tripartite arrangement of bank and financial supervision, that broadly defines the style of supervision mentioned earlier (Chapter 8).

An underlying issue here is how a country that traditionally relied on a rather informal regulatory structure and on self-regulation moved away from it, into one of the most striking pieces of statutory regulation of the banking and financial industry, the Financial Services and Markets Act. It is to note, in this regard, that the debate on regulation versus self-regulation has not been totally set aside: even not considering the Combined Code, which affects the whole corporate sector, the current debate about regulation of hedge funds and private equity means that the door has been left open even in the financial domain.

The Combined code of corporate governance: one may wonder why a topic of interest for the whole corporate world, and not specifically for the financial sector, is the subject of a chapter of this book (Chapter 9). The reason is that, while in other countries, mainly of civil law tradition, other stakeholders interests weight heavier on the companies (banks), the British, and American, scheme of corporate governance accepts that maximizing the shareholders interest is the main day-to-day objective. As a consequence, in a bank-based, civil law system (on these definitions, see later in this preface), stable conditions of employment, workers codetermination, cross-shareholdings, long-term relations with one bank are more relevant than in a market-based, common law system. Hostile takeovers are more difficult and rare. These factors are important in order to characterize, and differentiate from other systems, the banking systems of the UK or America. In Britain, the relevance of self regulation *vis-a vis* the statutory legislation makes the mentioned code particularly important.

Another issue shortly explored is that of competition legislation. Competition in banking, in Britain, does not fall within the perimeter of FSA supervision, is subject to the competition authorities (Office of Fair Trading [OFT] and Competition Commission). However, the relevance of the problem in the banking industry, and the interactions between the FSA and the competition authorities, explain why a chapter of the book is devoted to this theme (Chapter 10).

Some conclusions are drawn or – rather – new questions are raised in the final chapter (Chapter 11).

* * *

Going back again to the matter of 'exclusion', it will be noticed that the book focuses mainly on the banking industry. Less attention is dedicated to other financial institutions, like securities firm, asset managers, insurance companies. The issue that arises is whether this focus is justified, which means whether banks are (still) 'special'. A short digression may be useful in this regard.

For a long while, banks have been considered as a very specific category of financial intermediaries, at the centre of the financial system, being the mechanism by which funds can be transferred between the two basic sectors of the economy, the household and the business sectors.

Banks' intermediation is more limited where households and businesses meet together in the marketplace, so that equity or debt securities are directly exchanged. While the existence of 'complete' markets is only a theoretical construct, there is no question that the banks' role has been larger in some economies, and smaller in others. In addition, there is evidence that businesses have generally been moving away from intermediated finance through banks, towards raising funds directly from capital markets.

We shall not try to explain why a certain financial system is more bank-oriented or market-oriented. Sometimes, this alternative is related to different phases of economic growth. The market-oriented, or securitized, system would represent a more mature economy, linked to industrialization, to the growth of big corporations and then, even in a de-industrialized phase, to the great level of economic restructuring associated with the development of large and sophisticated service industries. But in some countries these phases of economic development have not seen a significant shift from bank to capital market financing.

Another view, known as 'law and finance' links each of the two models not to stages of economic growth, but to different legal and institutional frameworks: countries with better protection of property rights and private contracts increase the investors' propensity to hold financial assets other than bank deposits, facilitating the accumulation of capital and the economy's financial deepening. On the contrary, countries with weaker investors' protection (in terms of rules and their enforcement) tend to have smaller capital markets. Common law and civil law countries are, in this view, the prototypes of market-based and bank-based systems. The purpose of this exercise is to reverse the causality argument that economic/financial development causes legal development, which is a supra-structure over the underlying economic structure. More specifically, the theory is associated with the view that civil law systems have a heavier government hand than common law ones, and that this hand is in turn associated with adverse impacts on the markets.

It should be stressed that this theory does not point to an overall superiority, in terms of higher economic performance, of common law. This is an unanswered question, and whether the two systems will in the end converge is open to debate. Globalization and competition are factors pushing towards the market-oriented system; major disturbances may tilt the balance in the other direction.

Not entering this high-level and very specialistic debate, suffices is to say that the market-oriented financial system is generally associated – as we have just mentioned above – with the Anglo-Saxon economies, specifically the American and the British, while bank-oriented systems appear more rooted in Continental Europe (even if pieces of legislation as the Glass-Steagall and Sarbanes-Oxley in the US, or the Financial Services and Markets Act in the UK, do not easily fit into this simplified scheme).

A related issue is whether, in both systems, the two sectors are strictly separated, or whether the respective borders are blurred (or do not exist at all). Britain is an interesting case. Historically based on demarcation between different types of financial institutions – differences that came out more of tradition and self regulation, and less of precise statutory borders – for a long time this separateness between depository institutions and non-bank intermediaries went on, unchallenged. The banks followed the 'real bills' doctrine developed by Adam Smith, according to which prudent banks must only extend short-term, self-liquidating loans. Economic development relied largely on financial markets. Restricted practices in both bank and non-bank sectors protected their respective turfs.

However, it can be safely said that the banking sector was considered the bulk of the financial system. Some reasons for putting banks at the centre were – and are – common to every financial system: banks are strictly interrelated with a country's monetary policy: any policy impulses coming from the central bank are immediately felt by the banking system and so transmitted to the sectors of the real economy. The fiduciary nature of the bank deposit as 'money' creates a precise problem of public trust. The domino effect of a bank crisis has a potential systemic impact probably larger than other financial intermediaries. In Britain other reasons for the centrality of banks were connected more specifically with London as a financial centre: there was a huge inflow of foreign banks, related to the development of the euro-dollar market in the 1960s that contributed to a bank assets 'explosion'; the first competitive pressures introduced by the Bank of England in the early 1970s were applied to banks.

It might be objected that – following the internationalization of the City – the establishment of big financial conglomerates where banking activities mix up with securities activities and insurance services; the growth of pension funds and life assurance (less of unit trusts), associated with a remarkable shift of household assets from bank deposits to other non-bank assets – the 'franchise' of banks has been reduced and the notion of banks as deserving a 'special' position in the financial industry is obsolete.

This is the approach underlying the tendency, common to an increasing number of countries, to concentrate regulation and supervision in a single body, independently from the specific activity (activities) carried out by financial institutions, and more focussed on the risks involved in each category of financial intermediaries.

There are, anyway, at least three reasons why banks continue to deserve a 'special consideration' in the financial system:

- the above mentioned features of the banking sector (their close association with monetary policy, as its key-conduit; their capacity to generate liquidity in condition of stress; the relevance of their liabilities to the payment systems; their role as depository of public trust) remain unaffected, and so the public interest related to them (recent developments, however, have put in question the capacity of the banking system as liquidity provider; viceversa, the financial system has previously been able to generate liquidity independently from the impulses of the central bank);
- the role of banks has, in turn, developed and a distinction must now be drawn between their traditional lending activities and an expanding function of assets and risk facilitators and transformers. The 'commoditization' of credit risk is perhaps one of the most striking expressions of the changing role of banks, particularly in the UK. The strong characterization of the UK system as a market-based has not, in substance, disintermediated banks: rather, has prompted them to enter new fields of activities, to take new risks, more similar to other intermediaries';
- even if the banking sector is now, in relative terms, a smaller section of the financial intermediation, this is due to an increasing financial deepening of the UK economy (historically, already very large), but the 'grip' of the banking sector on the real economy is not less than before: the ratio of financial assets to GDP is, over time, remarkably stable or increasing.

Acknowledgements

We would like to thank, first of all, Pierluigi Ciocca (former Deputy Director General of the Bank of Italy) who started the ball rolling by asking us to write a report on the UK banking system and supervision; that report was the original, shorter Italian version of this book. We are also grateful to David Green: then at the FSA, he cleared the way to the English version of our research.

We are indebted to several colleagues and friends who, in several ways and different circumstances, offered their valuable comments. In particular, our gratitude goes to: Roberto Cardarelli, Michael Moore, Alexander Tieman, John Kiff, and Luisa Zanforlin of the International Monetary Fund; Magda Bianco, Francesco Cannata, Stefano Cappiello, Agostino Chiabrera Alessio De Vincenzo, Roberta Fiori, Antonella Foglia, Francesca Greguolo, Mariano Loddo, Laura Santuz, of the Bank of Italy; Ian Tower of the IMF and the FSA; Simon Hall of the Bank of England; Forrest Capie of the Cass Business School and the Bank of England; Steven Haberman of the Cass Business School; Phebe Olcay of the University of London and Massimo Marelli of Clifford Chance, London and the European Court of Justice, Luxembourg. We thank also Aldo Stanziale of the Bank of Italy who assisted us in drafting some notes used for a Working Paper on the same topic published by the Ente per gli Studi Monetari, Bancari e Finanziari Luigi Einaudi (Rome). A special thank also to Paolo Garofalo of the Bank of Italy (Representative office, London).

Lastly, our appreciation to John C. G. Smith, Stephanie Siciarz for their translation of some parts of the book and to Daniel Mishel for editorial assistance. The opinions expressed in the work are those of the authors and do not represent those of the Bank of Italy or the IMF.

C. G. and A. R.
Washington – Rome – Oxford

List of Acronyms

ABCP	Asset-backed commercial paper
ABSs	Asset-backed securities
AIM	Alternative Investment Market
APACS	Association for Payment Clearing Services
ARROW	Advance Risk-Responsive Operating frameWork
BBA	British Bankers' Association
BCCI	Bank of Credit and Commerce International
BIS	Bank for International Settlements
CA	Competition Act
CaR	Capital-at-Risk
CAT	Competition Appeal Tribunal
CC	Competition Commission
CCAB	Consultative Committee of Accountancy Bodies
CCC	Competition and Credit Controls
CDOs	Collateralized debt obligations
CDS	Credit Default Swap
CGAA	Coordinating Group on Audit and Accounting
CHAPS	Clearing House Automated Payment System
CLS	Continuous Linked Settlement
CRD	Cash Ratio Deposit
CRMPG	Counterparty Risk Management Policy Group
CRT	Credit Risk Transfer
DGFT	Director General of Fair Trading
DTI	Department of Trade and Industry
EA	Enterprise Act
ECB	European Central Bank
EEA	European Economic Area
EU	European Union
FIN	Financial Intermediation Ratio
FIR	Financial Interrelation Ratio
FOS	Financial Ombudsman Service
FRC	Financial Reporting Council
FRS	Financial Reporting Standards
FSA	Financial Services Authority
FSAP	Financial Services Action Plan
FSCS	Financial Services Compensation Scheme

FSF	Financial Stability Forum
FSMA	Financial Services and Market Act
FSSA	Financial System Stability Assessment
FTA	Fair Trading Act
GDP	Gross Domestic Product
HBOS	Halifax Bank of Schotland
HHI	Herfindahl–Hirschman Index
HMSO	Her Majesty's Stationery Office
HSBC	Hongkong and Shanghai Banking Corporation
IFRS	International Financial Reporting Standards
IFSL	International Financial Services London
IIP	International Investment Position
IMF	International Monetary Fund
IMRO	Investment Management Regulatory Organization
IOSCO	International Organization of Securities Commissions
IPO	Initial Public Offering
ISDA	International Swaps and Derivatives Association
ISMA	International Securities Market Association
JMB	Johnson Matthey Bankers
LCFIs	Large Complex Financial Institutions
LCH	London Clearing House
LGD	Loss-given default
LLP	Limited Liability Partnership
LSE	London Stock Exchange
M&A	Mergers & Acquisitions
MBBG	Major British Banking Groups
MFI	Monetary and Financial Institutions
MiFID	Market in Financial Instruments Directive
MIR	Market Investigation Regime
MMC	Monopolies and Mergers Commission
MPC	Monetary Policy Committee
MTF	Multilateral Trading Facilities
NAO	National Audit Office
NPSS	National Pensions Savings Scheme
NS	National Statistics
NYSE	New York Stock Exchange
OECD	Organization for Economic Co-operation and Development
OFT	Office of Fair Trading
OMO	Open market operation
OPRA	Occupation Pensions Regulatory Authority
OTC	Over The Counter

PAYE	Pay as You Earn
PIA	Personal Investment Authority
PPF	Pension Protection Fund
RAO	Regulated Activities Order
RBS	Royal Bank of Scotland
RCHs	Recognized Clearing Houses
RIEs	Recognized Investment Exchanges
ROA	Return on Assets
ROE	Return on Equity
RPBs	Recognized Professional Bodies
SEC	Securities and Exchange Commission
SERPS	State Earnings-Related Pension Scheme
SFA	Securities and Futures Authority
SIB	Securities and Investment Board
SIV	Structured Investment Vehicles
SME	Small and Medium Enterprise
SPV	Special-purpose vehicle
SRO	Self-Regulatory Organization
SSLR	Sterling Stock Liquidity Ratio
SSNIP	Small but significant non-transitory increase in price test
TPR	The Pension Regulator
UTCCRs	Unfair Terms in Consumer Contract Regulations
VaR	Value-at-Risk

Part I
Banking and Financial Markets

1
The Structure of the Banking System Between the 1960s and the 1980s

This chapter can be really defined as 'historic', because of the great changes that have affected the British banking system after the 1980s. Even if no gap can be found in the evolution – institutional, structural, operational – of the system (*'historia non facit saltus'*), it's undeniable that the present configuration bears only a thin resemblance to the previous morphology, legislation, functions. At the same time, this retrospective view of the banking and financial industry, also in its interactions with public policy issues and cultural frameworks then prevailing, is useful in order to put in focus the situation of today, and to understand better the most recent turmoil and its possible (not necessary) outcomes.

To be sure, we cannot take the whole period from the 1960s through the 1980s as a single bloc. After a long and relatively undisturbed post-war phase, an evolution occurred that, broadly speaking, meant the passage from an oligopolistic banking structure, an interest rate cartel, a rather protective environment, where banks could almost be considered as public utilities, and from a mostly informal supervision by the central bank, to a more dynamic environment, where the seeds of competition were sowed, and regulation and supervision became more articulate and statutory-oriented. The driving forces of the change can be found in some sectors of the banking system, less bound by the 'constraints' of the central bank, still very focused on the narrow group of the clearing banks, and in the openness of London as a financial centre, that increasingly attracted international banks (particularly American, but also branches of European banks).

This factor was closely connected with the development of the eurodollar market, in turn stimulated by the American foreign accounts difficulties and by a regulatory arbitrage between the United States and the United Kingdom (a recurring factor in the competition between the two financial centres of New York and London). However, the most enduring legacy of that long period can probably be found, from a regulatory – or, better, de-regulatory point of view – in the Big Bang of 1986, that deeply affected the financial markets, taking any protective or 'clubby' attitude out of them, and attracting, again, foreign banks, in particular American investment banks, restricted at home by the Glass-Stegall boundaries, to the London market. London was to be considered as their hub, or stronghold, inside the 'fortress Europe'. This happened at the expense of domestic institutions, often taken over by their American competitors: a relevant development, because it reinforced the view that the UK authorities were keeping an open view on the nationality of the entrants, rather focusing on maintaining the City international competitiveness.

The most important regulatory reform affecting banks and, in general, financial institutions occurred only during 1997–2000, after few grave, but not systemic, banking crises, when the whole structure of financial regulation and supervision was changed, and the monetary policy decision-making process was also revised.

One might wonder why this chapter ends with the 1980s, and not, for example, with the creation of the Financial Services Authority (FSA) and the approval of the Financial Services and Markets Act (FSMA) of 2000, that will be dealt with in a subsequent chapter.

The periodization is always a matter of discretion, if not an arbitrary choice; but after the Big Bang and during the 1990s a series of developments occurred that shaped the banking and financial system in a way not far from today's environment, for example in terms of internationalization, use of 'exotic' financial instruments, diversification of household assets in a broad range of financial products, blurring of distinctions between different types of financial intermediaries. The legislation of 1997–2000 systemized this whole matter, and we live now within that framework, and with the features just mentioned. In addition, our main database, that covers the period 1990–2005, appeared the best suited to give a fairly comprehensive and deep perspective of the economic and financial trends underway.

1.1 A fragmented banking system

Without an all encompassing banking law to provide a uniform framework, up to the beginning of the 1970s the literature describing the structure of the British banking system adopted – depending on the various authors – different partitions or classifications.[1]

These aimed at ordering a system which has been defined as highly structured, with a clear demarcation between different types of institutions. At the centre was the City, traditionally organized on a highly specialist basis, with the strong support of the Bank of England.[2]

Of the various classifications, that proposed by Revell has the benefit of comprising in just three segments a set of institutions characterized by a few but nonetheless significant common traits, and by many, equally significant, specialist features:

1. deposit banks;
2. secondary banks;
3. so-called near-banks, or retail secondary banks.

All three segments comprise institutions that took deposits (therefore 'banks' in the common meaning of the term). However, category (1) also includes specialist and unusual intermediaries such as discount houses, and the Bank of England itself (its Banking Department as distinct from the Issue Department); categories (2) and (3) differ from the first in that the institutions included did not participate in the UK clearing system. Category (3) differs from category (2) in that it was heavily biased towards retail operations.

Deposit banks were the core of the banking system. Banks belonging to this segment were essentially represented by the so-called clearing banks, which were authorized to operate fully in the payments system. Apart from some Scottish and Northern Irish banks, the segment was to a large degree dominated by the so-called 'Big Five' (Barclays, Lloyds, Midland, National Provincial and Westminster). This situation remained unchanged for a long time: the transition from the war economy to the post-war period had not brought about an attenuation of the – quantitative and qualitative – state controls on the banking system. Up to the early 1970s there was an official use of a 'directed' deposit banking sector.

However, in 1967 the Treasury and the Bank of England made it clear they intended to discontinue official control over the structure of retail deposit banking. This triggered attempted mergers between the major banks mentioned above. And so, while in 1968 the Monopolies Commission blocked the merger between Barclays and Lloyds, that same year Westminster and National Provincial launched the merger process which, two years later, was to lead to the formation of NatWest, reducing the major clearing banks to the 'Big Four'.[3]

The deposit banks could rely on a vast network of branches enabling them to spread risk geographically, fully exploit economies of scale in the provision of payment services and enjoy a certain degree of market power at local level. They adopted a traditionally conservative policy, offering mainly short-term loans and deposits that were almost exclusively sight deposits denominated in sterling. The oligopolistic structure of the deposit banks was long reinforced by an interest rate cartel. This situation prompted several writers to go so far as to liken the clearing banks to public utilities and to observe that they were likely to have contributed very little to the investment needs of Britain's industrial companies. Deposit banks, it was said, had evolved from suppliers of credit to become instruments for the execution of monetary policy, mere managers of the money supply.[4]

Despite the considerable differences in the way they operated, discount houses are included in this segment because they served to meet the requirements of deposit banks. Discount houses were money market institutions, whose liabilities consisted of 'sight' loans, primarily obtained from the clearing banks as part of their treasury management, and whose assets consisted of short to medium-term securities issued by the British government and commercial bills; securities that were given as collateral to the financing banks. If banks were to need liquidity and withdraw their 'sight' funds, the discount houses could turn to the Bank of England as lender of last resort. The reasons for this 'cushion' between the deposit banks and the central bank are essentially of a historical and traditional nature: in short, the reluctance of banks to seek finance in cases of necessity from a sister bank, even a special one like the central bank.[5] This explains why the development of an active and liquid inter-bank market gradually squeezed out the discount houses.

The secondary banks segment, primarily comprising accepting houses, overseas banks and foreign banks, appears considerably more heterogeneous. As mentioned earlier, the common factor distinguishing them from the first segment was their lack of direct access to the payment mechanism and the clearing arrangements. Moreover, unlike deposit banks, secondary banks took the bulk of their deposits on the wholesale market rather than the retail market.[6]

The accepting houses, originally devoted to financing UK foreign trade through the acceptance of bills of exchange, greatly expanded their activity in financing export credit, especially in relation to its insurance by the Export Credit Guarantee Department. In addition to this, accepting houses – through merchant banking – underwrote securities issued by foreign countries for placement on the London market. The organization of underwriting syndicates and the provision of financial advice to sovereign entities and commercial companies expanded as investment banking took root.[7] Accepting houses, with their large exposure abroad, were the first to organize the Eurobond market in London.

Overseas banks (established under English law but with most of their assets overseas), foreign banks (primarily American, especially with the development of the Eurodollar market in the 1960s[8]), subsidiaries of deposit banks (established by the latter to ensure a broad presence on the inter-bank money market without being subject to the operational limits of their parent undertakings), and consortium banks (established by consortia of English and foreign banks) completed the secondary banks segment. Overseas banks, together with the accepting houses, greatly contributed to the growth of the inter-bank money market.[9]

The third segment was made up of the near-banks. These were similar to secondary banks in that they were not qualified to participate in the payment mechanism, but differed from them in that they were primarily concerned with retail banking. This segment included finance banks, building societies and savings banks: the first were specialized in consumer credit, the second in residential property mortgages, and the third constituted a particular form of financial circuit that channelled households' savings towards public sector loans.

The balance sheets of the banks operating in the three segments provide a measure of the scale of their activities in the various sectors outlined above. A comparison of these balance sheets over a decade – from 1960 to 1970 – reveals the different dynamics of the individual categories of banks and of the three segments into which they are grouped. In fact, Table 1.1 reveals a substantial morphological change, in part induced by obsolete legislation and in part spurred by market forces.

The left-hand part of Table 1.1 shows that in 1970 deposit banks were primarily exposed to firms and the public sector and secondary banks to the foreign sector, while finance houses combined a significant degree of exposure to households (consumer credit) with substantial exposure to firms. Building societies were the major providers of finance to households through property mortgages, and savings banks channelled their resources almost exclusively towards the public sector.[10]

This said, these balance sheet items must also be assessed in light of the various categories' importance in the banking system as a whole, as reported in the right-hand part of Table 1.1. In this respect, by 1970 secondary banks had emerged as the dominant force: quantitatively they became the barycentre of the system with total assets of approximately £28 billion, equal to 46 per cent of the system total and mostly denominated in foreign currency, as against 13 per cent in 1960.

Table 1.1 UK banks: selected items from their balance sheets

	1970 (% of their total assets)				*Total assets (£ bn)*			
	Business	*Households*	*Public sector*	*Foreign*	*1960*	*%*	*1970*	*%*
Deposit banks	37.5	7.7	29.1	4.2	9.9	46.9	14	22.7
Discount houses	–	–	–	–	1.1	5.2	2.4	3.9
Secondary banks	12.2	0.9	11.0	71.9	2.8	13.3	28.4	46.1
Finance houses	47.3	33.1	–	13.9	0.9	4.3	1.4	2.3
Building societies	–	80.5	15.7	–	3.2	15.2	11	17.9
Savings banks	–	–	96.6	–	3.2	15.2	4.4	7.1
Total					21.1	100	61.6	100

Source: Authors' calculations based on data in J. Revell, *The British Financial System*.

Building societies also showed strong growth: in terms of total assets the financing of households through property mortgages accounted for approximately 18 per cent of the system total, as against 15 per cent in 1960.

By contrast Table 1.1 shows how the importance of deposit banks and discount houses declined. In 1960 they were the primary component of the system with assets of £11 billion, equal to almost 52 per cent of the total. Ten years later this percentage had dropped to around 27 per cent while building societies had begun to catch up with deposit banks (it should not be forgotten, however, that deposit banks had participated in the considerable expansion of secondary banks though their own subsidiaries).

If one considers that in 1970 the foreign sector accounted for 71.9 per cent of the assets of the secondary banks, it follows that this foreign exposure amounted to approximately £20.4 billion and exceeded the total assets of the deposit banks.

One can conclude that the 1960s ended with two 'winners': the secondary banks and the building societies, thanks respectively to the expansion of foreign activity and the boom in credit to households. In terms of market share the 'losers' were the deposit banks.

This fundamental change in the banking system's morphology was due to various reasons and at the same time paved the way for the developments of the following decade.

Turning to the reasons for the change, the growing role of secondary banks had a lot to do with the increase in the branches of foreign banks, especially American, which in turn was linked to the birth and development of the Eurodollar market in the 1960s. By keeping the door open for foreign competitors to enter the London market, the British authorities created the conditions for this to happen. They appeared keen to foster the competitiveness of London's financial centre, compared with the old structure based on the clearing banks and the discount houses, even if this meant making control of the money market as a whole much more complex.

The relative eclipse of deposit banks can be explained by various factors, of which the main ones appear to have been a shift of households away from banking deposits towards non-bank financial assets and the low competitiveness of deposit banks within the banking sector.

As regards the first factor, one indication of the growth of non-bank financial assets can be observed by comparing the growth of bank deposits with that of funds managed by unit trusts, insurance companies and pension funds. Once again, the sources available do not permit detailed comparisons, but they do allow rough indicators of the main trends to be identified. At the start of the 1960s the ratio of deposits with banks and building societies to the funds held by unit trusts, pension funds and life insurance companies was estimated at around 19, by the start of the 1970s it had fallen to 2.3, and it was to fall to 1.5 in the middle of the 1980s.[11]

As for the low competitiveness of the deposit banks, their firmly established specialization prevented them from taking part in the property mortgage boom, since they traditionally engaged in short-term credit provision. But the deposit banks were also 'enmeshed' by the demarcation lines that had long protected them from other segments of the banking system. Up until the 1970s a system of public controls on loans, together with an asset ratio and interest rate cartel among deposit banks, which had long accounted for the bulk of deposits and loans, had given the Bank of England a tight grip on the money supply. In exchange, the banks had suppressed price competition, to the detriment of their efficiency,[12] while the more dynamic sectors of activity had eluded them.

The expansion of mortgages and building societies was linked in part to growth in income and in part to rising house prices. Indeed, in its Report of 1980 the Wilson Committee (set up to review the functioning of financial institutions), attributed the success of building societies to the growing demand for residential property, a favourable fiscal treatment that lowered the cost of mortgages and permitted better returns on deposits, and the possibility for investors to rapidly liquidate their savings held with them.[13]

The fragmentary nature of the banking system was matched by an equally fragmentary structure of the supervisory bodies. It may be useful to observe that in the contemporary literature on banking, the word 'supervision' did not even occur.[14]

The Bank of England was responsible for the system's stability. It acted as lender of last resort and imposed certain asset ratios on the deposit banks. But its powers of supervision were few. Rather, it tended to rely on informal agreements with the deposit banks, the discount houses and the accepting houses; but the agreement's focus was not so much on assuring stability as on delivering an efficient government securities market and implementing the Bank's credit policy.[15] An only slightly different opinion contended that the central bank's institutional interest in maintaining the stability of the banking system could be linked to its responsibility as government banker and to its consideration of deposit banks as clients towards which it had a protective duty.[16]

The advantage of maximum flexibility was offset by the limited size of the supervised area (which became increasingly evident with the growth of the secondary banks) and by the uncertainty surrounding the legal basis of the Bank's powers.[17]

Finance houses were subject to a multitude of regulations, regarding among other things, the duration of the credit they granted, and, from 1965 onwards, the lending ceilings assimilated 'by Governor's letter' to those of the deposit banks. Such was the heterogeneousness of the regulations that, in 1971, the government felt it necessary to establish a committee to report on their reform, the Crowther Committee, which proposed the unification of controls under a Consumer Credit Commissioner.[18]

In view of their mutualistic and non-profit nature, the building societies were under the supervision of the Chief Registrar of Friendly Societies.[19]

Since some of their deposits were guaranteed by the State, the savings banks were subject to a degree of supervision by the National Debt Commissioners and the Trustee Savings Banks Inspection Committee.[20]

Lastly, there was no organized oversight structure for the sector's most dynamic segment, that of the secondary banks, even though they had been formally granted bank status pursuant to Article 123 of the

Companies Act 1967, through certification by the Board of Trade. This certification was handed out in a liberal fashion, despite the requirement to consult with the Bank of England before authorizing its issue.[21]

This panoply of regulation, which was extremely disjointed and erratic, helps us to understand not only the very different dynamics of the three segments in the 1960s, but also the series of regulatory shake-ups that affected the banking system in the United Kingdom from the early 1970s onwards. The 1970s and 1980s were also characterized by significant episodes of banking instability, accompanying a gradual liberalization of the banking system.

1.2 The 1970s: more competition, secondary banks' crisis, the Banking Act 1979

One of the system's most distinctive traits, the deposit banks' interest rate cartel, was abolished in 1971 with a series of measures following on from the Bank of England's consultation paper 'Competition and Credit Controls' (CCC), aimed at increasing competition in the banking system and reviewing the *modus operandi* of monetary policy.[22] As a matter of fact in the same year the Bank of England decided to replace the quantitative limits imposed on all banks and the liquidity ratio imposed on clearing banks with a new system requiring all banks to hold minimum reserve assets equal to 12.5 per cent of their eligible liabilities.[23]

The 1971 measures removed the partition separating the two market segments of deposit banks and secondary banks and permitted the full entry of deposit banks into wholesale banking (previously they had had only indirect access to the wholesale market through subsidiaries).[24] This had an impact on the functioning of the money market. In fact, prior to the CCC, one area (the discount market) fell within the operational scope of the deposit banks, which through the discount houses 'made' the money market and had access to central bank discounting; the second area (the parallel money market) fell within the scope of the secondary banks, was not covered by the central bank's 'safety net' and was primarily concerned with the Euromarket. The two areas had been kept separate to prevent the foreign sector from interfering with the domestic money market, in accordance with a structure which was deemed to meet the needs of monetary policy.

The absence of supervision by the Bank of England allowed the secondary banks to collect large amounts of unsecured funds on the secondary market and to use them to provide finance, including long-term loans, for the construction of non-residential property, a market that was booming in those years. The removal of quantitative limits for banks in 1971, together with the expansionary stance of monetary policy despite the high point of the cycle, fuelled a speculative bubble in the building sector. The decision, taken towards the end of 1973, to raise the discount rate led to a problem of maturity mismatching for many secondary banks.[25] In just a few months both house prices and the share market fell. 25 secondary banks paid the price, but were subsequently saved thanks to the intervention of the Bank of England and the support of the clearing banks, which bought 16 of the banks involved in the crisis.[26] The Bank of England bore approximately 10 per cent of the cost of the bailout.[27] According to an estimate, although the Bank of England didn't provide figures, it had to put aside 'a remarkable total of about £100m for the possible cost to itself of the whole rescue strategy'.[28] The crisis of the secondary banks is significant because, after decades of stability, it marked the central bank's début in a systemic bailout. 'The fact that the central bank, a state-owned body, accepted responsibility for potential losses of such a scale, with a resultant drop in its payments to the Nation's Exchequer, alone makes the measures taken to deal with the secondary bank crisis a matter of major public interest'.[29]

During the 1970s the international openness of the banking system increased further with the arrival of new foreign banks. As mentioned earlier, the Euromarket had found fertile ground in London starting in the previous decade, fuelled by massive outflows of dollars from the United States and the benevolent attitude of the UK authorities, which did not impose controls on foreign currency deposits held in London.[30] The growing demand for funds by developing countries was largely satisfied through 'syndicated loans', often organized by American banks with branches in London and with the participation of English banks and the branches of other foreign banks. The market procured funds through foreign currency deposits from countries running a surplus, especially members of OPEC. In 1979, the scrapping of exchange controls gave new impetus to operations of this kind.

The changes described led to a more open and competitive market in vast spheres of banking activity. After many years of lasting stability, often seen as linked to the non-competitive and relatively 'cartelized' nature of the system (described earlier[31]), the crisis of the secondary banks ushered in widespread changes to the structure of supervision, hitherto characterized by the informal model of the Bank of England with ample room left for self-regulation (the two main bodies of self-regulation were the Accepting Houses Committee and the London Discount Market Association[32]). From the 1970s onwards, the strong drive for innovation in the system, coming in part from the authorities themselves and in part from the market, and the crisis of the secondary banks, revealed the discrepancy between the system's changing structure and an untouched supervisory regime. Following the secondary banks' crisis, in 1974 reporting requirements to the Bank of England were stiffened and the scope of supervision widened. In 1978, in a note for the aforementioned Wilson Report, the Bank of England underlined how little banking and financial activity was subject to statutory regulation and, by contrast, to what a large extent it relied on non-statutory regulation (in terms of the Bank's own exercise of its 'traditional powers as central bank') and self-regulation.

The episode of the crisis of the secondary banks highlighted how, in the absence of appropriate forms of supervision, the removal of constraints – and therefore increased competition – could be associated in the short term with instability.[33] In all likelihood, competition in itself was not to blame for instability as much as the changing system, and therefore the process of transition from a restricted to a more liberal context. A regulatory earthquake, after that of 1971, occurred in 1979. The Banking Act 1979 extended the supervision of the central bank to the secondary sector (licensed deposit takers), and formalized supervision in the primary sector (recognized banks), thus creating a kind of two-tier system. This Act is anyway a watershed, since before that bank supervision was conducted on an essentially non-statutory basis.[34]

1.3 The 1980s: further into statutory bank supervision: the Banking Act 1987

A snapshot of the banking system at the beginning of the 1980s reveals a picture that is still evolving, even if the sources do not allow us to make a homogenous comparison with Table 1.1 since the variations in the classification of banks make it difficult to interpret the data. This is especially true of data before and after 1975, when significant variations in statistical classifications were made.[35]

Based on figures from Grady and Weale, Table 1.2 illustrates the relative weight of the various segments of the system and their performance in the decade from 1975 to 1984.

The difficulties involved in making a comparison with Table 1.1 are evidenced by the unavailability of the important group of building societies, while the secondary banks segment has become more detailed.

The predominance of secondary banks (especially foreign) is nonetheless confirmed since their total assets are now four times those of the

Table 1.2 UK banks: total assets (£bn)

	1975	*1984*
Deposit (clearing) banks	36.0	153.0*
Discount houses	2.7	7.8
Secondary banks:		
– accepting houses	5.8	26.6
– other banks	20.5	91.7
– foreign & Commonwealth banks	77.4	488.2
Total	142.4	767.3

Note: * The data for 1984 refer to all retail banks.
Source: Authors' calculations based on data from Grady and Weale, *British Banking*.

clearing banks; the role of the discount houses is on the wane. The central role of foreign banks in the Eurocurrency market is confirmed: this market, established by the accepting houses, has become the dominion of foreign banks (of the £488.2 billion assets, approximately £433 billion were denominated in currencies other than sterling).[36]

The new style of supervision introduced by the 1979 Banking Act appeared designed to avoid instances of moral hazard, which risked occurring in the wake of the rescue of the secondary banks. But in fact in 1984 the Bank of England intervened again in the crisis of Johnson Matthey Bankers. The crisis – caused by a rapid and over-concentrated expansion of the loan portfolio, problems in recovering some of the largest loans, inadequate internal controls, and organizational shortcomings, together with inaccurate reporting to the supervisory authority – led the Bank of England to intervene in the autumn of that year, despite the bank's small size, because it saw a potential systemic risk due to the fact that JMB was one of the five members of the London bullion market. The Bank of England intervened on a major scale by buying JMB together with a number of other financial institutions, replenishing its capital and subsequently selling it to an Australian company.

This episode gave rise to a further rethinking of supervision. In particular, there was criticism of the two-tier system of banks created by the 1979 Act. The most relevant distinction between recognized institutions and licensed deposit-takers was that a bank, to obtain recognition, must demonstrate that it provided a wide range of services and possessed a high reputation and standing. The style of supervision of the two types of institutions developed differently, because supervision of the former relied strongly on mutual trust and cooperation. Paradoxically, therefore, the fact that JMB was a recognized institution was a factor of delay in the supervisor's being aware and reacting to its crisis.[37] This led to a new banking law, the Banking Act 1987, which included all banks in the single category of authorized institutions and increased the information-gathering powers of the Bank of England. The previous year the Building Societies Act 1986 had deregulated the sector and made it possible for building societies to compete on a major scale with deposit banks in the market for retail financial products.

1.4 The capital markets: the Big Bang, the Financial Services Act 1986

One year before the Banking Act 1987 another reform had an enormous impact on the capital market. A number of different factors contributed to its enactment: (i) the wave of privatizations under the Thatcher government; (ii) the growth in the presence of foreign, especially American, banks, which had made secondary banks into the largest and most dynamic segment of the banking system, although their operations were mainly restricted to the Eurocurrency market; (iii) the abolition of exchange controls in 1979, which had boosted cross-border capital movements significantly; and (iv) the revolution in information technology. All these factors widened the gap between rapidly evolving financial structures and governance arrangements based largely on self-regulation, which had created a protected and relatively closed system of relationships between financial intermediaries.

Unlike the United States, which had enacted the Glass-Steagall Act in 1933, the United Kingdom had not introduced legal separation between commercial banking and investment banking after the 1929 stock market crash. However it had achieved a comparable result – following a pragmatic approach with no legal backing – in two ways: on the one hand the deposit banks had long restricted their activity mainly to short-term lending, while long-term loans were granted by specialist intermediaries (such as building societies); on the other hand the capital market had isolated itself through clubby regulations that provided participants with a high degree of protection.

Strictly speaking, the so-called Big Bang (27 October 1986), which liberalized important aspects of the capital market, was the result not of a law but of a reform introduced by the London Stock Exchange. In reality, however, it was in response to the pressure brought to bear by the Conservative Government through the Office of Fair Trading, which had decided to challenge the LSE's clubby regulations in court following the extension to services of the Restrictive Practices Act and its anti-cartel provisions.

The previous regime had hinged on just a few participants: acceptance houses, which played a role similar to that of investment banks, did the deals; brokers carried out the transactions; and separate jobbers, acting as market makers, had to take positions in securities to ensure orderly trading conditions while being allowed to do business only with stock-brokers and other jobbers. In general jobbers and brokers had the legal form of partnerships (only towards the end were jobbers allowed to be companies), their number was limited and they could not be owned by persons outside the Stock Exchange. A system of fixed commissions was in operation.

Big Bang totally reversed this situation: entities outside the Stock Exchange – especially banks, many of which were foreign and prevalently American – bought (or entered into alliances with) brokers and jobbers; fixed commissions were abolished and commissions fell substantially, from about 2 per cent to as low as 0.2 per cent, as a result of the competition that followed. Computerized communications permitted the switch from open outcry trading to an electronic screen-based system and the introduction of the Stock Exchange Automatic Quotation System (SEAQ); the floor of the Stock Exchange was soon empty.[38]

This deregulation contributed to increasing the large American banks' interest in the London market, not least because at home they continued to suffer under the constraints imposed by the Glass-Steagall Act, which was not repealed until 1999. Rather than make costly acquisitions of local brokers, these banks often preferred to build up their presence organically. They imposed an increasingly transactions-driven business approach instead of the relationship-based approach typical of the old acceptance houses. With the implementation of the European single market in mind, the American banks chose London as the base for the expansion of their operations in Europe.[39]

Not surprisingly deregulation led to the creation of large and complex banking and financial conglomerates engaged in the whole range of universal banking business. The growth in securities trading permitted the development on a major scale of banking and financial groups with integrated operations in the fields of commercial banking, investment banking and fund management.[40] One consequence of these trends was the considerable expansion of non-bank intermediaries, which continued in the 1990s.

This powerful anti-protectionist drive and the consequent increase in competition inevitably has a potential for serious conflicts of interest as a by-product, conflicts that the authorities are required to regulate and curb.

In parallel with deregulation it was therefore felt necessary to legislate to avoid abuses involving market confidence, transparency and investor protection. In a report commissioned by the Treasury, Professor Gower examined the possibility of introducing a sort of 'English SEC'. In the event, the report came down in favour of a more structured form of self-regulation.[41] The legislative outcome was different, however: the Financial Services Act 1986 broadened the scope of legislation at the expense of self-regulation. The measure's importance lies in its having been approved at a time when the City was still calling for a reform that would continue to be based on self-regulation. The 1986 Act provided for a system of controls in which self-regulation maintained a major role but it also established the Securities and Investment Board (SIB), a formally private body that was to perform the public function of supervising the existing self-regulatory organizations and ensuring that they performed their regulatory activity in a manner consistent with the public interest.

The main self-regulatory organizations (SROs) that survived in the new structure were: the Securities and Futures Authority (SFA), the members of which were mainly brokers and dealers in securities, financial instruments and commodities; the Investment Management Regulatory Organization (IMRO), the members of which were portfolio managers for private customers, pension funds and collective investment undertakings; the Personal Investment Authority (PIA), the members of which were companies selling life insurance, investment funds and other investment services to the public.[42] Other entities, such as the Stock Exchange, LIFFE and the London Clearing House, had to be recognized by the SIB, but did not come under its supervision.

Within the banking and financial industry the distinctions between the different categories of intermediary were being eroded by mergers, acquisitions and the conquest of positions of control involving banks, building societies, non-bank intermediaries and insurance companies. The blurring of the boundaries between these categories – which, in any case, the English legal framework had never established rigorously and, where they did exist, were being dismantled – brought pressure to bear for a concourse of the regulators; self-regulation appeared rooted in the notion of the City as a 'club' and the Financial Services Act 1986 had sent a clear signal of the legislator's intention to abandon this model. As for the central bank, on the one hand it did not have a firmly established tradition of supervision, while on the other new legislation, the

Bank of England Act 1998, by making the Bank entirely independent in its conduct of monetary policy (although not in the establishment of the inflation target), strengthened the case of the advocates of a clear separation between the functions of banking supervision and monetary policy.

2
The UK's Financial Structure and Economic Sectors

Before examining the structure and regulatory framework of banking and financial intermediation in the last fifteen years, it appeared desirable to provide an analysis – albeit with a broad sweep – of the country's financial structure, in view of the powerful influence this exerts on the activity of intermediation. Looking at these aspects also implies mentioning some major economic and political issues that have been a feature of the United Kingdom over the years and exercised a major influence on its financial structure, especially as regards the effects of policies – some going back to the 1980s – such as the privatization process, pension reform and the deregulation of the building societies sector.

Looking at the main financial aggregates in the period 1990–2005, it can be seen that the financial structure has been marked by:

- a considerable and growing financial deepening of the economy;
- a high propensity of households to invest in life insurance and pension funds. This has been accompanied by growing exposure with the banking system, mainly in the form of secured lending;
- a high propensity of firms to finance themselves on the capital markets, with equities and debentures, rather than through bank credit;
- a considerable external openness of the economy with an increase in assets and liabilities in relation to Gross Domestic Product (GDP) owing to a significant increase in both direct and portfolio investment and in inward and outward bank transactions;
- a strengthening of the 'market-based' nature of the financial system, where most financial transactions are conducted with a higher degree of arm's length and less through banking relationships. This does not mean that banks have become marginal; their role as multifunctional

financial entities has remained of key importance. If anything, it is their business that has changed, with a further increase in their foreign orientation, a contraction in the share of corporate loans and an expansion in that of lending to households. Above all there has been a large-scale entry, especially of foreign banks and subsidiaries of foreign banks, into investment banking and an increase in the use of innovative financial instruments, which have permitted credit risk to be transferred. This has tended, as will be seen in more detail in chapter 6, to turn banks from risk holders into risk originators and distributors. Most of the risk, however, remained within the banking system.

2.1 The economy's financial deepening and its implications

This section contains a short overview of the main financial aggregates of both the economy as a whole and its main sectors, while those that follow explain the factors underlying the evolution of the balance sheets of thee sections: households, non-financial corporations and the foreign sector.

As regards the financial deepening of the economy as a whole, the main indicator is the Financial Interrelation Ratio (FIR), i.e. the ratio of total gross financial assets to GDP (FIR 1) or to the total real assets of the economy (FIR 2). The ratio to GDP rose from about 7 in 1990 to 12.5 in 2005. The ratio to real assets is also very high and rising, having increased from 1.5 to 2.5 (Table 2.1).

Another indicator is the Financial Intermediation Ratio (FIN), which is the ratio of the financial assets of banking intermediaries (banks and building societies) to the total financial assets of the economy. This ratio remained stable at around 37 per cent, with a decline towards the end of the 1990s that was subsequently made good.[1] The assets of banks and building societies decreased instead in relation to the total assets of the financial system (which includes other financial institutions,[2] life insurance companies and pension funds), declining from 66 to 57 per cent (Table 2.1). The assets of banking intermediaries nonetheless increased in relation to GDP over the period considered, with the ratio rising from 2.6 to 4.7. Taken together, these indicators suggest that banks' role in the real economy did not diminish but that they lost ground in the financial sector to insurance companies, pension funds, securities firms and unit trusts.

Turning to the household sector, over the past fifteen years there has been a substantial increase in households' financial assets and liabilities, a significant shift to forms of private retirement provision, and

Table 2.1 The UK's financial assets

	As % of GDP	*As % of UK non-financial assets*	*% of UK financial assets*			*% of total assets of financial intermediaries*			*As % of GDP*			
	Total UK financial assets FIR 1	*Total UK financial assets FIR 2*	*Banks and building societies FIN*	*Insurance and pension funds*	*Other financial intermediaries*	*Banks and building societies*	*Insurance and pension funds*	*Other financial intermediaries*	*Banks and building societies*	*Insurance and pension funds*	*Other financial intermediaries*	*Total financial assets of the financial sector*
1990	7.14	1.5	36.8	12.5	6.2	66.3	22.5	11.2	2.63	0.89	0.44	3.97
1991	7.23	1.6	34.2	13.9	6.6	62.5	25.3	12.1	2.47	1.00	0.48	3.95
1992	7.75	1.8	34.2	14.5	7.2	61.1	26.0	12.9	2.65	1.13	0.56	4.33
1993	8.55	1.9	30.7	16.1	9.1	55.0	28.8	16.2	2.63	1.38	0.77	4.78
1994	8.03	1.9	32.9	15.0	8.3	58.6	26.7	14.7	2.64	1.20	0.66	4.51
1995	8.62	2.2	32.4	15.6	8.6	57.3	27.5	15.3	2.80	1.34	0.75	4.88
1996	8.73	2.2	31.9	15.9	9.9	55.2	27.6	17.2	2.78	1.39	0.87	5.04
1997	9.66	2.4	32.1	16.1	9.9	55.2	27.7	17.1	3.10	1.56	0.96	5.62
1998	9.81	2.4	31.8	16.9	9.1	55.0	29.3	15.8	3.12	1.66	0.89	5.67
1999	10.63	2.5	28.8	17.5	9.6	51.6	31.2	17.2	3.07	1.86	1.02	5.95
2000	11.05	2.5	30.9	15.7	10.4	54.2	27.5	18.3	3.41	1.74	1.15	6.30
2001	10.71	2.4	33.1	14.4	12.0	55.6	24.2	20.2	3.55	1.54	1.29	6.38
2002	10.05	2.1	35.7	13.2	11.8	58.8	21.8	19.4	3.58	1.33	1.19	6.10
2003	10.69	2.2	36.3	13.2	12.6	58.5	21.2	20.3	3.88	1.41	1.35	6.64
2004	11.16	2.2	37.2	13.1	13.2	58.5	20.7	20.8	4.15	1.46	1.48	7.08
2005	12.52	2.5	37.3	13.1	14.4	57.5	20.2	22.3	4.67	1.64	1.81	8.11

Source: Authors' calculations based on National Statistics data: Financial Balance sheets, UK Economic Accounts.

a relatively modest role played by mutual funds. On the liabilities side, households' already large exposure to the banking system has been growing, above all in the form of mortgages.

In particular, households' financial assets rose from 2.1 to 2.9 times GDP over the period considered, while their liabilities rose from 75 to 102 per cent of GDP. Accordingly, their net financial wealth was always positive and, up to 1999, almost always rising.

Analysis of households' financial assets over the period shows, above all, an increase in the share of life insurance companies and pension funds, from about 44 to 54 per cent. This was accompanied by a drop in shares and equities issued in the United Kingdom (from 16 to 10.5 per cent); an increase in mutual funds issued in the United Kingdom (from 2 to about 4 per cent); and an increase of the role of shares, equities and mutual funds issued abroad (from 0.5 to 1.9 per cent). Meanwhile the share of liquid assets (currency and deposits), fell from about 30 per cent to 25.6 per cent. On the liabilities side, the share of long-term loans secured on dwellings rose from about 70 to 75 per cent, while that of short-term loans fell from about 18 to 15.5 per cent (Table 2.2).

As regards non-financial corporations, it can be seen that the ratio of financial assets to GDP almost doubled (from 0.7 to 1.3), while liabilities, including equity, rose from 1.8 to about 2.7 times GDP. The breakdown of the sector's assets reveals a sizeable increase in shares and other equities (from 31.5 to 42.7 per cent). This was mainly due to purchases of foreign shares and other equities (which accounted for over 38 per cent of the sector's financial assets in 2005), probably in connection with mergers and acquisitions (Table 2.3).

In terms of firms' financial liabilities, what is most evident is an increase in the share of bonds as a percentage of total liabilities, from 5 to 10.3 per cent. This increase was not reflected in any reduction in the share of equity capital (which has always played a very important role, albeit with wide fluctuations), but rather in that of short-term loans and other accounts receivable (primarily trade credit). These two forms of finance declined substantially, from over 30 per cent of liabilities to just over 20 per cent, probably due to the more effective liquidity management.

Examination of the foreign sector reveals an even larger increase in assets and liabilities: in the fifteen years up to 2005 the stock of foreign assets increased from 1.6 to almost 4 times GDP; for their part liabilities rose from 1.5 to 4 times GDP.

The financial flows (net borrowing or net lending) of the different economic sectors reflect some aspects of the dynamics of the stocks described above and indicate how the nature of intermediation has changed in the

Table 2.2 Households' financial balance sheets: % of total assets and liabilities

	Currency and deposits	*Securities other than shares*	*Shares and equities issued in UK*	*Shares equities and mutual funds issued abroad*	*UK mutual funds*	*Life ins. and pension funds*	*Other assets*	*Total assets*	*Short-term loans*	*Long-term loans secured on dwellings*	*Other liab.*	*Total liabilities*
1990	30.3	1.7	16.0	0.5	2.0	44.5	5.0	100	17.9	70.1	12.0	100
1991	29.1	1.7	15.2	0.5	2.0	46.6	4.9	100	16.7	71.0	12.3	100
1992	27.7	2.1	15.3	0.5	2.1	47.9	4.5	100	15.5	72.5	12.0	100
1993	24.0	1.9	15.6	0.5	3.0	51.1	3.9	100	14.2	73.9	11.9	100
1994	25.2	2.0	15.4	0.9	3.3	49.2	4.1	100	14.3	74.3	11.4	100
1995	23.7	2.1	15.2	1.0	3.6	50.6	3.7	100	14.6	73.7	11.7	100
1996	23.7	2.0	14.8	1.0	3.9	51.2	3.5	100	14.6	74.2	11.2	100
1997	21.6	1.7	16.3	0.8	4.0	52.5	3.0	100	15.1	73.2	11.7	100
1998	21.3	1.7	15.8	0.9	3.7	53.6	2.9	100	15.6	72.9	11.5	100
1999	19.1	1.5	18.2	0.9	4.8	52.9	2.6	100	16.2	73.0	10.9	100
2000	20.3	1.5	17.4	0.9	4.9	52.2	2.9	100	16.9	72.8	10.3	100
2001	23.3	1.6	13.0	0.9	4.6	53.4	3.2	100	17.4	72.8	9.8	100
2002	27.1	1.7	10.2	1.0	4.0	52.6	3.4	100	17.1	72.5	10.4	100
2003	27.0	1.6	10.3	1.2	4.0	52.5	3.3	100	15.6	73.8	10.6	100
2004	27.1	1.4	10.2	1.4	4.4	52.1	3.3	100	15.6	74.7	9.6	100
2005	25.6	1.2	10.5	1.9	3.9	53.8	3.0	100	15.5	75.1	9.3	100

Source: Authors' calculations based on National Statistics data: Financial Balance sheets, UK Economic Accounts.

Table 2.3 Private non-financial corporations: financial balance sheets

	% of total financial assets						% of total financial liabilities					
	Currency and deposits	*Loans*	*Shares and other than equities*	*of which shares and other equities of the rest of the world*	*Other accounts receivable*	*Total financial assets*	*Securities other than shares*	*Loans*	*of which short-term loans*	*Shares and other equities*	*Other accounts receivable*	*Total financial liabilities*
1990	28.9	13.6	31.5	*23.6*	20.2	100	5.1	*31.0*	*21.2*	53.2	10.7	100
1991	29.3	13.0	31.8	*23.3*	19.6	100	5.4	*28.3*	*19.3*	56.4	9.9	100
1992	27.7	12.6	35.2	*27.1*	19.1	100	5.1	*27.0*	*18.2*	58.8	9.1	100
1993	29.1	12.0	34.5	*26.7*	17.9	100	5.4	*23.7*	*16.0*	62.8	8.1	100
1994	29.5	12.4	34.2	*26.2*	17.5	100	5.8	*23.7*	*15.7*	62.0	8.5	100
1995	28.7	13.3	35.1	*27.3*	16.1	100	6.3	*22.6*	*15.3*	63.5	7.6	100
1996	30.0	13.4	34.8	*26.5*	15.3	100	6.1	*22.4*	*14.9*	64.4	7.1	100
1997	30.9	13.4	35.9	*26.6*	14.3	100	6.1	*21.2*	*13.8*	66.4	6.3	100
1998	27.7	16.3	38.6	*29.3*	12.4	100	6.6	*21.3*	*12.9*	66.5	5.6	100
1999	24.1	14.9	47.3	*36.3*	9.4	100	6.6	*19.5*	*11.5*	69.3	4.6	100
2000	22.3	12.2	50.1	*42.6*	9.5	100	7.9	*21.2*	*12.4*	66.4	4.5	100
2001	24.1	13.2	47.2	*41.5*	9.3	100	8.9	*25.5*	*14.7*	60.8	4.9	100
2002	25.9	13.9	45.6	*41.7*	8.8	100	11.1	*31.2*	*17.9*	52.3	5.4	100
2003	27.8	12.5	45.5	*41.4*	8.2	100	10.6	*30.0*	*17.4*	54.4	4.9	100
2004	30.7	13.5	42.2	*38.1*	8.1	100	10.3	*30.3*	*17.9*	54.7	4.7	100
2005	31.7	13.2	42.7	*38.5*	7.9	100	10.3	*30.2*	*17.3*	55.3	4.2	100

Source: Authors' calculations based on National Statistics data: Financial Balance sheets, UK Economic Accounts.

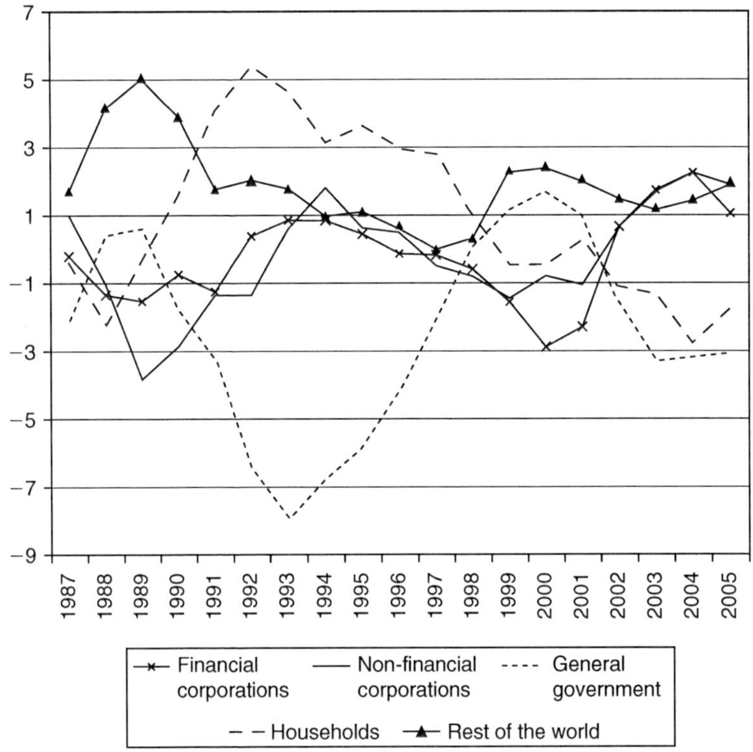

Source: National Statistics, *Blue Book*.
Figure 2.1 Sectoral financial balances: net borrowing or net lending (% of GDP)

United Kingdom.[3] Since the beginning of the 1990s there has been a contraction in general government net borrowing and a reduction in households' net lending. In recent years, households have become net debtors, while non-financial corporations have become net creditors (Figure 2.1). In 2004, private non-financial corporations boasted the highest financial surplus relative to GDP since 1969. This phenomenon, which is also to be found, to a more marked degree, in other countries, and has been linked to low interest rates, improved profitability, and a prudent investment policy.[4]

More than the government, it is interesting to consider the two real sectors of the economy (non-financial corporations and households) and the rest of the world. In fact the factors underlying the changes in sectors' financial assets and liabilities are reflected in the demand for financial instruments, their composition, and therefore ultimately in the role of banking and financial intermediaries. An attempt will also be made to indicate some macro-prudential implications of these changes.

2.2 The evolution of households' balance sheets

The performance of households' balance sheets can be viewed from three different perspectives: the propensity to save; debt and its technical form; and the aggregate portfolio composition of total financial assets. The latter aspect, in turn, can be seen in the context of the evolution of retirement provision (see Chapter 3).

The propensity of households to save, measured as the ratio of gross savings to disposable income, fell sharply, albeit with wide fluctuations, from 11.7 per cent in 1992 to 5.5 per cent in 2005. In 2004 it dropped to 3.7 per cent, the lowest level since the beginning of the 1960s.[5] Various factors explain savings trends in the United Kingdom. Among the different aspects underlying intertemporal consumption choices were improved income and employment prospects, the fall in inflation and its greater stability (Figure 2.2), the healthier state of the public

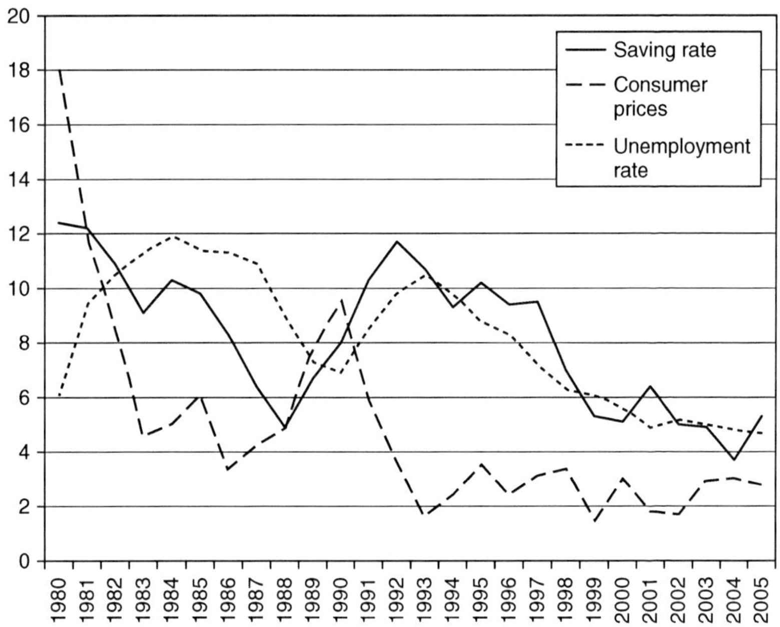

Source: National Statistics, *United Kingdom Economic Accounts*.

Figure 2.2 Propensity to save and the economic cycle

finances (and accordingly the prospect of less burdensome taxation in the future), the growth in real and financial wealth and, more generally, less uncertainty about the economic situation. Another factor, which was the subject of broad debate in the early 1990s, regards the effects on the propensity to save of the deregulation in the banking system during the 1980s.

It has been observed that banking deregulation, described in the previous chapter, by increasing the potential supply of credit, enabled consumers to reduce their liquidity constraints, and hence their propensity to save. This was reflected in increased demand for mortgages and consumer credit. In fact in the most advanced financial systems, savers are more likely to use their real wealth as collateral for consumer credit and mortgages, thereby relaxing their credit constraints. In other words, permitting the use of housing as collateral made previously illiquid assets more liquid and reduced credit rationing.[6]

It should be noted that the use of property as collateral is facilitated in the United Kingdom by an efficient legal system. In fact, when judicial procedures are faster and cost less, creditors find it easier to recover the real asset (the collateral). By contrast, in countries with a less efficient legal system banks usually require substantial down payments, which means forcing customers (often the younger generations) to have accumulated more savings in order to obtain a mortgage and buy a house.

It could be said that these liquidity constraints have been further (indeed even too much) relaxed in recent years thanks to the development of credit risk transfer, from the simplest forms, such as asset-backed securities (used for the securitization of mortgages and consumer credit) to more complex arrangements, that make use of derivative instruments (such as collateralized debt obligations). These instruments have enabled banks to manage credit risk more efficiently, by increasing diversification and permitting the transfer of the related risk, including to non-bank entities (such as insurance companies, pension funds and hedge funds). However, in addition to reducing the risk premium, this process has reduced the incentives to maintain rigorous criteria for assessing creditworthiness, as we will see more extensively in Chapter 6.

Regarding the evolution of households' liabilities, two factors need to be taken into consideration: the degree of indebtedness and the breakdown of the financial liabilities into their various technical forms (short term, long term, secured and unsecured).

In 2005 household debt was about 165 per cent of disposable income, from a minimum of around 122 in 1995 (Table 2.4). It is also found to be concentrated in the medium and high income cohorts of the

Table 2.4 Households' balance sheets: assets and liabilities as a % of disposable income

	Currency and deposits	*Securities other than shares*	*Shares and equity issued in the UK*	*Shares equities and mutual funds issued abroad*	*UK mutual funds*	*Life ins. and pension funds*	*Other assets*	*Total financial assets*	*Short-term loans*	*Long-term loans secured on dwellings*	*Other liabilities*	*Total financial liabilities*	*Net financial assets*	*Total non-financial assets*
1990	105.1	6.1	55.7	1.8	7.0	154.5	17.2	347.4	21.8	85.6	14.7	122.0	225	433
1991	101.9	5.9	53.1	1.7	7.0	162.9	17.2	349.6	19.9	84.5	14.6	119.1	196	391
1992	99.3	7.5	54.7	1.7	7.5	171.7	16.2	358.6	17.6	82.6	13.7	113.9	209	338
1993	96.7	7.6	63.0	2.0	12.1	206.0	15.7	402.9	15.8	82.0	13.2	110.9	227	329
1994	96.6	7.5	58.9	3.5	12.6	188.4	15.6	383.0	16.0	83.3	12.8	112.1	277	311
1995	97.7	8.6	62.5	4.3	14.9	208.3	15.2	411.4	16.2	81.6	12.9	110.8	250	292
1996	97.9	8.2	61.4	4.1	15.9	211.8	14.5	413.8	15.9	80.9	12.2	109.0	280	304
1997	99.9	8.0	75.4	3.7	18.5	242.7	14.0	462.3	16.5	80.1	12.8	109.4	280	308
1998	101.6	8.3	75.6	4.1	17.9	255.5	14.0	476.9	17.5	81.7	12.9	112.1	332	336
1999	103.4	8.1	98.2	4.6	26.0	286.2	14.2	540.7	18.8	84.8	12.7	116.3	342	368
2000	103.6	7.7	89.0	4.4	24.8	266.6	14.6	510.7	20.3	87.3	12.3	119.9	393	397
2001	104.2	7.0	58.4	4.1	20.8	239.5	14.2	448.3	21.6	90.3	12.2	124.1	355	399
2002	108.6	6.9	41.1	3.9	16.1	210.8	13.6	401.0	23.4	99.5	14.3	137.2	298	466
2003	112.7	6.8	43.2	5.0	16.9	219.5	13.8	417.9	23.2	109.9	15.7	148.8	235	496
2004	118.2	6.2	44.7	6.3	19.1	226.8	14.5	435.8	25.4	121.1	15.6	162.0	244	539
2005	121.4	5.6	49.8	9.0	18.4	254.9	14.4	473.5	25.6	123.7	15.4	164.7	251	533

Source: Authors' calculations based on NS data: financial balance sheets, UK economic accounts; *Blue book*, non-financial balance sheets.

population.[7] An international analysis conducted by the Organization for Economic Co-operation and Development (OECD) shows, however, that this ratio is far lower than that reported, for example, in the Netherlands (246 per cent), Denmark (260 per cent) and New Zealand (181 per cent), but that it is higher than in the United States (135 per cent) and Japan (132 per cent).[8]

The sustainability of this debt can be analysed using two indicators: the ratio of interest payments to disposable income and that of financial liabilities to financial assets that are 'disposable' or easily liquidated if necessary.

The first indicator assesses the ability of households to respond to an increase in the cost of debt servicing. This shows a sharp fall in the early 1990s, followed by a stabilization due in part to low interest rates but mostly to better employment conditions and higher incomes. The second indicator was constructed by excluding claims on pension funds and life insurance companies from households' financial assets. This provides an indication of the potential for debt restructuring, in the event of difficulty, through the sale of part of the assets. In fact, like real assets, pension fund and life insurance assets cannot be easily liquidated. As can be seen from Figure 2.3, in recent years the situation has clearly deteriorated and the index has risen above the level of the early 1990s.

When it comes to the composition of household debt, it was pointed out earlier that long-term loans secured on dwellings (primarily mortgages) are the most common form (accounting for 75 per cent of the sector's liabilities). A form of secured lending that traditionally plays an important role in the United Kingdom is so-called mortgage equity withdrawal. This consists of mortgages granted for purposes other than the purchase or extension of a property and exploiting the value of the property owned. The strong growth in this type of credit needs to be set in relation to the sizeable increase in property values and the more advantageous credit conditions that this instrument offers compared with other forms of finance.

Short-term and mostly unsecured loans increased in the period under consideration from about 22 to 25.6 per cent of disposable income. Long-term loans secured on dwellings rose, instead, from about 85 to 124 per cent (Table 2.4). As noted, the most important factor of such dynamic has probably been the 'increase in the number of owner-occupied dwellings per person of working age. This is partly due to the rise in the total number of occupied dwellings, reflecting smaller households, and partly to the increasing owner-occupation rate'.[9]

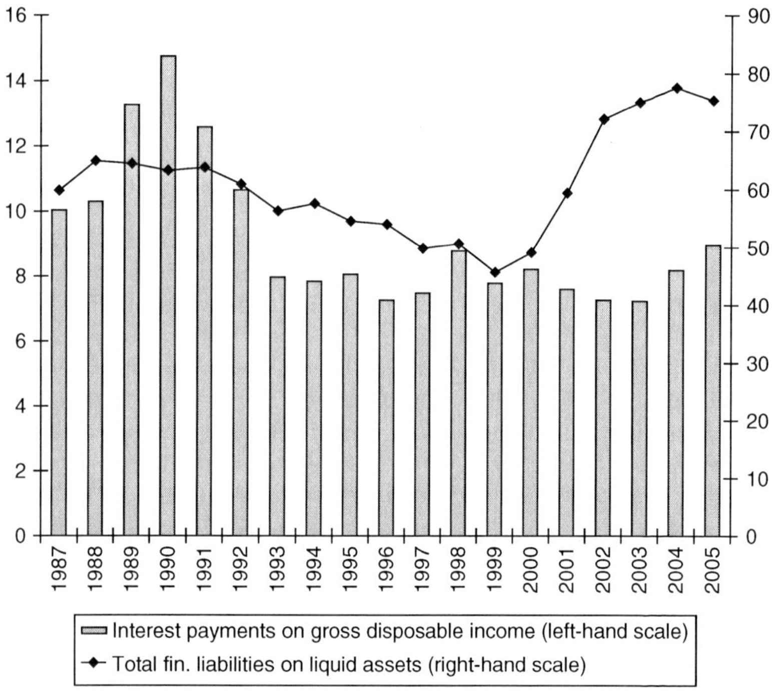

Source: National Statistics, *United Kingdom Economic Accounts*.
Figure 2.3 Household sector: financial ratios

Structural changes on the supply side have probably also played an important part in these developments. As we shall see in Chapter 4, which examines the structure of the banking market, the dismantling of operational barriers between banks and building societies has increased competition. This can be seen less in reduced spreads with respect to borrowing rates than in more advantageous offers in terms of contractual clauses or means of financing, and through the growth of credit cards as a means of payment.[10] The increase in lending to households for property purchases also led to banking intermediaries being highly exposed to the household and real estate sectors. In fact, if we exclude interbank lending, in 2005 over 60 per cent of total lending to the economy was to households and 17.6 per cent was to the real estate sector.

In conclusion, while the high level of household debt has been an opportunity for the banking sector and allowed households to bring forward consumption, it could nonetheless entail serious problems in the event of an erosion in the value of collateral or of real and financial assets, slowdown of disposable income, or a combination of these factors.

Moving to the allocation of household savings, as is well known, a sweeping programme of privatizations was launched during the 1980s, resulting in the sale to the market of numerous industrial companies and public utilities.[11] It was held that this programme had attracted a large number of investors to the stock market, so much so that it was dubbed 'popular capitalism'. According to a sample survey, in the household sector the percentage of stocks as proportion of total financial assets declined from about 14 per cent in 1980 to 11.3 per cent in 1985 and increased to 17 per cent in 1995.[12] Another, more recent, survey shows how the percentage of households holding shares peaked at the end of the 1990s at 29 per cent, subsequently declining gradually and continuously to about 20 per cent in 2006.[13] That the spread of popular capitalism was only modest – at least after the privatization and demutualization phases – is confirmed by the data on households' direct ownership of equity (Table 2.5).

In the fifteen-year period under consideration, direct equity ownership peaked in nominal terms at the end of the 1990s, then declined, and has only given signs of renewed vitality in recent years. This trend quite closely mirrors the performance of the London Stock Exchange (LSE), with one proviso: that it is constantly lower, as can be seen by comparing the index number of the value of the shares owned with the performance of the stock market. This appears to indicate public disaffection with the stock market, which, moreover, would be consistent with the survey referred to above showing a decline in the number of households directly exposed.

If we consider the ratio of households' equity holdings to GDP, it can be seen – by way of further confirmation of the above – that the figure at the close of the fifteen-year period was not dissimilar to the opening figure (about 35 per cent, despite the much higher peak of almost 66 per cent recorded in 1999).

Quite different conclusions are reached if, ignoring the propensity to invest directly in shares, we also calculate indirect equity ownership, i.e. shares owned by institutional investors to which households entrust their savings: pension funds and life insurance companies.[14] This shows that the total number of shares owned – directly and indirectly – by households, generally keeps step with the performance of the stock market, even overtaking it. The closing value of the ratio of these shares to GDP is higher than the opening value (about 104 per cent, as against 89 per cent).

Table 2.5 Householdings of shares (direct and indirect)

	Shares owned by households		*Shares owned by pension funds and insurance companies*		*Total*		*FTSE 100*		*GDP*	*(A)/(I)*	*(E)/(I)*
	£bn	*index (1990 = 100)*	*£bn*	*index (1990 = 100)*	*£bn*	*index (1990 = 100)*	*(end of year)*	*index (1990 = 100)*		%	
	(A)	*(B)*	*(C)*	*(D)*	*(E)*	*(F)*	*(G)*	*(H)*	*(I)*	*(J)*	*(K)*
1990	196.2	100.0	298.4	100.0	494.6	100.0	2143.5	100.0	558.2	35.1	88.6
1991	206.3	105.2	369.9	123.9	576.2	116.5	2493.1	116.3	587.1	35.1	98.1
1992	230.0	117.3	425.9	142.7	655.9	132.6	2846.5	132.8	612.0	37.6	107.2
1993	281.0	143.3	556.7	186.5	837.7	169.4	3418.4	159.5	642.7	43.7	130.3
1994	279.1	142.3	505.5	169.4	784.6	158.6	3065.5	143.0	681.0	41.0	115.2
1995	316.5	161.4	592.1	198.4	908.6	183.7	3689.3	172.1	719.7	44.0	126.2
1996	328.1	167.3	633.7	212.3	961.8	194.5	4118.5	192.1	765.2	42.9	125.7
1997	422.8	215.5	757.7	253.9	1180.5	238.7	5135.5	239.6	811.2	52.1	145.5
1998	443.1	225.9	828.1	277.5	1271.2	257.0	5882.6	274.4	860.8	51.5	147.7
1999	595.6	303.6	1019.9	341.8	1615.6	326.6	6930.2	323.3	906.6	65.7	178.2
2000	570.9	291.1	943.8	316.3	1514.7	306.3	6222.5	290.3	953.2	59.9	158.9
2001	406.9	207.4	812.3	272.2	1219.1	246.5	5217.4	243.4	997.0	40.8	122.3
2002	301.7	153.8	615.1	206.1	916.8	185.4	3940.4	183.8	1048.8	28.8	87.4
2003	337.8	172.2	683.9	229.2	1021.7	206.6	4476.9	208.9	1110.3	30.4	92.0
2004	366.6	186.9	735.7	246.5	1102.3	222.9	4814.3	224.6	1176.5	31.2	93.7
2005	439.5	224.1	837.3	280.6	1276.8	258.2	5618.8	262.1	1224.7	35.9	104.3

Sources: National Statistics, *The Blue Book*; for the FTSE 100 the source is Bloomberg.

This decline in direct equity ownership has meant that – as shown earlier (see again Table 2.2) – equity has declined as a percentage of households' assets, while forms of 'asset management' have increased (life insurance companies, pension funds and mutual funds).

The National Statistics data provide further confirmation of what was said earlier and a long-term perspective: as a percentage of the total value of shares held by UK residents and traded on the share market (the LSE), the proportion held by individuals fell from 39 per cent in 1975 to 21 per cent in 2004. Conversely, the proportion held by pension funds and life insurance companies (which, however, also invest on behalf of non-residents), gradually increased from 35 per cent in 1975 to about 49 per cent in 2004.[15]

In short, the role of institutional investors (and in particular of pension funds and life insurance companies) has expanded in relation both to the assets of the financial sector and to the portfolio the household sector. Households have therefore increased their equity capital ownership indirectly; in other words it is through the equity investments made by institutional investors that families have boosted their ownership of share capital. This has significant implications from a prudential and consumer protection perspective. On the one hand it makes the supervision of these intermediaries increasingly important, on the other it attenuates problems deriving from the direct, and at times inadequately diversified, acquisition of risk by households.

Finally, it is interesting to observe how the stock of real (largely residential) household wealth rose in the period under consideration from 4.3 to 5.3 times disposable income (Table 2.4) or from 2 to 2.7 times GDP. Figure 2.4 compares the property price index with nominal GDP growth and the stock exchange index (FTSE-ALL share, up to mid-2008).

2.3 The financial structure of the non-financial corporate sector

As with the household sector, both the structure and evolution of firms' balance sheets have an important impact on the banking and financial institutions operating in the United Kingdom. In particular, the demand for credit and other financial services and the degree of indebtedness have repercussions both on the operations of financial intermediaries and on systemic stability.

The financial structure of businesses depends on a series of cyclical and structural factors. These need to be seen in relation to investment policies, including acquisitions, the capacity to generate cash flow, tax rates,

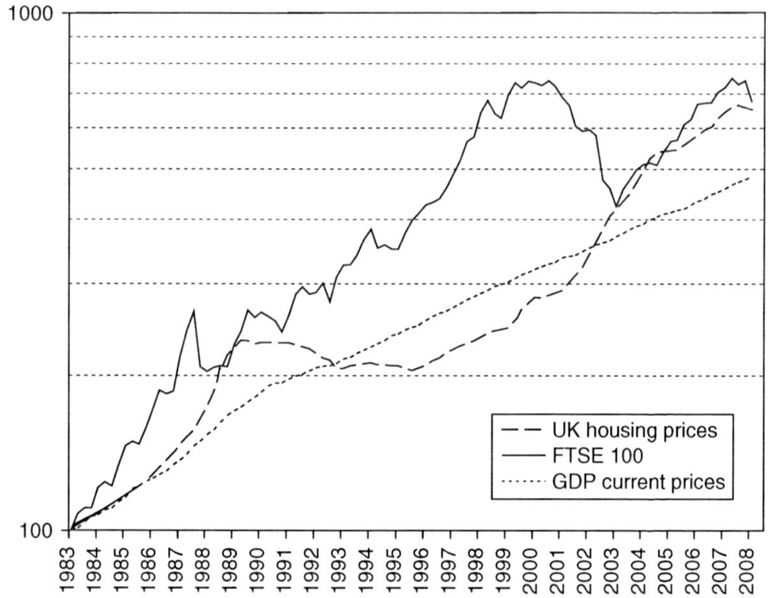

Source: Authors' calculations based on data from National Statistics, Halifax, London Data stream – Thomson Reuters.

Figure 2.4 GDP at current prices, housing prices and stock exchange index (indices: 1983 = 100; logarithmic scale)

dividend policies and the propensity to use equity capital and obtain a stock exchange listing.[16]

One feature of UK non-financial corporations[17] when compared with those of other European countries is the significant role played by share capital among the various forms of financing. As we saw earlier, in 2005 share capital was 55 per cent of firms' total liabilities; a figure that had fluctuated between 50 and 60 per cent and risen to almost 70 per cent at the end of the 1990s (Table 2.3).

In this regard, we have taken two aspects into consideration: i) the possibility to obtain a stock exchange listing; and ii) the relationship between debt and equity deriving from firms' financial policies, the corporate tax regime and market conditions.

One aspect that may have encouraged British firms to obtain a stock exchange listing was their size. While nowadays there are stock exchanges specialized in the listing of small and medium-sized enterprises, for a long time size was an important precondition for entry and in the UK it was met partly through specialization in industries with large economies of scale. In the early 2000s 50 per cent of turnover was concentrated in firms with at least 250 workers.[18] This means that a significant share of the country's economic activity was generated by firms which, in principle, were large enough to be listed on the stock exchange.

While a firm's size may have been an important precondition for listing, its corporate governance structure and especially the protection of minority shareholders were decisive.[19] As a result institutional investors were encouraged to enter the equity market.[20] This was reflected in greater separation between ownership and control and in a lower concentration of majority shareholders within companies. An examination of the ownership structure of a selection of firms listed in the United Kingdom in the latter half of the 1990s reveals that the leading 'ownership block' (main sole shareholder or group of individuals) held less than 10 per cent of the voting shares. This contrasts with 54 per cent in Italy, 57 per cent in Germany and 20 per cent in France. Only in the United States was the figure lower (5.4 per cent).[21] According to a joint research of the London School of Economics and the Bank of Italy, forthcoming, the mean percentage of ownership was in 2004, for the largest shareholder, 49.4 percent in Italy, 47.3 in Germany, 11.9 in the UK.[22]

In the United Kingdom the composition of equity capital is therefore less concentrated than elsewhere. On the other hand, the presence of institutional investors in the capital of firms, primarily pension funds and insurance companies, is much more marked: in the United Kingdom they hold 62 per cent of the 'ownership blocks', as against 24 per cent held by company managers, 8 per cent held by other companies and 5 per cent by individuals.[23]

Worth noting that the willingness of the UK companies 'to go public' is not new. There is a long tradition of British firms being predisposed to obtaining a stock exchange listing. While also present in other industrial countries, in the United Kingdom this practice was particularly widespread and persistent. In 1900 the ratio of stock market capitalization to GDP was 2.42; not dissimilar from the current value of 2.25. Lavington notes that between 1911 and 1913 there were 6,542 registered companies; 378 of these were listed (of which 165 on the LSE and the others on provincial stock exchanges).[24] Large capitalistic families' need to open up to forms of external capital – including by ceding control, while nonetheless retaining an important position in the ownership structure – was at the heart of this process.[25]

Other minor, though not negligible, factors in promoting access to the market were the rules and costs of listing, which were particularly favorable in the United Kingdom compared with other countries.

According to a recent study, that compares costs at London's equity markets (the LSE's Main Market and the AIM) with the other two major European stock exchanges (Deutsche Börse and Euronext) and with New York Stock Exchange and Nasdaq in the USA, issuing equity (IPOs) on the London markets is cheaper than on the American markets, mainly because of the higher underwriting fees charges for the US transactions. London's position in this regard is similar to the European exchanges. Legal, accounting and advisory fees in London tend to be higher than in Frankfurt or Paris, but lower than in New York. For trading costs, London is the most convenient market other than New York. On the other side, the UK – according to the study – is ranked as the leading country in terms of corporate governance: a listing on the London market delivers the greatest benefits. Even if the Sarbanes-Oxley legislation in the US may have improved governance standards, the benefits so delivered in terms of corporate governance do not appear superior to those achieved under the British regime, while compliance costs have substantially risen in the US as a consequence of that law.[26]

It should, however, be pointed out that in recent times there has been an inverse trend, with share buybacks and sometimes the delisting of companies, partly owning to the expansion of private equity (see Chapter 4).

The second aspect to be considered in examining how the structure of firms is related to the development of the banking and financial system is the relationship between debt and equity (or capital gearing).[27] This relationship has direct implications for the financial system, both through the demand for (bank and non-bank) debt financing and because excessive leverage may lead, especially in the event of an unexpected rise in interest rates, to an increase in the probability of default.

The factors that determine the level of capital gearing and its change over time are not immediately obvious. We know from economic theory that, in certain conditions, replacing one of the components with the other does not alter a firm's financial equilibrium. In fact shifting from equity to debt makes the firm's equities riskier and the resulting higher cost of equity finance offsets any benefit of having more debt (and vice versa). In practice, however, the tax deductibility of corporate interest payments on debt capital gives debt an edge. Accordingly, as corporation tax rates are lowered, the marginal advantage of debt financing decreases. This was true in the United Kingdom, especially in the mid-1980s, when the main rate of corporation tax was reduced from more than 50 per cent to about 35 per cent. Subsequently, it was reduced further and now stands at 30 per cent.[28]

As regards the degree of indebtedness, firms would appear to have a target level of capital gearing. This target, or equilibrium level, is a function of the trade-off between the tax advantage (the amount of interest deductible) and the probability of bankruptcy (which in turn is related to the expected cost of financial distress). It has recently been estimated that the long-run equilibrium level of UK private-sector non-financial firms' capital gearing at market price is about 16 per cent.[29] It has also been shown that firms adjust their balance sheets to eliminate excessive deviations from the equilibrium capital gearing by reducing dividend payments and increasing the volume of shares in issue. There is only weak evidence, however, that such firms adjust excessive debt situations through more restrained capital investment. This is consistent with the view that real adjustment, by reducing investment, only occurs when the dividends distributed to shareholders cannot be reduced any further.[30]

Other explanations have been sought for changes in capital gearing. In particular, it has been noted that in the absence of debt, companies would generate a larger amount of cash that would then be at the disposal of the management. Under such circumstances, shareholders might worry that the managers would use this liquidity for their own 'perks' (bonuses, benefits, etc.) rather than to maximize the return for shareholders. Debt is therefore a way to limit the free cash flow available to managers. Another explanation is based on the fact that since managers are more informed about the firm than outsiders, the decision to issue equities instead of debt may signal that the quality of the firm is weak. This, in turn, reduces the price that outsiders are willing to pay for the equity (and, therefore, the market-to-book ratio).[31]

In the last few years there has been a pronounced divergence from what was considered the equilibrium level of debt, with a peak towards the end of 2002, followed by a correction. In 2005 capital gearing was 24 per cent (Figure 2.5). It is difficult to determine whether this rather high level of debt is due to factors of a transitory nature or to a permanent increase in the equilibrium level.

It is worth noting in this respect that the acquisition activity of British firms has been very intense, both in the UK and abroad, with exceptional years such as 1999 (£137 billion) and 2000 (£288 billion) and subsequently a high level (£56 billion per year on average), far above the average of the early 1990s (about £12 billion per year). Most of the domestic transactions were financed with cash (65 per cent on average) or ordinary shares (32 per cent).

As for the division of the debt between banks and securities, the growth in bond issues is set in relation to the stable and credible process of

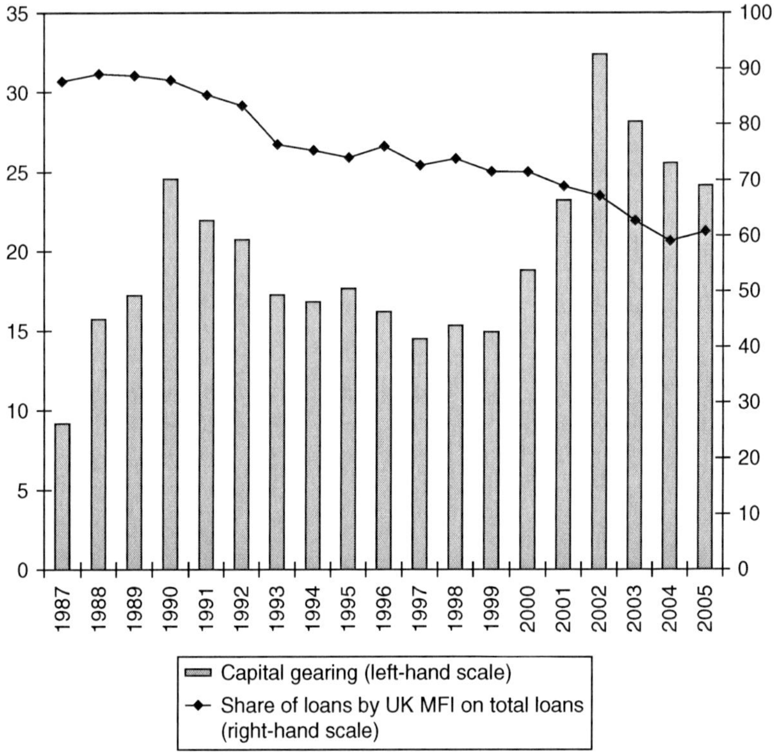

Source: based on National Statistics data: *Financial Statistics*.
Figure 2.5 Private non-financial corporations: financial indicators

disinflation and the parallel reduction in the risk premium and thus in interest rates. The new institutional arrangement based on central bank independence and inflation targeting, accompanied by a favourable international context, has played a crucial role in this respect. In recent years net issues of bonds and comparable instruments have doubled as a percentage of firms' total liabilities, rising from 5 to more than 10 per cent over the period considered (Table 2.3).

The relationships between the variables referred to above have important implications for monitoring financial stability because firms' financial sustainability affects the quality of banks' assets. In the event of divergence from the equilibrium situation, firms must reduce their debt by following a low dividend policy or by issuing new shares. However, if the debt were to rise further or if conditions on the share market were not favourable, the adjustment may be complicated (e.g. to the detriment of investment) or take a long time. The objectives of macro-prudential supervision therefore include that of carefully monitoring corporate debt and, if possible, estimating its equilibrium value.

In doing this it is necessary not to forget the international dimension, which has steadily grown in importance. Firms' greater exposure abroad allows them to diversify their sources of finance. At the same time, however, they become exposed to sudden changes in external financial conditions and to exchange rate risk if the positions are not appropriately hedged.[32]

To conclude this section, the following points thus emerge regarding the corporate sector:

- the sector's financial deepening has increased, with equity capital continuing to play a major role and an increase in bond issues. The factors important for share capital, apart from those of a historical nature, have been the average size of firms and the corporate governance system. An important element for debt capital has been the fall in inflation expectations, fostered by the new institutional setting of the central bank and the international context;
- capital gearing has risen in the last few years, probably due in part to Mergers & Acquisitions (M&A) activity. It is difficult to determine whether the recent level of capital gearing is the consequence of a permanent increase in the equilibrium level or of factors of a transitory nature;
- firms' recent greater propensity to incur debt despite the low tax rates on corporate income has been reflected only in part in an increase in the demand for credit from domestic banks since a growing share of firms' financing needs has been met through the issue of bonds and a growing share of the demand for credit has been directed towards foreign intermediaries.

2.4 The role of the financial sector in external balance

The growing globalization and financial deepening of the economy have also been reflected in the main items of the country's balance of payments and of the international investment position (IIP).

We shall focus in particular on the following aspects: (1) the contribution made by exports of financial services to the current account of the balance of payments; (2) the net income generated by foreign direct and portfolio investment and banking intermediation; (3) the sectoral and

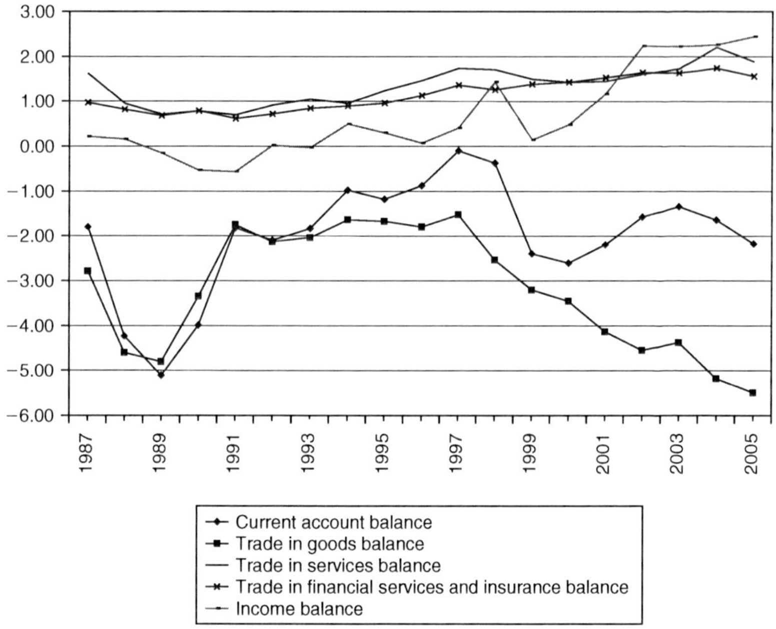

Source: National Statistics, *The Pink Book*.
Figure 2.6 The current account balance: components (% of GDP)

geographical composition of IIP; and (4) the 'valuation effect' deriving from changes in the value of the stocks of foreign portfolio assets and liabilities. These aspects throw light on the nature of the country's growing financial flows and the stock of assets and liabilities with the rest of the world and make it possible to assess, albeit only in part, the potential exposure of the economy to financial shocks through the foreign channel.

Compared with the late 1980s and early 1990s, when the current account deficit was more than 5 per cent of GDP, the country's external unbalance has improved, although it is still negative. The improvement has been mostly due to exports of financial services and in the last few years to a sizable surplus on the income account, which has exceeded the surplus on financial services since the turn of this century (Figure 2.6). More specifically, the balance on merchandise trade deteriorated in the period considered and reached 5.5 per cent of GDP in 2005 owing to a series of factors such as the delocalization of production and the decline of manufacturing, the gradual erosion of the surplus on oil, the strength of the pound sterling and the weak growth of some of the country's main export markets, especially in the euro area. Part of the deterioration was offset by the uninterrupted surplus on services of 1–2 per cent of GDP. The balance of the financial services and insurance contributes for 83 percent to the services' total surplus, in 2005 (specifically, the financial services and insurance surplus is 19 billion pounds, the services total surplus is 23 billion, against a trade deficit of 67 billion pounds).

The second aspect, net income flows such as dividends on foreign direct investments and interest earned on portfolio investments, reflects the greater international openness of financial and non-financial firms and the expansion of the City of London as a world financial centre. These flows played an even more important role than exports of services in containing the external imbalance. As can be seen in Table 2.6, the balance on investment income swung from a deficit at the beginning of the 1990s to a substantial surplus (of about £30 billion in 2005) thanks to the contribution of direct investment income and to a much smaller extent of portfolio investment income. These income flows more than offset the substantial deficit (of more than £16 billion) on bank interest.

The substantial surplus on investment income – in the presence of a negative international investment position – can be explained by the fact that a relatively large portion of British assets abroad consists of direct investments, while the foreign assets in the United Kingdom consist mainly of bank deposits, held as low-risk, low-return assets in a country deemed to be safe. Table 2.7 shows the performance of the British banks' foreign business. The direct and portfolio investment income of the banks and other financial institutions (excluding insurance companies) shows a large surplus.

The third aspect concerns the international investment position (IIP). For an economy that has undergone considerable financial deepening, the analysis of the stocks of financial assets and liabilities is especially important insofar as it shows the country's exposure to potential sudden portfolio shifts by domestic and international investors or changes in asset prices.

At the outset we should note that the UK net foreign asset position shows an imbalance of 11 per cent of GDP in 2005. This is relevant, though less pronounced if compared to the US (−18 per cent of GDP). Note on the contrary the relevant positive position of Germany (20 per cent of GDP) and Japan (36 per cent of GDP).[33] A database launched in 2001 by the IMF makes it possible to analyse the counterparties of portfolio investment and its technical forms, aspects that are especially useful from the macro-prudential standpoint because they highlight the potential exposure to a 'country risk'.

Table 2.6 Balance of Payment: investment income (£m)

	Direct investment income balance	*Portfolio investment income balance*			*Other investment income: mainly payments on loans and deposits*	*Reserve asset income*	*Total investment income balance*
		Earning on equities	*Earning on debt securities*	*Total portfolio investment*			
	A	*B*	*C*	*D*	*E*	*F*	*A + D + E + F*
1990	8328	−1160	−5967	−7127	−5802	1732	−2869
1991	8266	−1548	−3202	−4750	−8416	1656	−3244
1992	8177	−551	−177	−728	−8728	1456	177
1993	6228	−331	2794	2463	−10442	1525	−226
1994	11367	−1000	242	−758	−8668	1577	3518
1995	11012	−1161	286	−875	−9363	1686	2460
1996	11954	−2591	−926	−3517	−9525	1551	463
1997	14554	−3152	440	−2712	−9983	1372	3231
1998	21334	−3869	3714	−155	−9981	1132	12330
1999	16141	−5769	562	−5207	−11026	1161	1069
2000	17607	−27	1990	1963	−16165	985	4390
2001	25304	−3328	3735	407	−15074	961	11598
2002	35457	−3524	3952	428	−13329	820	23376
2003	33174	−3289	4235	946	−10324	791	24587
2004	36506	−2782	3110	328	−11014	705	26525
2005	44572	−2037	3148	1111	−16545	659	29797

Source: United Kingdom Balance of Payments: The Pink Book.

Table 2.7 Balance of payment: investment income – banks and other financial institutions

	Banks and other financial institutions (£ million)					
	Direct investment income balance			*Portfolio income balance*		
	Credits	*Debits*	*Balance*	*Credits*	*Debits*	*Balance*
1990	–220	–654	434	3457	6602	–3145
1991	–141	–770	629	3981	5020	–1039
1992	631	331	300	4784	3430	1354
1993	1506	4143	–2637	6723	2990	3733
1994	2162	690	1472	7733	3715	4018
1995	2025	2530	–505	10467	5440	5027
1996	3949	3382	567	11359	6152	5207
1997	3954	1649	2305	13148	7093	6055
1998	3891	–2661	6552	17957	8365	9592
1999	5603	3594	2009	13846	6787	7059
2000	6656	7254	–598	18987	9247	9740
2001	7520	6660	860	20229	10470	9759
2002	7696	3174	4522	18302	7656	10646
2003	9993	4740	5253	18595	7030	11565
2004	10938	5557	5381	21570	8820	12750
2005	14914	7994	6920	26351	12286	14065

Credit: Earnings by UK residents on direct or portfolio investment abroad
Debit: Foreign earnings on direct or portfolio investment in the UK
Note: 'Other financial institutions' excludes insurance companies.
Source: *United Kingdom Balance of Payments: The Pink Book.*

It emerge that the United Kingdom's exposure to emerging markets is relatively modest and well diversified. The United States, however, plays a major role, which could have adverse effects if there were to be a disorderly adjustment of the global imbalances accompanied by a large fall of the dollar, American domestic demand or further deterioration of the mortgages sector, as indeed started happening in 2007. In particular, the structure of the portfolio of assets (equity and debt) issued by non-residents and held by UK residents indicates that at the end of 2005 the greatest exposure of British investors appears to have been *vis-à-vis* the United States (25 per cent of the total stock of foreign portfolio assets), followed by Germany and France (7 per cent), Japan (6 per cent), and Italy and the Netherlands (6 per cent). Some 40 per cent of the portfolio is held by banks, 34 per cent by insurance companies and 10 per cent by mutual funds (Table 2.8). The exposure in relation exclusively to debt securities, mostly sovereign bonds, is also mainly *vis-à-vis* the United States (24 per cent), followed by the Netherlands (7.6 per cent) and Italy

Table 2.8 UK portfolio investment assets by sector of holder country of non-resident: year end 2005

Country	Total (%)	Banks	Insurance	Mutual funds
		% of total assets		
Finland	1.01	0.23	0.27	0.10
Belgium	1.07	0.61	0.25	0.10
Denmark	1.07	0.45	0.13	0.12
Korea, Republic of	1.14	0.35	0.38	0.27
Hong Kong SAR of China	1.38	0.22	0.49	n.a
Sweden	1.54	0.69	0.37	0.17
Switzerland	2.04	0.26	1.00	0.47
Spain	2.51	1.11	0.57	0.27
Australia	2.54	1.00	1.04	n.a
Luxembourg	2.57	0.85	0.99	n.a
Ireland	3.79	1.58	n.a	0.34
Italy	5.57	3.74	0.83	0.33
Netherlands	5.92	2.39	1.70	n.a
Japan	6.10	1.67	2.77	0.98
France	7.09	2.45	2.32	0.87
Germany	7.26	3.26	2.15	0.69
United States	25.32	9.71	10.99	2.70
Jersey	1.80	0.84	n.a	0.03
Cayman Islands	3.95	3.27	0.34	n.a
International organizations	2.86	0.84	1.51	0.02
Other countries	13.46	5.27	6.27	2.92
Total (equity and debt securities)	100	40.76	34.37	10.38

Source: Authors' calculations based on IMF data: Portfolio Investment: Coordinated Portfolio Investment Survey (CPIS).

(5.8 per cent). In 2005 the exposure to emerging market debt instruments was well diversified across a large number of countries (Table 2.9).

The last aspect concerns the 'valuation effect' in relation to capital gains and losses on portfolio investments.[34] In this case the country is subject to an external adjustment even with zero financial flows. Since a large portion of assets and some liabilities are likely to be denominated in dollars, the 'valuation effect' has been estimated in that currency. As can be seen in Table 2.10, a capital gain on the assets side is often accompanied by a capital loss on the liabilities side, thus attenuating the net effect on the economy. The values are nonetheless fairly substantial (similar to the annual portfolio investment inflows and outflows) and extremely volatile.

Table 2.9 UK portfolio investment debt securities: assets by country of non-resident issuer (%)

	2001	*2005*
Colombia	0.10	0.20
Philippines	0.10	0.20
Taiwan Province of China	0.04	0.24
Iceland	0.06	0.27
Malaysia	0.14	0.35
India	0.08	0.36
Hong Kong SAR of China	1.15	0.45
Argentina	0.12	0.47
Russian Federation*	0.33	0.48
Turkey	0.11	0.55
South Africa	0.33	0.69
Mexico	0.57	0.82
Canada	2.97	1.44
France	6.12	1.48
Denmark	1.00	2.54
Australia	1.47	2.91
Sweden	1.51	3.03
Luxembourg	2.00	4.03
Japan	5.56	4.07
Germany	11.58	4.15
Spain	1.57	4.24
Ireland	1.39	5.21
Italy	9.96	5.82
Netherlands	5.14	7.61
United States	24.11	24.04
Cayman Islands	5.69	6.45
Jersey	0.76	1.70
International organizations	3.68	2.97
Other countries	12.36	13.23
Total value of debt securities	100.00	100.00

Note: * = 2004; 2005 preliminary.
Source: IMF, Portfolio Investment: Coordinated Portfolio Investment Survey.

From what has been said it is possible to draw some conclusions: in the first place, it has become ever more important in the United Kingdom to maintain and increase competitiveness and innovation in the financial sector, the exports of which have become an important component of the current account of the balance of payments; in the second place, given the size of the country's external position, it could be a source of

Table 2.10 UK total portfolio: investment equities and debt securities (US$m)

	2000	*2001*	*2002*	*2003*	*2004*	*2005*
Stocks						
Total assets	1,352.0	1,359.0	1,360.0	1,670.0	2,109.0	2,292.0
Difference with respect to the previous year		*7.0*	*1.0*	*310.0*	*439.0*	*183.0*
Total liabilities	1,489.0	1,390.0	1,438.0	1,869.0	2,274.0	2,439.0
Difference with respect to the previous year		*−99.0*	*48.0*	*431.0*	*405.0*	*165.0*
Flows						
Total assets		124.7	−1.2	58.4	259.1	290.6
Total liabilities		69.6	76.2	155.6	159.8	230.6
'Valuation effect': variation of the value of stocks minus flows						
'Valuation effect' on assets		−117.7	2.2	251.6	179.9	*−107.6*
(+ is a capital gain for a UK resident)						
'Valuation effect' on liabilities		−168.6	−28.2	275.4	245.2	−65.6
(+ is a capital loss for a UK resident)						
Exchange rate $ per sterling (end of period)	1.49	1.45	1.61	1.78	1.93	1.72
Exchange rate (period average)	1.51	1.44	1.50	1.63	1.81	1.82

Source: Authors' calculations based on IMF data: International Financial Statistics.

fragility if the imbalance between assets and liabilities should increse or in the event of external shocks. We are nonetheless aware that, in the absence of disaggregated data, above all on the currency composition and possible hedging, it is very difficult to make an evaluation. Only simulations or stress tests on micro data would be able to provide an indication of the economy's exposure to the above-mentioned events; lastly, there is an aspect of broader significance that concerns the effects of financial deepening and globalization on the country's external imbalance.

In particular, the enormous stock of foreign assets and liabilities means that even with constant flows a small change in the values of these stocks, caused by capital gains or losses or by mismatching of the net positions in foreign currency, could have major effects on the net asset position.[35] Thus, as noted by Maurice Obstfeld, the performance of the current account has become increasingly inadequate for the purpose of evaluating a country's external imbalance. In addition, the policy implications of this new environment, where two-way cross-border claims are extraordinarily important, are far from clear.[36] The usual approach on the current account imbalance, which stresses the role of saving and investing in altering net foreign assets, and the implications of borrowing for future consumption should be complemented with an assessment of possible adjustments of the country's portfolio positions.

3
The Development of Private Pension Schemes and the Pension Reform

Earlier, we considered households' substantial and growing investment in pension saving. This investment is closely related to the limited role of public pensions. The interaction between public and private pensions is easier to understand if set against a historical background. UK private pension provision, both occupational and personal, has roots reaching far back into the past. Its growth was subsequently influenced to a considerable extent by the birth and successive reforms of public pension provision.[1] These reforms have become stratified over time, making the pension system extremely complex and very difficult to reform radically. In this respect reference has been made to the path-dependent nature of pensions and stress placed on the 'problem of history for any radical reform of British pensions'.[2]

3.1 The problem in an historical context

The roots of the problem are considered to lie in the reluctance of the state to place the financial burden of pensions on the shoulders of the collective and in the development, starting in the 19th century, of private institutions explicitly devoted to the payment of old-age and disability pensions, the result of an ideological reliance on voluntarism rather than public intervention. This situation contributed to the development of the expertise necessary for the assessment of long-term liabilities, to the growth of financial markets in which to invest the funds accumulated, to the creation of authorities to regulate these markets and to the widespread use of the typically Anglo-Saxon legal concept of the trust. In the same historical period, Bismark's Germany gave the signal to continental Europe for the establishment of a very different form of social security based on the state pension system.

The shift in the United Kingdom to a state-run universal contributory pension paid at a flat rate until death did not occur until the National Insurance Act 1946, after two schemes, launched respectively in 1911 and 1925, that saw the involvement of the state into the social security system. Although the idea of its designer, William Beveridge, was for the system to be a fully funded one in which employees' contributions would pay for their benefits, the solidaristic environment then prevailing and the social belief in the state's intervention reduced the political cost of immediately paying full pensions, without the necessary transitional period for accumulating contributions. The resulting system was therefore unfunded, a pay-as-you-go system where current pensions were paid, not out of a previously accumulated fund, but out of other people's current contributions. In addition, the flat-rate approach linked contributions to the level the poorest workers could afford. The Treasury became aware of the impending deficit of the National Insurance Fund and, while GDP was growing substantially in the good years of the post-war period, was reluctant to concede pension increases: more specifically, to allow pensions to be linked to earnings rather than prices.

The demand for pensions linked to earnings was met by the private 'pillar' of the pension system: specifically, by the occupational schemes. During the 20th century the development of large firms as the dominant form of industrial organization, which brought long-term stability of employment relationships, had been conducive to the proliferation of company pension schemes. Nonetheless, whereas before the war occupational pensions were the preserve of a minority, subsequently they expanded enormously, so that in 1967 the membership of such earnings-related, private schemes was equal to about 53 per cent of the working population.

In 1957, a Labour proposal to link state pensions to earnings, funding this link with higher contributions to be invested in stocks, was dropped. At the same time, the National Insurance Fund moved into deficit. The Conservative government adopted a new sub-scheme introducing a limited earnings-related element in the state pension (the 'graduated state pension' – note that this also included the feature of contracting out); the higher contributions needed went in fact to subsidize the National Insurance deficit: solving the emerging deficit issue created a longer term problem. Plans were also made to allow occupational schemes to 'contract out' of the new earnings-related state pension, encouraging the growth of these schemes.

The existence of a link between contributions paid to the National Insurance Fund and the pensions and other benefits was questionable from the beginning in a pay-as-you-go system such as Britain's. The emergence of a National Insurance Fund deficit in 1957 triggered the series of reforms referred to above, which further weakened the link. Broadly speaking, the aim of the reforms was to curb the cost of state pensions by shifting part of the burden of pension provision on to occupational schemes and later personal schemes as well, while seeking to keep the whole system reasonably fair.

The 'graduated state pension scheme' was followed in 1978 by the state earnings-related pension scheme (SERPS), designed for employed workers not covered by an occupational scheme. However, employers were to receive a rebate of social insurance contributions if they 'contracted out' and took over part of the state's pension obligation. SERPS was replaced from 2002 onwards by the Second State Pension, as distinct from the Basic State Pension. In 2001 the state had introduced an additional scheme, the stakeholder pension, based on employer and employee contributions paid into low-cost pension plans with both public and private components. All this occurred in a context of increasing complexity and cost and decreasing efficiency.

Together with the adoption of the Pay as you Earn (PAYE) system for income tax, the introduction of deduction at source of National Insurance contributions blurred the distinction between contributions and taxes and National Insurance appeared almost as an alternative form of income tax. The result was the return to a frequent and recently growing National Insurance Fund surplus (equal in 2005 to about £20 billion if unfunded social benefits are included in expenditure). In the long run the balance between contributions and expenditures is consistently maintained, not considering wide fluctuations due to cyclical factors related to the unfunded social benefit component (Figure 3.1)

Another result was the stabilization of social security benefits in relation to GDP after the sharp rise in the postwar years. In particular, from the mid-1970s onwards pension expenditure fluctuated between 7 and 8 per cent of GDP and in recent years has shown a downward trend (Figure 3.2).

With the curbing of state pensions, by the end of the last century occupational pension plans had become a crucial component of the UK pension system, together with the increased importance of products sold by life insurance companies, which entered the pension sector in a big way. Personal pension schemes grew in popularity over time, partly owing to the shift in occupational schemes from defined-benefit to defined-contribution. This reflected the deterioration in the financial situation of many large firms and obviously made occupational pensions

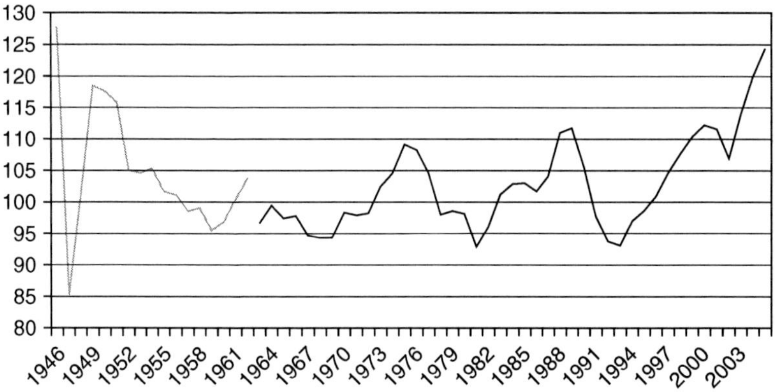

Source: National Statistics.

Figure 3.1 Social security: coverage ratio

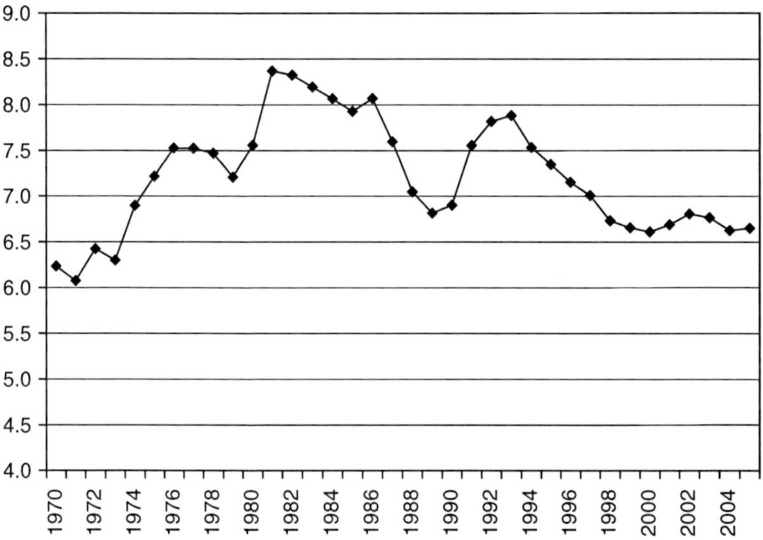

Source: National Statistics.

Figure 3.2 Social security expenditure as a % of GDP

less attractive to workers. Individually purchased retirement savings accounts thus accompanied the retrenchment of state pensions and private occupational pensions.[3]

In 2003 the state accounted for about 65 per cent of total pension expenditure in the United Kingdom and the private sector's occupational and personal schemes for about 35 per cent. For example, in Italy the pattern was different, with 97 per cent public and 3 per cent private.[4]

Since private plans are funded in advance, they shift resources from working years to retirement years; capital market investments have thus become an important source of income for the old. According to a recent estimate, in the 1990s investment income – of which about half came from company pension funds – provided more than 40 per cent of the total income of those aged over 65, not only in the UK but also in the USA and Canada. The figure is higher for medium-high income brackets, where such income serves to top-up the state pension, the basic source of financial security. In continental Europe, by contrast, investment income is a small component even for those with high incomes.[5]

The large disbursements of pension benefits by the private sector are matched by the assets accumulated by households with pension funds and insurance companies. Between 1990 and 2005 these assets grew by a factor of 3.5, rising from 1.5 to 2.5 times households' disposable income and from 44.5 per cent to 54 per cent of their total financial assets. Figure 3.3 also shows the pronounced fall in the value of these assets after the share market bubble burst in 1999.

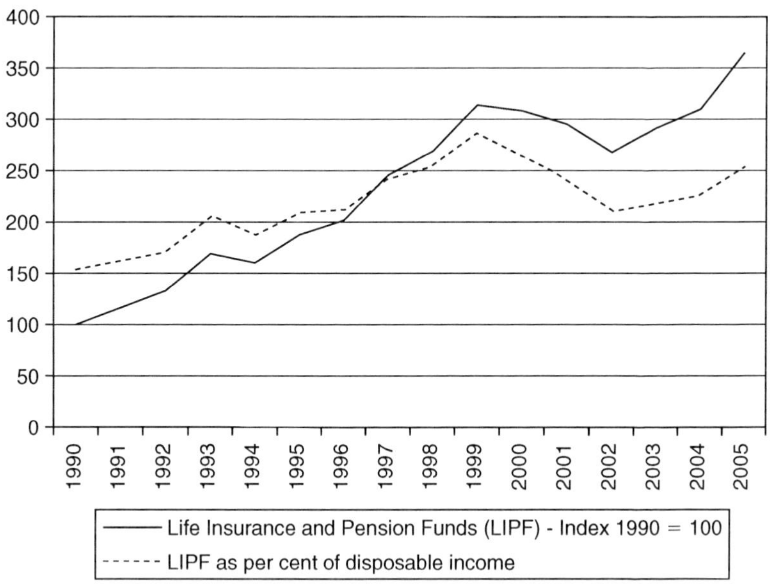

Source: Based on National Statistics data.

Figure 3.3 Households' financial assets in life insurance and pension funds

The investment of this enormous volume of financial resources stimulated the development of the activities needed for their management. The search for yields able to cover long-term financial liabilities undergoing rapid expansion, both now and in the future, led to investment in innovative asset classes and in particular strengthened the demand for financial products with very long maturities. Among other things, this encouraged several countries, including the United Kingdom and France, to issue 50-year Treasury bonds.

More generally, new issues came to the fore regarding financial stability and transparency. To some extent, the growth of private pension schemes did not solve the macroeconomic problem of the imbalances in the pension system, but transferred it from the public sector to the private sector.

3.2 The revision of the pension system

It is in this context that at the beginning of this century the need for a radical revision of the pension system emerged clearly and led to the creation of a Pensions Commission in 2002 and to new legislation on the occupational pension schemes. The main factors that generated this need were:

- the rapid ageing of the population, which increases the demands on state pay-as-you-go systems such as that of the United Kingdom, precisely when economic policy is calling for smaller government with less taxes. The old-age dependency ratio is rising as a consequence of the increase in life expectancy;
- a macroeconomic environment characterized by growing competition and globalization, creating problems for firms' financial stability and thus for their occupational pension schemes. Moreover, in recent years the instability of financial markets, especially share markets, has decreased the value of pension funds, thereby creating or aggravating their deficits. The phasing-out of the dividend tax credit for pension funds, introduced by the Labour government in 1997 in a period of a booming stock market, has contributed to the decline of the pension funds value, according to many observers. In addition, new accounting standards (FRS17) have led to an increase in the present value of future pension liabilities reported in company accounts. This situation has increasingly led to firms closing defined-benefit schemes and replacing them with defined-contribution schemes, which obviously lower the pensions payable to retirees. The attractiveness of such

advance-funded schemes has naturally had to take account of these developments;

- it has proved hard to go down the path of personal pension schemes sold by insurance companies using products that are difficult for users to understand. Partly owing to their complexity and partly as a consequence of inappropriate and fraudulent selling practices, on several occasions these products have caused savers to incur substantial losses. Several employees contracted-out of the Second State Pension, or moved their holdings from occupation to personal schemes, but their performance has been worse than the schemes' they had left. The crisis of the insurance company Equitable Life has been a case in point, as an example of poor risk management.

Occupational and personal supplementary retirement provision, which continues to constitute one of the pillars of the pension system, has thus suffered from problems related to market confidence and consumer protection and awareness. The phenomenon of mis-selling has undoubtedly contributed to the general reform of financial supervision. 'The state plans to provide decreasing support for many people in order to control expenditure in the face of an ageing population and the private system is not developing to offset the state's retreating role. Instead it is in significant decline.'[6]

The complex issue of pension provisioning has been addressed by the Labour government in two main ways: in regard to the private schemes, with a new legislation on occupational schemes, while the need for a state pension system reform led to the creation of an *ad hoc* Pensions Commission, chaired by Adair Turner.

The Pension Act 2004 introduced a new regulator, The Pension Regulator (TPR), taking the functions of the previous Occupation Pensions Regulatory Authority (OPRA) and entrusted it with a more extensive range of powers. The main objectives of TPR are the protection of private schemes, the promoting of a better understanding of these schemes (consumer awareness), the mitigation of risks which may lead to payment of compensation by the Pension Protection Fund (PPF).

The PPF, created by the same Act, pays compensation – within certain limits – to pensioners of a defined-benefit scheme, when their pension fund is unable to meet its obligations. The PPF is funded by the pension funds themselves, through levies which are risk-based: their amount depends on the size of the pension fund deficit and the likelihood that the fund becomes insolvent. The levy climbs in line with the level of risk, but weaker funds have a cap, in percentage of their liability. No risk factor is in the levy, as related to the investment risk run by the pension fund on its investments. In fact, the PPF is in itself an investor in the financial markets (in 2006 it became a shareholder in a company whose pension liabilities had been placed in the PPF). According to the Act, every scheme has a 'statutory' funding objective, in terms of sufficient and appropriate assets to cover, on an actuarial basis, its liabilities.

The Act has been criticized since its inception. A moral hazard risk, by employers that, counting on this safety net, might not manage their pension fund appropriately, has been mentioned. The risk-based levies and limits to compensation should however contain this moral hazard, together with the supervisory powers granted to TPR. In addition, the fear has been raised that, in case of extensive pension fund crisis, the PPF itself could be depleted and – even in a 'private' safety net arrangement as the one envisaged by the Act – a 'government' bail-out might follow for systemic reasons.

These fears have been eased by the turnaround of pension funds from huge deficits, coming from a rising stock market, cash transfers by companies to plug deficits, raising contributions from employers and employees, better management of the funds investments. The Act has also created a new special tribunal, the Pension Regulator Tribunal, which may confirm, vary or revoke the Regulator's determinations and a PPF Ombudsman, as distinct from the Financial Ombudsman[7] (see Chapter 8).

The problem of the occupational schemes is compounded by the government involvement in their regulation. In 2006 the Parliamentary Ombudsman found the government guilty of maladministration of the occupational schemes regulation and in 2007 a High Court confirmed that the government had to pay the workers damaged by the insolvency of their schemes.

As regards the state pensions, the Pensions Commission put bluntly forward four options: the impoverishment of pensioners compared with the rest of society; an increase in the National Insurance burden; an increase in the savings rate; and an increase in the retirement age. The solution it proposed was a mixture of the last three options.

The Commission[8] took the view that the English state pension system did not run the risk of an immediate crisis (as indicated above, there is not an imbalance in National Insurance pension provision) but that there could be a crisis in the future owing to an inadequate savings rate, a worsening of the demographic problem and insufficient private retirement provision. The Commission proposed that the public pension system should be simplified and strengthened, partly by indexing pensions to earnings instead of prices, and that the retirement age should be raised in the long term, and taxation increased. Overall the Commission forecasted an increase in state pension expenditure under its proposed reform to 7.5–8 per cent in the third decade of the century, depending on whether the retirement age gradually rises to 67 or 69 in 2050.[9] The most innovative aspect of its proposals was the creation of a National Pensions Savings Scheme (NPSS).

The idea of the NPSS was in response to the evidence that the state system, even if reformed as above, was not sufficient and that only some workers will enjoy adequate private pension provision. Turner remarked that the percentage of private sector workers with no private pension provision in addition to that provided by the state had grown from 44 per cent 56 per cent in 2004.

The NPSS is based on the idea that additional savings to finance pensions cannot be compulsory, which would be too much like a tax, but can nonetheless benefit from incentives for interested workers; employee and employer contributions would be invested in the financial markets, with low fees, within a single national scheme which purchases fund management services at wholesale level, and invests each individual's account according to his choices. This was a most controversial point of the Turner Report, because it involves critical choices, both of asset managers and of asset allocation.

The Report was followed by two government White Papers,[10] and the Pensions Act 2007 has put into law the reforms set out in the first of them. This law links cost of living increases in the Basic State Pension with earnings rather than prices, and gradually raises the state pension age to 68 for both men and women between 2024 and 2046, so making the state pension system more affordable in connection with the increased longevity of the population, along Turner's proposals. The second White Paper, devoted to the above mentioned personal accounts, has a follow-up in another Pensions Bill, announced by the government in July 2007.

4

The Configuration of the Banking System in the Last 15 Years

Before going on to describe the structure and the performance of the banking industry in the last fifteen years or so, four considerations are necessary.

The legislative reforms described in Chapter 1, and in particularly the Building Societies Act of 1986, which allowed for the demutualization of the building societies, underpins the evolution of the banking system's configuration in the period here considered. These changes took place predominantly in the 1990s and the early 2000s in large part through greater contestability and the search for economies of scale.

The second consideration concerns the peculiarity of the City: in the course of the 1990s and the first few years of the present decade, we have witnessed, on the one hand, the completion of the process of consolidation in the domestic market, and on the other, the strengthening of the City as a principal market in the international financial and banking system, thanks to the great increase in both stock market and OTC transactions.

The third point is that the banking system in the United Kingdom is characterized by the presence of two distinct market configurations in which, at times, the same intermediaries operate: on one side, the retail market, aimed generally toward domestic activity (credit to households and to small and medium sized enterprises, often belonging to the real estate and services sectors); on the other, the wholesale market, with an offer of more complex products – from corporate finance to securities intermediation in the primary and secondary market, as broker/dealers, to advising on corporate transactions – where competition among intermediaries is fierce, and where customers are mostly international.

Finally, this marketplace is characterized by a great openness, with the presence of numerous foreign banks (both branches and subsidiaries) operating in large part in the City of London. In this regard, the breakdown of assets held by British banks versus those held by foreign-controlled banks is significant: more than 50 per cent of the total bank assets refers to foreign banks. This represents a slight decline with respect to the maximum levels of more than 60 per cent reached at the beginning of the 1990s but is still quite relevant.

4.1 The banking system: structure, conduct, performance

The consolidation under way in the British banking system is evident in the evolution over time of the number of banks present in the United Kingdom (Table 4.1). There has been a progressive reduction in both the number of UK incorporated banks (from 289 in 1990 to 157 in 2007) and the number of branches of foreign banks (from 259 to 169 in the same period). Other significant trends emerge, however: the decline in UK incorporated banks concerns only banks that are British owned or controlled (from 209 to 72). Furthermore, among the foreign banks, European ones now surpass non-European.

Although the demutualization of building societies happened in 1986, it was only in the following decade that a reciprocal 'field invasion' between banks and building societies was truly witnessed. This increased market competition, which had previously been dominated by the 'Big Four' (Barclays Bank, Lloyds Bank, Midland Bank and National Westminster Bank). A process of consolidation took place mainly

Table 4.1 Number of banks in the UK

	1990	*1995*	*2000*	*2005*	*2007*
Banks with headquarters in the United Kingdom (UK incorporated) (1) *of which:*	289	224	189	165	157
– UK owned	209	142	112	78	72
– foreign-owned (a)	80	82	77	87	85
Banks with headquarters abroad (non-UK incorporated) (2) *of which:*	259	257	242	177	169
– UK branches of an European Economic Area (EEA) firm (b)	–	102	115	95	90
– branches of banks outside the EEA (c)	–	155	127	82	79
UK service of an EEA firm	–	–	–	–	5
Total banks (1 + 2)	548	481	431	342	331
Total foreign banks phisically located in the UK (a + b + c)	339	339	319	264	254

Source: International Financial Services London (IFSL), *Banking*, City Business Series.

through non-hostile operations concerning to a large degree domestic banks.[1]

After the demutualization of Abbey National, which took place in 1989, various building societies became banks. Among these: Cheltenham & Gloucester, in 1995 (later acquired by Lloyds); Halifax, Northern Rock, Alliance & Leicester, Woolwich, all in 1997 (the latter acquired by Barclays in 2000). Bradford and Bingley was demutualized in 2000.[2]

As in other countries, the process of consolidation happened gradually. In 1992, Hong Kong and Shanghai Banking Corporation – HSBC acquired Midland Bank, becoming a British bank. Later, various building societies were consolidated amongst themselves, for example, Halifax with Leeds Permanent Building Societies (1995), or with medium-large banks, like Lloyds with TSB (1995). Royal Bank of Scotland with National Westminster merged in 2000, while Halifax and the Bank of Scotland in 2001. Table 4.2 shows both market shares and concentration ratio of major UK banks (December 2007).

With the process of consolidation well underway, an important cross-border operation took place with the acquisition, in 2004, of Abbey (known as Abbey National before 2003) by a Spanish banking group, Banco Santander.[3] Other small banks sold to foreign banks are Clydesdale Bank and Yorkshire Bank (both acquired by National Australia Bank) and Bristol & West Building Society (acquired by the Bank of Ireland).

Some operations were 'cross-sector', such as, for example, the acquisition by Lloyds–TSB Bank of the life insurance Scottish Widows, or the acquisition by Abbey National of Scottish Mutual and Scottish Provident. The takeover in 2007 of the Dutch bank ABN Ambro through an international consortium of the Royal Bank of Scotland, Fortis and Banco Santander is another important operation.

In general, the process of consolidation is not considered to have brought about an increase in market power, since at the same time there was an increase in contestability[4] in the banking sector, connected with the abolishment of the barriers between banks and building societies.[5] This could explain the decline in the profit margin relative to the activity of banking intermediation. Particularly, the net interest income as a percentage of total assets decreased from about 3 per cent to the current 1 per cent (Table 4.3).[6] This would emerge also from a comparison of the interest margin in the domestic and by the same banking groups in foreign markets: against the relative stability of margins in foreign markets, subject to international competition, we see a structural reduction in profitability in the domestic market (Figure 4.1).[7]

Table 4.2 Concentration of the banking market*

Total major banking groups	*Millions of sterling*		*Market share***	
	deposits	*loans*	*deposits*	*loans*
The Royal Bank of Scotland	682365	829250	38.3	35.3
Halifax – Bank of Scotland (HBOS)	243221	430007	13.7	18.3
Barclays	294987	345398	16.6	14.7
HSBC Bank	268269	227687	15.1	9.7
Lloyds TSB	156555	209814	8.8	8.9
Abbey National	69650	112147	3.9	4.8
Northern Rock	11563	98835	0.6	4.2
Alliance & Leicester	30758	53147	1.7	2.3
Bradford & Bingley	24153	40445	1.4	1.7
Total major banking group	1781521	2346730	100	100

Data refers to loans & advances to customers and customers deposits (so excluding the interbank market).

*Indices of concentration***	*deposits*	*loans*
Market share of the top 3 banks	68.5	68.4
Market share of the top 5 banks	92.4	87.0
Market share of the top 7 banks	96.9	96.0
Herfindahl–Hirschman index	0.18	0.17

Notes:
* Data refer to December 2007.
** % calculated over major banking groups: consolidated worldwide group operations, IFRS basis. Indices of concentration are purely indicative because they do not refer to the domestic market and include only major banking groups.
Source: Authors' calculations on British Bankers' Association data, 'Banking Business. The Annual Abstract of Banking Statistics', 2007.

As in other countries, banks tried to limit the effects of the competitive pressure in the sector of credit intermediation by moving toward types of activities less elastic to the price factor, such as, for example, the asset management. The breakdown of gross income into two components, 'interest income' and 'other income', therefore tipped in favor of the latter. At the beginning of the 1990s, the 'other income' covered 40 per cent of total income, versus 27 per cent at the beginning of the previous decade. In 2005 this percentage reached 57.6 per cent.[8] The contribution of the traditional credit intermediation activity to the composition of banks' income decreased greatly compared to the contribution generated by other activities, such as fees generated by the securitization of loans.

Table 4.3 Annual Abstract of Banking Statistics: Major Banking Groups in the UK

	UK branches	*No. of staff**	*Net interest income*	*Ratios as a % of average balance sheet assets*					
				Non-interest income (net)	*Gross income*	*Operating expenses*	*Net income*	*Impairment & other provisions (net)***	*Profit after tax*
			A	*B*	*C = A + B*	*D*	*C − D*		
1987	15915	465.5	3.1	1.8	4.9	3.2	1.8	1.5	0.1
1988	15775	497.3	3.3	1.8	5.1	3.3	1.8	0.3	0.9
1989	15495	502.0	3.1	1.9	5.0	3.3	1.8	1.6	0.1
1990	14942	521.2	2.9	1.9	4.8	3.2	1.6	0.9	0.4
1991	14125	509.5	2.9	2.0	4.9	3.2	1.6	1.3	0.2
1992	13463	508.2	2.6	1.9	4.5	3.0	1.5	1.2	0.1
1993	14362	489.8	2.5	2.0	4.5	2.9	1.7	0.9	0.5
1994	13950	286.9	2.4	1.8	4.3	2.7	1.5	0.3	0.8
1995	13621	279.3	2.4	1.8	4.2	2.7	1.5	0.3	0.8
1996	12793	274.0	2.3	1.5	3.8	2.3	1.4	0.2	0.8
1997	12200	320.7	2.2	1.4	3.6	2.2	1.4	0.2	0.8
1998	11846	312.6	2.2	1.4	3.6	2.0	1.6	0.3	0.9
1999	11497	322.9	2.2	1.5	3.7	2.0	1.7	0.2	1.0
2000	11026	307.3	2.0	1.5	3.5	2.0	1.6	0.2	0.9
2001	10875	321.2	1.9	1.5	3.4	2.0	1.4	0.3	0.8
2002	10754	322.8	1.7	1.3	3.0	1.9	1.1	0.3	0.5
2003	10600	327.4	1.6	1.5	3.1	1.8	1.3	0.3	0.7
2004	10388	330.7	1.2	1.6	2.8	1.8	1.0	0.2	0.6
2005	10232	325.7	1.1	1.6	2.7	1.6	1.0	0.2	0.6
2006	10052	317.1	1.1	1.6	2.7	1.5	1.1	0.2	0.6
2007	9696	315.2	0.8	1.1	1.9	1.1	0.8	0.2	0.5

Notes: Figures may be affected by changes in the sample.
Excluding long-term assurance funds before 2004.
IFRS were adopted for end-2005. For comparative purposes, 2004 accounts were re-stated on a pro-forma IFRS basis.
* Figures include staff of certain subsidiaries and are for Great Britain only.
** Prior to 2004, specific and general provisions as defined by the UK GAAP.
Source: British Bankers' Association, *Banking Business. Annual Abstract of Banking Statistics*, various years.

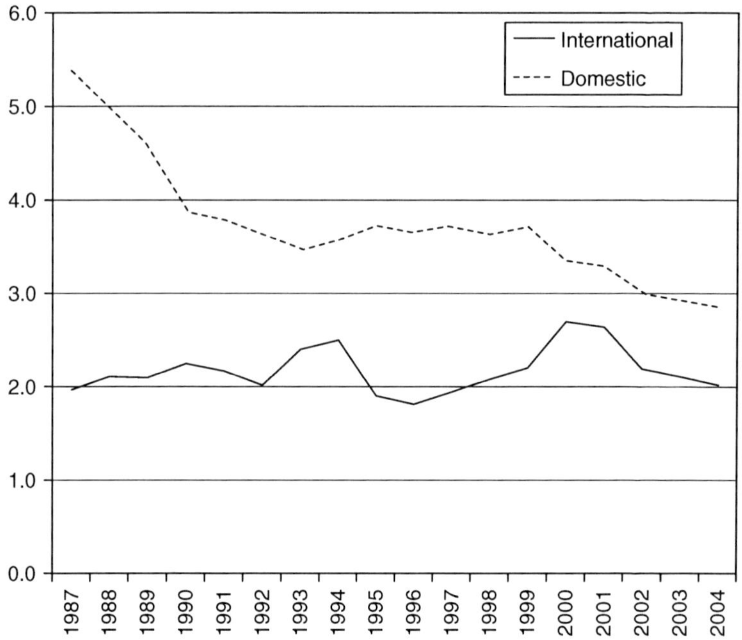

Source: British Bankers' Association data.
Figure 4.1 Net interest margin as percentage of average interest-earning assets in the domestic and foreign markets (*weighted average of the four principal banks in the United Kingdom*)

Non-interest income reached about 2 per cent in the early 1990s (again Table 4.3). After that, the greater competition witnessed in this type of operations, too, led to a reduction in the margins from services, which remained, since the end of the last decade, along the lines of 1.5 per cent. As a consequence, gross income as a percentage of total assets decreased in the course of the 1990s, from about 5 per cent to 2 per cent. It was necessary to act on the cost side, by containing labour costs, further reducing the number of branches, and implementing other cost-cutting strategies, among which the consolidations described above, aimed at attaining economies of scale.

The incidence of labour costs, calculated as a proportion of gross income and equal to about 35 per cent in the mid-1980s (already much reduced compared to 46 per cent in the early 1980s), was below 25 per cent in 2005. This contributed to reduce operating expenditures, again as a proportion of total assets, from about 3 per cent at the beginning of the 1990s to around 1 per cent in 2007 (Table 4.3). This also happened, as mentioned above, through the closing of a large number of branches (from about 15,000 at the beginning of the last decade to the current 9,700, approximately). It can be said in this case that the competitiveness pressures 'hit the mark and more': there was in fact the problem of the low competitive tenor in some market segments, not to mention the 'desertification' of banking service offerings in some areas of the country, made up for, in part, with banking services offered by the postal network.

To conclude, the blurring between banks and building societies reshaped the configuration of the banking market in the United Kingdom. What ensued was a system both more concentrated and more competitive, in which the differences between intermediaries disappeared. Increased competitiveness brought about an erosion in interest margins; banks found themselves forced to turn to other sources of revenue and to increase their operating efficiency through policies to contain and cut costs, and through mergers and acquisitions. The branch network and operating costs were gradually reduced. The cost reduction made it possible to maintain the overall profitability of banking enterprises. Even so, as we will see extensively in the next section, in some market segments and in some geographical areas problems arose of excessive market power, to the detriment mainly of households and small and medium sized enterprises.

4.2 Steps to strengthen competition in the domestic market

As we have already mentioned, one of the strategies adopted by banks in response to the increased competitive tenor has been to seek economies of scale through the processes of aggregation. This creates in certain environments, particularly retail banking, signs of excessive market power. For this reason, in 1998 the Treasury promoted an independent evaluation to determine if there were elements warranting investigation by the Competition Commission.[9]

The evaluation, which concluded with the publication in March 2000 of a Report (the so-called 'Banking Review' or 'Cruickshank Report', after the name of the author, Don Cruickshank), analyzed competition in the retail sector (expressely excluding investment banking) in three specific contexts: (1) money transmission through the payment system; (2) banking services offered to consumers; and (3) financing conditions of small and medium-sized enterprises (SMEs).[10]

On the first point, the Report revealed that unregulated payment networks were for the most part controlled by the same large banks that dominated the services markets for SMEs and consumers. In the sector of credit and debit cards, it emerged that three financial institutions were controlling 85 per cent of the market. The Report noted that this structure bore elevated costs for retailers who accept credit cards, and high costs for some services, such as cash withdrawals from automatic tellers, equal to even as much as six times the cost of production.[11] The Report recommended, in this regard, the creation of a new regulator, the PayCom, independent of competition authorities[12].

Regarding the second aspect, the Report uncovered symptoms of low competition in the offering of banking services, in particular bank current accounts, home mortgages, and credit cards. In these sectors the concentration was deemed 'high' or 'rather high'.[13]

Lastly, as far as the offering of services for SMEs (enterprises with less than 250 employees or with sales revenue of less than £10 million), the market was even less competitive and very concentrated, especially at the local level. While in the sector of credit to households the Report noted an improving trend in terms of competition, in the sector of credit to SMEs the Report showed the presence of high entry barriers, such as the difficulty for potential entrants to obtain adequate information on the economic conditions of enterprises to finance. The Report therefore recognized the need for a formal investigation of the competitive situation in the banking services markets. The government, subscribing to this recommendation, handed the matter over to the Competition Commission (CC), which in 2000 launched a review, focusing however on only one of the three aspects mentioned above: banking services to SMEs. The related Report was produced in 2002.[14]

The Report is interesting in that, not only does it provide an analysis of the state of competition in broad sectors of domestic banking activity, but it also offers a representation of the *modus operandi* of the authority presiding over competition. The CC analysed the operations of 16 clearing banks[15] belonging to 12 banking groups. Only certain banking services were considered.[16] Then 'relevant markets' were determined for small and medium-sized enterprises (as defined by the business-volume criteria: less than 25 million).[17] It emerged from the investigation that in all the 'relevant markets', with the sole exception of certain types of loans ('other loans'), concentration was high, and in fact greater than the Herfindahl–Hirschman Index (HHI) safety limit of 0.18.

The concentration analysis was complemented by an analysis on restrictive and distortionary practices on the part of banks: numerous practices emerged that were reducing competition and restricting clients switching from one bank to another. Above all, the market appeared to be characterized by the presence of a number of entry barriers (thus confirming the evidence of the Cruickshank report) for potentially competing banks, such as: (1) the necessity on the part of potential entrants to acquire a vast network of branches; (2) difficulty in attaining those relevant skills arising from long-term relationships with clients; (3) the offering of free services to new enterprises ('start-ups'), a policy that potential entrants would be not be readily able to adopt; (4) scarce information available on the small and medium-sized enterprises compared to that possessed by banks already present in the market; and (5) the policies of negotiation or of extending the time necessary for switching to another bank.

Since the analysis of concentration and strategies was providing a number of elements to indicate the presence of possible monopolies, the CC made an estimate, if indirect, of the extra-profits. This estimate revealed that there existed a difference between actual prices and 'theoretical' prices, which are what would have been recorded in the presence of perfect competition. This gap materializes when the prices of the services considered (and consequently the return of capital) are significantly and stably higher than the cost of the capital proportionally utilized to offer these same services. The Commission estimated that the average return of capital in the period 1998–2000 was 36 per cent, versus a cost of capital of 15 per cent. On the basis of this evaluation, the CC introduced various 'adjustments' to take into account a series of factors, such as 'intangible assets' (costs of recruiting and training of personnel, costs of acquiring new clients, information technology costs, etc.), and the average long-term levels of non-performing loans and of the higher risk factor associated with small and medium-sized enterprises. For the four main clearing banks (Barclays Bank, HSBC Bank, Lloyds TSB Bank, and the Royal Bank of Scotland group) profits in excess of the cost of capital and appropriately 'adjusted' were, on average for the period 1998–2000, of 13.5 percentage points.[18]

Lastly, the CC was called on to verify if with reference to the banking services in question there had been any situations of 'scale monopoly', or of 'complex monopoly'[19] The analysis identified a 'scale monopoly' situation for the Royal Bank of Scotland group and two cases of 'complex monopoly'[20], though not such as to be considered prejudicial to the 'public interest'.[21]

The Commission considered two types of remedies: first, 'behavioural', with regard to eight clearing banks, in order to foster conditions of competition and of true choice on the part of the clientele, introducing more price transparency and facilitating the switching of accounts. Other measures, of a 'structural' kind, were also considered, such as the divesting of branches, or divestment of SMEs businesses to new clients, tax or licence fees on banks dealing with SMEs, but these were discarded in so far as they would not have, even while limiting extra-profits, fostered the entrance of new banks and/or improved the conditions practiced in small and medium-sized enterprises.[22] All the same, because it was clear that 'it was necessary to give the level of prices a decisive and significant shift towards what we consider to be the competitive levels',[23] the CC recommended a remedy concerning banking charges. It was thus suggested that the above mentioned four main banking groups would, for four years, have to remunerate business current accounts at a rate equal to at least the base rate of the Bank of England minus two-and-a-half points. Alternatively, banks could offer free money transmission services. The motivation behind this choice was the fact that a large part of the excessive prices came from the segment related to bank current account and demand-deposit account offerings.[24] These remedies were agreed by the Office of Fair Trading (OFT) with the banks in December 2002.[25] In December 2007, the Competition Commision decided to lift price controls, considered 'no longer necessary'. It however mainted in place the 'behavioural undertakings'.

While with reference to the Cruickshank proposal for a new regulator for the payment systems networks the government decided in 2005 not to proceed, a decision that angered Cruickshank,[26] the third context affected by Cruickshank, that of consumer banking services has been the subject of the Office of Fair Trading investigation. In this respect, we must remember that bank current accounts and related services (credit and debit cards, issuance of checkbooks, ATM access, phone and internet banking) are free or at a low cost. Banks, however, tend to apply very high fees in case of a customer default on his payments.

From a competition standpoint, the central issue is the possible abuse of market power; from a legal standpoint, the problem is focused on the applicability of the Unfair Terms in Consumer Contract Regulations (UTCCRs) to consumer banking.

In April 2006, the OFT stated that penalties imposed by credit card providers for failure to make required payments or for charges in excess of contractual agreement could not exceed a limited amount, considered to be fair in the light of a reasonable estimate of the management costs related to the customer default. In this decision, the OFT considered those charges as subject to the general test of fairness set out in the UTCCRs.[27]

The OFT wanted this statement as generally applicable to other analogous defaults charges in consumer contracts, including bank overdrafts, mortgages and store card agreements, that means beyond the specific case of credit cards, but the banks did not in fact adjust their penalties. This gave rise to a long series of complaints, particularly in reference to the fees for unauthorized checking overdrafts.

Banks, in fact, apply very high fees for these overdrafts. In particular, in addition to the debit interest rate, fees are charged that can range from about £20 to £40 per overdraft, regardless of the reason behind it (for example, a bad check or a direct debit without funds). The client can end up paying hundreds of pounds if in the course of a few days he or she conducts transactions hitting an account in the red. The reaction of the public was particularly strong, when it was noticed that in 2006 total gross profits for the nine principal banking groups in the United Kingdom amounted to about £32 billion with an increase of 16.4 per cent compared to 2005 and 52.3 per cent compared to the average for the period 2000–2005.[28]

The OFT started, in March 2007, an investigation into the fairnass of the level and application of unauthorized overdraft charges. But the investigation broadened soon into a market study because the OFT wanted to consider those charges in the wider context of other charges and any interest payments that are made for the bundle of services provided by the current accounts. The final aim of the market study would be to have well informed and active customers as drivers of bank competition, and a fair customer treatment by the banks.

In the meantime, tens of thousands of complaints flooded the OFT and the Financial Ombudsman Service (FOS) in respect to the unauthorized overdraft charges. In the fundamental disagreement between the OFT and the banks about the application of the unfairness rules of the UTCCRs, which would obviously lead to lower charges, the issue was brought in July 2007, as a test case, to the High Court of Justice, whose decision is expected in early 2008.[29] The market study of the OFT will be published after the test case hearing.

In this context, the FSA[30] conducted an investigation into the fees applied by banks for exiting a mortgage loan (mortgage exit administration fees). The FSA established that these fees cannot be higher than those set forth in the contract, unless the contract expressly provides for the discretion to increase said fees and the increase is justified by an increase in management costs for early exit.[31]

To conclude, the results of these investigations brought to light the fact that even a banking system traditionally open to international competition and innovation, such as that of the United Kingdom, can show areas in which market power is excessive. The authorities came to this conclusion by complementing the relevant traditional analysis based on market concentration with an analysis of potential entry-deterrent strategies or of oligopolistic behavior. Cases of oligopoly have been confirmed in some segments of the market, associated with the presence of extra-profits, and for this reason provisions have been introduced to promote more competitive pricing. Under the general policy framework related to competition, as we will see extensively in Chapter 10, we should highlight the more general attention being paid to the protection of competition and the safeguarding of consumers' welfare.

4.3 The foreign banks and the role of the City

Within the United Kingdom's banking system, there is a heterogeneous whole comprised of banking, financial, and insurance institutions, oriented in large part toward the international market and situated in a dense network of contacts and relationships. It is a sort of sub-system unto itself, with a configuration, dynamics and behaviours different from those of operators oriented toward retail for the domestic market. Thus, a banking group could find itself, at the same time, competing strenuously with large international banks and, on the home front, operating in a context where this situation does not fully materialize.

The configuration of the London marketplace is that of a 'financial district,' characterized by a high degree of competitiveness and an inclination for innovation. Within this 'district', there is equal room for British banks and foreign ones, which – in terms of total assets – occupy a space equal to about half of the overall total. The 'district' is reminiscent of Marshall-type industrial districts,[32] where competitive advantages come from 'environmental' economies of scale, from positive externalities, which all economic agents cultivate and to which they all have access. As underscored by Krugman, there is an important difference between traditional comparative advantages, where countries trade in order to take advantage of their differences in factor endowments or productivities, and the increasing returns approach, where countries trade because there are inherent advantages to specialization (in our case the positive externalities of the financial district).

This specialization advantage arises not only from the pool of highly specialized labor, but also from the increasing returns associated with a high volume of transactions, which guarantees the liquidity and, therefore, the efficiency, of the market. Both of these aspects contribute to cultivate a cumulative virtuous cycle that allows the system to maintain advantages of agglomeration even in the presence of high congestion costs.[33] All the same, differently from the industrial districts, we can observe a potentially more precarious equilibrium, in which important historical roots could lose value in a context where the results of technological innovation spread rapidly. The development, too, of integrated electronic platforms at the global level, based on a grid-like structure rather than a centralized one, could act in this direction. Furthermore, differently from traditional districts, London's is characterized by extreme mobility of qualified labor, drawn from the international market of experts in financial instruments. For this reason the competitive advantage is not necessarily 'enclosed' within the area, as in the traditional district, but rather could be dispersed, were it not constantly renewed. Thus the continuous inclination toward innovation.

The City, from the very initial phases of its development, has always drawn advantage from the regulatory imperfections and restrictions present in other places. In every district there is a specific, endogenous, economic factor, such that – in the presence of path-dependency – *history matters*. This factor seems to be comprised of both a regulatory context unlike that of competing financial marketplaces and a policy careful not to impede market development. At times deregulation has been necessary to protect its role, preserve its capacity to adapt, or re-launch its development in moments of decline.

A recent inquiry conducted among senior decision makers in the international financial services industry, about the key components of the competitive advantages in the banking sector, seems to confirm what we have said. It shows that the first three factors, in order of importance, are: availability of skilled personnel; regulatory environment; access to the international financial market. Other aspects, such as the quality and availability of commercial property, the culture, and the language were revealed to be much less important.[34]

Looking at the news from this financial marketplace, we see how the City has on various occasions feared losing its international supremacy. In reality, however, the force of attraction exerted by the economies of scale described above has always prevailed, as has the favorable regulatory and institutional context.

At the beginning of the 1990s it was feared that the deregulation in other important financial centers might re-shape the City's role. It was also feared that technological developments might make the presence of this marketplace less necessary. In 1991, in an article significantly entitled 'No longer a necessity', *The Banker* magazine concluded: 'In short, London may no longer be able to count on its traditional magnetism to pull growing numbers of foreign banks'.[35] These fears were not unfounded, since in an economic context characterized by low 'exit costs', it is easy for congestion costs (which in London are certainly high) to more than compensate for the 'positive externalities' of the district. Exogenous factors can also have very significant effects, as demonstrated by the re-shaping of the presence of Japanese banks in London, after the banking crisis in Japan that took place during those years.

In the second half of the 1990s, when the date was nearing for the start of the euro, fear spread in the City that the euro would move the center of gravity for financial activities toward continental Europe.[36] In fact, the start of the European currency did not affect the supremacy of the City; on the contrary, removing the exchange risk increased the opportunities of this financial marketplace, with the development of an integrated credit and debt market denominated in only one currency. It was necessary, in this case as well, to rapidly adapt to the new context, which, for example, saw a large drop in transactions in currency, both in cash and in volume terms, following the reduction of 11 currencies into just one.

In 2007 the number of foreign banks operating in the London marketplace was 254, down 85 from 1990, due to the process of consolidation in the banking sector that took place globally. There is no up-to-date data on the number employees of foreign banks. In 2004, according to an unofficial source, employment in this sector was at around 69,000 (of which 24,000 with American banks), 10,000 with Japanese, 7,000 with Swiss, 6,000 with French, and 3,000 with German banks.[37] Unofficial data from the Bank of England on the total assets of foreign banks allow us to make some considerations: particularly we note that the 'market share' of Japanese banks decreased drastically, from 34 per cent in 1990 to about 3 per cent in 2007. The data show, on the whole, an increase in European banks, particularly German – on the rise until 2002, but then in decline – Dutch, and, recently, Spanish. The asset share of American and Italian banks, on the other hand, decreased by about 3–4 percentage points. Nevertheless, we must point out that the aforementioned data do not take into account off-balance sheet positions, an even more important part of foreign-bank operations (Table 4.4). It is easy to note that the worforce does not always reflect the balance-sheet size.

Regarding investment banking, first we must note that the strong economies of scale led to a high level of concentration globally. Estimates are that at the international level the top five banks hold 38 per cent of the global investment banking market (2005 data).[38] The main source of revenue of investment banks comes from merger and acquisition advisory activity, which, again in 2005, generated 46 per cent of the fee

Table 4.4 Total assets of foreign banks in the United Kingdom (% share over the total of foreign banks in the UK)*

	*Other foreign banks***	*Italian*	*Dutch*	*French*	*German*	*Japanese*	*American*	*Spanish***	*Total*
1990	27.7	6.4	1.7	5.6	9.4	34.0	15.3	–	100
1991	28.4	6.7	1.7	5.5	10.2	31.6	15.7	–	100
1992	31.7	7.5	1.8	6.2	12.6	29.1	11.1	–	100
1993	29.1	7.1	1.6	7.7	15.6	26.6	12.3	–	100
1994	27.6	6.4	1.9	7.1	16.9	27.2	12.7	–	100
1995	27.4	5.1	2.6	6.4	21.4	24.2	12.9	–	100
1996	29.9	4.9	2.6	8.2	22.5	17.8	14.0	–	100
1997	32.5	4.5	3.3	7.9	21.0	15.7	15.0	–	100
1998	32.4	4.4	6.3	8.0	23.2	10.7	15.0	–	100
1999	32.9	4.2	7.0	8.7	26.2	7.8	13.1	–	100
2000	33.2	3.9	7.1	7.9	24.6	8.3	15.0	–	100
2001	31.4	3.4	7.3	8.7	25.8	8.4	15.0	–	100
2002	32.9	2.8	8.2	9.1	25.3	6.9	14.8	–	100
2003	39.0	2.2	8.3	9.3	23.3	5.5	11.9	0.5	100
2004	42.3	1.7	8.5	8.5	22.5	4.1	11.6	0.7	100
2005	40.1	1.3	8.9	8.0	20.8	4.0	11.1	5.8	100
2006	43.1	1.9	9.5	5.5	19.0	3.3	11.8	6.0	100
2007	42.8	1.8	10.2	6.4	18.6	3.0	12.0	5.1	100

Notes:
*Data refer to the second quarter.
**Before 2003, Spanish banks are included in Other foreign banks.
Source: Compiled from unpublished Bank of England data.

revenues of the sector, versus 34 per cent of the fixed income underwriting and 20 per cent of equity underwriting. The activity of merger and acquisition advising and of equity underwriting is highly cyclical, with significant fluctuations even from year to year. No British bank is present in the 'top ten' international investment banks. The presence of British banks has in fact decreased for some time, leaving room for American banks and a few big European groups. Even so, although the United Kingdom generates only a part of European investment banking fee revenues (27 per cent in 2005), about half of such activity is conducted in the London marketplace.[39]

4.4 Fund management and hedge funds

The British fund management market is in large part situated in London, though the marketplaces of Edinburgh and Glasgow are also well established. It is estimated that at the end-2005 the total funds under management in the UK was equal to £3.4 billion. (globally, around £30 billion). Institutional funds (mostly insurance funds and corporate pensions funds) accounted for almost 66 per cent of funds under management, retail fund (mostly unit trusts, investment trusts, open-ended investment companies) for 15 per cent. The residual percentage is made up of 'alternative funds' (hedge funds, private equity funds, property funds) and private client funds (funds managed by stockbrokers or private client departments of banks).

The main managers in Britain, at the end of 2004, were: Barclays Global Investors (about £48 billion of assets under management); Aviva (about 289), HCBC Holdings (261). Worldwide, Barclays Global Investors is ranked third, preceded by the Swiss bank UBS (£1085 billion) and by the German group Allianz (£801 billion). The UK has the second highest ratio of managed funds as a percentage of GDP (178 per cent), after the United States only (213), at end-2005.[40]

Both sectors, that of investment banking and of fund management, are characterized by the presence of very high fixed costs, especially in the areas of research and of development and engineering of complex financial instruments and electronic platforms for trading activities. In this context, only those enterprises that manage to take full advantage of economies of scale through large volumes of production survive. Therefore, this market too is dominated by a small number of global players.

The hedge fund industry has grown rapidly in recent years. Although there does not exist any universally accepted definition of a hedge fund, they are off-shore investment corporations (open-end investment firms) or on-shore investment limited partnerships. They manage asset pools and are characterized by the practice of short selling, the ample use of derivatives for investment purposes, a high level of leverage. Hedge funds follow different strategies or investment styles. Some of the major strategies fall into three categories: 'directional', which take positions based on market or securities trends (macro funds and long/short funds); 'event-driven', which seek to exploit mispricing caused by events related to specific firms; 'arbitrage' and 'statistical or quantitative' funds, which seek to exploit even small pricing inefficiencies between closely-related securities.[41] Although they are managed in the principal financial marketplaces, and sometimes quoted in stock markets, often they are domiciled in off-shore markets, for tax reasons.

It has been estimated that at the global level the assets managed by the hedge-funds industry have increased from about US$150 billion in 1996 to about US$1.5 trillion ten years later. In the same period, the number of funds tripled, reaching more than 9,000 units. London is the second largest global centre for hedge fund managers, with a global market share estimated at about 21 per cent, doubled with respect to just four years earlier. According to the International Financial Services London at end-2006, four-fifths of European hedge fund investments were managed in the UK. In that same year, the two largest UK hedge funds were Barclays Global Investors and Man Investment Limited, each with about US$19 billion under investments, as compared with more than US$34 billion of JP Morgan Asset Management and more than US$32 billion of Goldman Sachs Asset Management. Man Investment and HSBC are among the largest funds of hedge funds (with, respectively, US$35 billion and US$20 billion under management).[42]

London's predominance in the hedge funds sector at the European level derives above all from the presence of specific professional features, such as closeness to institutional investors, a solid industry of fund management, and a favorable regulatory environment.

In the UK law, there is no definition – either statutory or regulatory – of hedge funds. They are included within the 'unregulated' collective investment schemes. Although they are generally off-shore, the fund manager is located in Britain and is therefore subject to authorization and regulation by the FSA. Under Section 238 (6) of the FSMA, hedge funds, as unregulated schemes, can be promoted only to institutional investors and high net-worth individuals. Recently, however, the FSA has taken steps to open hedge funds to the retail market, through funds of hedge funds: they would be UK regulated funds, that invest in 'alternative investments' (not only in hedge funds), with certain limits aimed at a better consumer protection.[43]

The relationship between hedge funds and banks is very close: the latter (investment banks, or prime brokers) offer settlement services, clearing, risk management, and lending (including securities lending for financing leveraged positions of hedge funds). Big hedge funds tend to conduct some of these activities for themselves, internally.

As to the stability aspects, the FSA maintains, along a widespread opinion, that hedge funds play an important role in increasing market efficiency and liquidity. Still, certain aspects should be monitored, such as adequacy of risk management, both by prime brokers, especially in the presence of high counterparty leverage, and by hedge funds, and the valuation process of illiquid assets, as well as the size of the 'side pockets'. Among the various aspects potentially critical from a surveillance point of view are the liquidity risks connected with the closing of positions following similar investment strategies; operational risks, especially with regard to delays in confirmations; insider trading problems (early exploitation of market events); and market manipulation in cases where the size of the fund is relevant.[44] However, no direct supervision is deemed necessary. Instead, the regime adopted by the FSA is essentially based on indirect supervision through the prime broker, and industry's self-regulation.

On the first aspect the attention has been focused on prime brokers (investment banks) that provide technical and financial support. The FSA approach is based on the belief that information about the prime brokers' exposure to their hedge fund manager client is the most useful and efficient. In order to attain this, the FSA carries out surveys every six months of large dealers' exposures to hedge funds of about 15 institutions.[45] The survey makes it possible to identify the credit exposure to hedge funds and to examine the relationship between prime brokers and hedge fund managers. It also makes it possible to assess factors such as net equity, long/short market value, and excess collateral. This helps the FSA to gauge the risk appetite of both hedge funds and prime brokers.

A technical aspect, whose weight will emerge more clearly in the Chapter 6, is that the prime broker assesses hedge fund exposure on a daily basis in order to calculate initial and variation margins, and monitors the mark-to-market valuation changes and assesses risk exposure by applying stress-testing. However this can only be done in accordance with the prime broker's position; but the prime broker cannot observe the same hedge fund's exposure to other brokers, which means that the capacity to assess the fund's concentration risk across the entire portfolio is limited. Both the FSA and the industry are seeking to improve risk management and practices of disclosure and margining, in order to implement and broaden best practices.

In addition, the FSA has put forth various initiatives regarding hedge funds themselves. For the major – around 35 – hedge funds it has created a relationship management team, that keeps a frequent contact with them, including informal meetings; review of stress-testing techniques; thematic projects are developed for the rest of the industry, considered as low-impact from a stability point of view.

There is much debate as to the level of information and transparency to require from market players (hedge funds and prime brokers). On these aspects the Chairman of the FSA has considered that there are various areas where transparency should be improved.[46] In particular, concerning transparency for investors, he underscored, among other things, the difficulties of valuing positions in illiquid assets or markets, which could lead to valuation errors to the detriment of the investor and, in extreme cases, to fraud resulting from deliberately misleading valuations. Policies and procedures such as the separation of duties between portfolio managers and offices, and a better reconciliation of value between the fund manager, the prime broker, and the administration, are essential.

Finally, on transparency to the public, the FSA has a very strong position, namely that the hedge fund should not disclose proprietary information: 'The FSA is strongly opposed to the general requirement for hedge fund (or other asset managers or proprietary traders) to disclose positions, either to regulators or to the general public'.[47] Not only it would it be difficult to use such information for regulatory purposes, but also, disclosing it to the public could 'prove damaging rather than supportive of financial stability'.[48]

Recently, a working group chaired by a former Deputy governor of the Bank of England, Andrew Large, has been established by the industry itself, in order to explore five areas of concern, regarding disclosure, valuation, risk, governance, and activism in companies where hedge funds have a stake. The results, to be released in 2008, would bring to a code of best practice standards for the industry.[49]

4.5 Private equity

In the UK, private equity has been unofficially defined as a firm authorized by the FSA, as a collective investment scheme, that manages, or advises, funds which own, or control, one or more British companies.[50] The funds are generally structured as limited partnerships, basically for tax reasons.

The UK private equity sector is the largest in Europe, and second only to that of United States, both in terms of number of transactions and of equity invested. In 2004, the sector's equity was above 1.1 per cent of British GDP, much higher than the European average of 0.35 per cent.[51] The compound annual rate of growth in the decade ending in 2005 was 20 per cent. Table 4.5 shows current trends of the three categories, by stage, into which the sector is empirically divided: early stage, expansion, buy-outs.

A more comprehensive estimate of this sector can be found in the amount and provenance of the 'committed' (or 'raised') funds[52]. A large proportion of committed capital comes from foreign countries, 79 per cent in 2005. Increasingly, institutional investors (pension funds, insurance companies, funds-of-funds) are investors in the sector, as shown in Table 4.6.

The private equity sector is greatly affecting the listing of companies. The last few years have seen an increase of the relative weight of capital invested in the sector, *vis-à-vis* the amount raised through Initial Public Offerings (IPOs) at the London Stock Exchange. In 2004, the figures were respectively £9.7 billion and £16.1 billion, but in the first half of 2006 these figures were 11.2, *vis-à-vis* £10.4 billion.

These trends raise important issues in term of efficiency of the public market (reduction of liquidity, 'discovery' of the right price of the target companies as compared with the exchange's price), even if the London market appear to be deep and broad enough to sustain an increasing de-listing; of corporate governance (efficiency of a closely held company, where agency problems typical of a public company are less deeply felt, but where transparency is equally less, for example in terms of ownership and corporate accounts); and of financial stability.

This issue is linked to the high leverage of buy-out transactions; for top deals, around 97 per cent is debt-financed. Sharp increases in interest rates or, in general, the repricing of risk, can make these transactions particularly vulnerable. The banks' exposure to private equity funds is often parcellized and sold to other intermediaries, such as hedge funds or collateralized loan obligation managers, but the total risk may increase if banks, encouraged by the possibility of selling their exposure, lower their standards of lending and if – in difficult market conditions – banks cannot unload their exposure to investors.[53]

The issues of corporate governance have been tackled by a Working Group that has been created by some private equity firms and the trade body, the British Venture Capital Association, under the chairmanship of David Walker, following a pattern similar to the initiative, mentioned

Table 4.5 Private equity in the UK (£m)

	Early stage			*Expansion*			*Buy-outs*			*Total*		
	UK	*Overseas*	*Total*	*UK*	*Overseas*	*Total*	*UK*	*Overseas*	*Total*	*UK*	*Overseas*	*Total*
1997	159	31	190	907	345	1252	2000	742	2742	3066	1118	4184
1998	288	118	406	822	249	1071	2665	777	3442	3775	1144	4919
1999	347	117	464	1156	377	1533	4666	1184	5850	6169	1678	7847
2000	703	385	1088	2122	802	2924	3546	698	4244	6371	1885	8256
2001	390	141	531	1636	615	2251	2726	656	3382	4752	1412	6164
2002	295	109	404	1374	237	1611	2811	640	3451	4480	986	5466
2003	263	100	363	867	591	1458	2944	1592	4536	4074	2283	6357
2004	284	178	462	954	770	1724	4098	3395	7493	5336	4343	9679
2005	382	95	477	1951	1053	3004	4480	3715	8195	6813	4863	11676
2006	946	380	1326	2994	3602	6596	10198	7644	17842	14138	11626	25764
2007	434	249	683	3817	4615	8432	13047	114798	127845	17298	119662	136960

Source: BVCA, *Report on Investment Activity*, various years

Table 4.6 UK private equity funds raised by source

		(£m)			*as a % on grand total*		
		2003	*2004*	*2005*	*2003*	*2004*	*2005*
Pension funds	UK	781	359	1,502	9	11	5
	overseas	2,080	512	7,175	23	15	26
	total	2,861	871	8,677	32	26	31
Insurance companies	UK	208	74	558	2	2	2
	overseas	513	148	3,136	6	5	12
	total	721	222	3,694	8	7	14
Corporate investors	UK	30	72	423	–	2	2
	overseas	138	119	928	2	4	3
	total	168	191	1,351	2	6	5
Banks	UK	473	108	822	5	4	3
	overseas	676	373	854	8	11	3
	total	1,149	481	1,676	13	15	6
Funds of funds	UK	1,054	98	1,131	12	3	4
	overseas	925	497	3,244	10	15	12
	total	1,979	595	4,375	22	18	16
Government agencies	UK	47	95	517	1	3	2
	overseas	1,163	75	3,196	13	2	12
	total	1,210	170	3,713	14	5	14
Academic institutions	UK	32	5	65	–	–	–
	overseas	180	96	1,279	2	3	5
	total	212	101	1,344	2	3	5
Private individuals	UK	67	220	562	1	7	2
	overseas	75	78	1,019	1	2	4
	total	142	298	1,581	2	9	6
Other sources	UK	117	79	292	1	2	1
	overseas	330	291	611	4	9	2
	total	447	370	903	5	11	3
Total from UK sources		2,809	1,110	5,872	32	34	21
Total from overseas sources		6,080	2,189	21,442	68	66	79
Grand total		8,889	3,299	27,314	100	100	100

Source: BVCA, Report on investment activity, 2005.

earlier, by the hedge funds sector. These initiatives have been largely driven by concerns, by the authorities and the public opinion in general[54], about the increasing role of these funds in the UK economy and the potential risks they may pose to corporate governance, financial stability, market integrity, consumer protection. In fact, the initiatives are taken also to prevent primary legislation or regulatory action by establishing codes of self-regulation.

The code, in the case of private equity, has been released in November 2007 and is based on a larger disclosure, both by the 'portfolio company', i.e. the company owned or controlled by the private equity firm, and by the firm itself[55]. The ensuing guidelines for the industry have already been a target of criticism, both from the many observers, as inadequate to promote transparency, and by the industry itself, that may feel now a competitive disadvantage *vis-à-vis* investors that operate in the same way, but would not be subject to the code not being private equity firms (like Sovereign Wealth Funds or wealthy private individuals).

5
The Stability of the British Banking Sector

This chapter is divided into two sections, the first deals with a short survey of the main banking crises in Britain completing the information already given in Chapter 1 (related to the crises of the 1970s and 1980s) with an illustration of the crises that occurred in the 1990s, mainly the small banks crisis of the early 1990s – the Bank of Credit and Commerce International (BCCI) and the Barings bankruptcies of 1991 and 1995, respectively.

We observed that short-term lending, the geographical diversification connected to their large size, and the cartelization of the system are important factors in explaining the stable performance of the banks, but possibly at the expense of an underlending to the industry. We are not emphasizing the supervisory role of the Bank of England, which was due mainly to a kind of protective duty towards the banking system, whose smooth functioning was deemed to be essential for the working of the money market.

We also note that the seeds of competition and increasing international presence created a more dynamic, if less stable market, in the early 1970s. On the whole, five banking crises can be detected between the 1970s and the 1990s: two with a strong domestic component and both related to the mortgage market and to money market funding; three having an international dimension.

All these episodes did not greatly affect the public purse (as crises in other countries did). The protection schemes, funded by the financial industry – the Deposit Protection Scheme that started in 1982, and the subsequent Financial Services Compensation Scheme (FSCS), that started in 2001 – suffered a not excessive net cost for bank failures, taking into account recoveries from the liquidation procedures.

The second section is devoted to the approaches presently followed by the British authorities, the FSA and the Bank of England, in monitoring the stability of individual banks and of the system as a whole: prudential indicators, market-based indicators and stress-testing. The first indicator of financial soundness seems to point to a comparative advantage of British banks on an international basis, probably due, at least in part, to the size of the banks, permittings relevant economies of scale. The second, the Credit Default Swap (CDS) indicator, shows a strong correlation among large international banks. The third methodology, still under consideration, offers a useful device to assess the resilience of the system.

5.1 A long-run perspective

It is widely believed that the British banking system has traditionally been relatively stable. Even the crisis that led to the Great Depression in 1931 affected it only slightly in comparison with the experiences of other industrial countries. One important factor concerning the stability may have been that the bulk of the deposit banks' business was restricted to the short term. Size may have been another factor; for example, comparing the British system (a few banks with many branches) with that of the United States (many local banks, prevented for a long time by law from undertaking interstate expansion), has suggested that a presence stretching across the country may have shielded English banks from severe local crises. 'If, in the interwar period, the [Depression] stricken towns of the industrial north-west had had their unit banks, it is inconceivable that the English banking system would have escaped serious internal crisis.'[1] It has also been noted that stability was promoted by the long-term collusion among banks, that is by the cartelization of the sector by the system of price fixing described in Chapter 1.

In short, functional specialization, consolidation, geographical diversification and limited competition are factors associated with the stability of the system; a stability that may have imposed a cost for the economy, however, and led to the economic system being underlent, in other words to a curbing of its intermediation in the financing of the economy. In this survey of the factors of stability, the role of the Bank of England as supervisor, always primarily on an informal basis, is not particularly emphasized. It is nonetheless easy to link the Bank's interest in maintaining financial stability with its responsibility as the government's banker and lender of last resort. The smooth functioning of the money market, with the Bank of England at its centre, served to promote the stability of the entire banking system, towards which, according to Sayers, the Bank had a sort of protective duty.[2]

This view of the British banking system as basically stable is more controversial for the period after the easing of credit controls, starting in 1971.[3] The subsequent episodes of instability were accompanied by reforms of banking supervision. A system that was basically self-regulated, but subject to strict quantity and price controls, was replaced by a liberalized system that was subject to more supervision by the central bank.

It is possible that the move away from oligopolistic banking structures characterized by price-fixing, towards structures marked by more competition was not always accompanied by higher standards of risk management, controls and care within individual credit institutions. Competition stimulates progress and in the long run innovation in the banking industry fosters efficiency, but in the short term it may cause crises by exposing the inefficiencies that protection had previously concealed.

Notwithstanding the crisis episodes, in the last few decades of the 20th century the banking system confirmed that it was relatively robust and unaffected by problems of a systemic nature.

In Chapter 1 – which gives a historical background related to the period between the 1960s and the 1980s – the crises of the secondary banks (1973–76) and Johnson Matthey Bankers (JMB (1984) were mentioned. In the 1990s there were three other important episodes of banks in difficulty: the crises of a group of small banks (the early 1990s), the collapse of Bank of Credit and Commerce International – BCCI (1991) and that of Barings (1995). Of these five crises, two were purely domestic: the secondary banks and the small banks. They were both linked to developments in the property market and to a huge funding on the money markets. The other three crises were at least partly international. In the last two cases – BCCI and Barings – fraud was the underlying cause of the crisis.

In general, the costs of crises can be met, alternatively or jointly: by depositors; by the public purse (the central bank and/or the Treasury); by the private sector of the economy. The latter can either involve the banking system itself, when a salvage is organized by one or more banks or when there is a scheme for the protection of depositors financed by the industry, or, more rarely, by non-banking investors, if permitted by legislation (this is not the case where a separateness between banking and industry is mandated by law). Public intervention – again, legislation permitting – is generally associated with cases of potential or actual systemic risk. Such a potential risk was deemed to exist in the JMB and the secondary bank crises and, again, in the crisis of the small banks in the early 1990s, but not in the BCCI and Barings crises, even though they were on a larger scale. The costs of crises – however measured – are difficult to determine exactly, not least because subsequent recoveries deriving from the sale of the failed bank's assets may offset part of the initial disbursement.

Of the five crises referred to above, that of the secondary banks, which followed the increase in competition in the banking system introduced by the Bank of England in 1971, occurred at a time when a deposit protection scheme still did not exist. In the face of substantial withdrawals of deposits, the Bank intervened, making allocations to provisions for possible losses that amounted to £30.2 million in the period 1974–76.[4] This was a very small fraction of the United Kingdom's GDP: in fact if the Treasury had made out a cheque to the Bank for the total amount, it would have been equal to 0.02 per cent of the GDP recorded in 1976.[5] But a substantially higher figure, close to £100 million, has also been quoted, even if unconfirmed by the central bank.[6]

In the case of JMB, the Bank of England intervened, despite the bank's small size, in view of the potential systemic risk because JMB was one of the five members of the London bullion market. The bank was sold for the symbolic figure of £1 to the Bank of England, which, as part of the safety net put in place with other banks and members of the bullion market, spent about £21 million and injected another £100 million of fresh capital. In total the Bank's intervention cost 0.03 per cent of GDP in 1985. The bulk of JMB's assets were subsequently sold to the Australian company Westpac.[7]

Another crisis – the third in order of time of those mentioned – involved small banks in the period 1991–94. It was the consequence of the bursting of the speculative asset price bubble in the late 1980s. A sizeable number of small banks who raised funds on the money market and granted property loans were hit hard by higher interest rates and the fall in property prices. The losses incurred were substantial, but met in large part out of capital. The Bank of England intervened by providing liquidity support in order to avert the systemic risk of contagion via the money market. In the event it kept 40 small banks under control and cooperated in their reorganization. It was only some years later that the Bank made this intervention known. Its impact, not announced, can be deduced from the outlays of the Deposit Protection Scheme, which amounted to £38.7 million net of recoveries[8] (this Scheme had been introduced in the UK in 1982).

5.2 Banking crises in the 1990s

In the early 1990s the single most important crisis was that of British Commonwealth Merchant Bank (1990), which led to the largest payment by the Deposit Protection Scheme after that for BCCI, but the entire amount was subsequently recovered.[9] BCCI had been created in Luxembourg in 1972. In 1974 a holding company was established, again in Luxembourg, with ramifications in that country and in the Cayman Islands. A network of branches and subsidiaries was set up in more than 70 countries; the branches in the United Kingdom were controlled by the Luxembourg holding company but were recognized by the Bank of England under the 1979 and 1987 Banking Acts. BCCI, and despite having its registered office in Luxembourg, was managed from London.

At the time of the crisis, in the United Kingdom BCCI had 25 branches, 1,100 employees and about 120,000 clients. The reasons for the crisis lay primarily in the fraudulent conduct of the management. The Bank of England ordered the closure of the bank in 1991. The Bank defended itself from the accusation of delay in acting on the grounds of an undertaking to recapitalize the bank by the government of Abu Dhabi, the reference shareholder. But following a report by Price Waterhouse commissioned by the Bank of England under Section 41 of the Banking Act, it was necessary to close the bank and freeze its assets in order to protect depositors. The closure was coordinated at international level and did not cause serious turbulence in financial markets or payment systems. It is estimated that the bank's capital fell short of creditors' claims by about US$3.5 billion[10] (corresponding to approximately £1.98 billion at the exchange rate of 1991).

The sterling deposits at the UK branches amounted to about £404 million and, starting in 1992, the Deposit Protection Scheme paid depositors 75 per cent of the first £20,000. The Scheme paid a total of £78.5 million, but recovered £77.4 million from the sale of BCCI assets. The losses incurred by depositors on their sterling deposits in Britain can therefore be calculated as £325.5 million.[11] Neither the Bank of England nor the public purse incurred a loss.

The collapse of BCCI was the subject of two inquiries in 1992, one by the Treasury Committee of the House of Commons and the other by a Committee chaired by Lord Bingham. The latter did not result in a radical revision of supervision, but the Bank of England accepted its conclusions and adopted measures aimed at improving its internal organization, the exchange of information with the government and the training of supervisory staff.[12]

The collapse of Barings in 1995 also highlighted the problems of a group with international exposure and was again due to fraud, although in this case primarily by a single trader who was arbitraging between the derivatives markets in Singapore and Osaka from a non-bank subsidiary located in Singapore. Barings' internal controls proved to be inadequate and the bank incurred losses of about £900 million. The Dutch bank ING bought Barings for a nominal amount and took over its assets and liabilities, so that Barings' depositors and other creditors were fully protected.[13]

In the same year the Bank of England's Board of Banking Supervision conducted an inquiry into the collapse of Barings and reported to the House of Commons. According to the inquiry, 'the events leading up to the collapse of Barings do not [....] of themselves point to the need for any fundamental change to the framework of regulation in the UK. There is, however, a need for improvement in existing arrangements', including the need for a better understanding of the non-banking (financial) businesses of a complex group; for improved coordination with the other regulatory authority, the SFA, responsible for supervising markets; and for close cooperation with regulators of other countries. For its part the Bank maintained its opinion that an increase in its inspectors' on-site visits to a level comparable with that practised by supervisory bodies in other countries would have entailed an unjustified increase in the costs incurred by the Bank (and ultimately by taxpayers): 'a wholesale change to this style of supervision' was not accepted.[14]

In total the Bank of England's interventions in the various crises in the 1990s involved provisions for loan losses of around £95 million and there was no support from the government's budget.[15] More specifically, in the two biggest failures, judged to be isolated cases and not of systemic importance, the losses incurred by BCCI were borne mostly by depositors and those incurred by Barings by the bank that acquired it.

As regards the Scheme for the protection of deposits, it should be remembered that the FSMA 2000 introduced a single scheme for the entire financial industry. The FSCS began operations in December 2001 and replaced the five pre-existing schemes, including the Deposit Protection Scheme for bank deposits.

In reference to the sub-scheme related to bank deposits, no bank default occurred from its inception in 2001 through 2006. Previously, between 1982, when the original Deposit scheme was created, and 2001,there were 31 bank failures, the last one in 2000.[16] Total compensation paid in regard to deposit-taking business amounted for the whole period 1982–2006 to £149 million while recoveries were £137 million.

Table 5.1 Financial Services Compensation Scheme sub-scheme accounts

(£000)	*2001/02*	*2002/03*	*2003/04*	*2004/05*	*2005/06*	*2006/07*
Accepting deposits						
Compensation costs	19	62	385	225	86	777
Recoveries	176	1109	2982	219	368	4854
Insurance business						
Compensation costs	26453	131295	131365	112984	93188	495285
Recoveries	7965	36411	96163	45270	106671	292480
Investment business and mortgages						
Compensation costs	14451	63023	65845	61501	107936	312756
Recoveries	1082	8488	7084	4756	1648	23058
General insurance						
Compensation costs	–	–	–	0	5	5
Recoveries	–	–	–	0	0	0
Total						
Compensation costs	40923	194380	197595	174710	201210	808818
Recoveries	9223	46008	106229	50245	108687	320392

Source: FSCS *Annual Report*.
Note: Mortgage Advice & Arranging with effect from October 2004;
General Ins. Mediation with effect from January 2005.

Table 5.1 gives an overview of the expenses and recoveries of the new Scheme, for all its sub-schemes, for the period 2001 (its inception) – 2006. It should be noted that there is a relatively high amount of compensation for insurance and investment business; however, these numbers are influenced by previous history. For example, in reference to deposit business, the low level of compensations reflects the fact of that there were no failures in the last few years, while the recoveries are related to insolvencies in the previous period. In reference to insurance, a Policyholders Protection Board was in existence from 1975 to November 2001, when the new Scheme took its place. Claims for protection during that period were considered under the Policy Protection Act 1975. The new Scheme, FSCS, assumed the responsibilities of the Board, but continued to apply the 1975 Act to claims related to the previous period. Twenty-eight insurance companies failed since 1975, two of them life-insurances, but no default occurred since FSCS assumed responsibility. Therefore, the high amount of compensation is related to failures of the pre-November 2001 period.

5.3 Monitoring financial stability and stress testing

The stability of financial intermediaries can be evaluated in three ways: first, by using traditional financial and prudential indicators, such as profitability, capitalization, non-performing loans, liquidity, etc. These are useful for representing the technical situation of financial intermediaries on the basis of accounting data or regulatory reporting; second, it is possible to use what is known as market-based indicators, which evaluate financial soundness by inferring the market's perception of risk. The main advantage in using these indicators is that they incorporate the expectations perceived by the market or the risk premium, through the pricing mechanism; third, it is possible to run simulations (stress-testing) aimed at measuring banking and financial systems' resistance to hypothetical scenarios characterized by extreme but plausible events.

The FSA collects firm-based information in the context of its surveillance activity that, however, is not published. In the future, with the implementation of Basel II, the FSA plans to release aggregate statistical data on key aspects of the banking sector, including credit risk, operational risk, market risk and supervisory actions and measures.[17] Financial soundness indicators for the United Kingdom are however collected by the International Monetary Fund, by the OECD and by the European Central Bank (ECB).[18] The latter provides both prudential and structural indicators. They have the advantage of allowing for some international comparisons, even if only for a limited number of variables.[19]

Table 5.2 compares some of these indicators for the United Kingdom, France, Germany, Italy, using ECB data based on the IFRS accounting standards.[20] It illustrates the existence of a rather significant comparative advantage of the UK banks. For example, it shows that the cost-to-income ratio is around 40 per cent for UK banks, much lower than for other competitors. This is not only due to the fact that the number of banks and branches in the United Kingdom is much lower, but also to the higher value of total assets, which makes it possible to take advantage of high economies of scale. The ability of containing operational costs is reflected in good profitability (both in terms of ROE and ROA). This, in turn, represents a good buffer in the case of adverse events.

If profitability is important to face temporary or cyclical downturns in the quality of the credit portfolio, the first line of defence in the case of more serious difficulties consists, clearly, in a good capitalization. As shown by Table 5.2, the solvency indices (the overall solvency ratio and the Tier 1 capital) are above the prudential requisites. In perspective, as noted recently by the FSA, banks' senior managers should

Table 5.2 Financial and structural indicators: all domestic banks (2006)*

	UK	*France*	*Germany*	*Italy*
Prudential indicators (1)				
Total expenses	0.99	1.33	1.14	2.04
Cost-to-income ratio	39.94	60.56	65.19	58.74
Net interest income	1.61	0.80	0.84	1.79
Net non-interest income	0.86	1.39	0.91	1.67
Net interest income (% of total income)	65.09	36.49	47.96	51.73
Net non-interest income (% of total income)	34.91	63.51	52.04	48.27
Profits (after tax and extraordinary items) (ROA)	0.80	0.62	0.31	0.81
Profits (after tax and extraordinary items) (ROE) (% of Tier 1)	19.04	20.24	10.24	17.68
Overall solvency ratio	13.66	11.22	11.67	10.08
Tier 1 ratio	8.24	8.43	7.69	7.03
Structural indicators (2)				
Number of credit institutions	401	829	2,050	807
Number of local branches	12,880	27,075	40,282	32,337
Population per branch	4,700	1,579	2,045	1,813
Number of employees of credit institutions	453,045	435,413	692,500	339,878
Total assets of credit institutions (million euros)	9,651,517	5,728,127	7,122,777	2,793,244

Sources: (1) ECB, *EU Banking Sector Stability*, November, 2007; (2); ECB, *EU Banking Structures*, October, 2007.
Note: *As % to total assets, if not otherwise indicated. Based on International Financial Reporting Standard (IFRS). All data are based on cross-border consolidation (branches and subsidiaries located abroad) and cross-sector consolidation (all financial institutions other than insurance companies).

ensure that their firms 'maintain an appropriate mix of capital so as to avoid becoming over-reliant on hybrid capital and other forms of innovative financing, which are less able to absorb shocks compared with core equity capital'.[21]

There are no data available to compare non-performing loans at the international level. However, the United Kingdom has always had a percentage quota of non-performing loans on total loans that is very low and in decline (between 2.5 per cent in 2000 and 1 per cent in 2005, also thanks to an extensive use of securitization; 7.45 per cent if net of provisions to capital).[22] This performance has been obtained despite the great increase of personal insolvencies in England and Wales, from about 5,500 in 2000, to about 15,700 at the end of 2006.[23]

Another aspect concerns the monitoring of the banks' 'large exposures' in the inter-bank market. These consist of relevant total exposures (both on and off-balance-sheet) toward the principal counterparties. 'Large exposures' are defined as any exposure that exceed 10 per cent of eligible capital (Tier 1 plus Tier 2, less any regulatory deductions, e.g. related to insurance subsidiaries) at any point in time during the reporting period.[24] In March 2006, the major UK banks' large exposure towards non-UK large complex financial institutions (LCFIs) was about 53 per cent of the banks' total exposure, against only 31 per cent of the exposure with other major UK banks.[25] This very close relationship between UK banks and non-UK LCFIs requires close monitoring by the regulator, since risks could be transmitted among institutions through counterparty exposure and mutual involvement in capital markets.

The assessment of the liquidity situation of intermediaries requires a more articulated analysis, as we will see extensively in chapter 6 discussing the surveillance requirements of the FSA and the Sterling Stock Liquidity Ratio (SSLR). A good liquidity position is essential to manage sudden and unexpected changes in market conditions. The sterling stock liquidity requirement relative to total assets of 'major UK banks' was 4.3 (median value) at the end of 1998, declined to 1.8 at the end of 2003, and was 2.1 at the end of 2006.[26] Other liquidity indicators monitored by the authorities are the 'liquid assets ratio' (cash and short-term government debt on total assets) and the ratio of 'liquid assets' (defined as debt securities, treasury bills, items in the course of collection from other banks, and cash) to 'vulnerable liabilities'. 'Vulnerable liabilities' are items in the course of collection, an estimation of debt securities issued with a maturity of under three months, and inter-bank deposits.

These liquidity indicators, however, offer only an initial assessment of the technical position of the intermediary. This derives from the fact that under stressful conditions, the liquidity situation can deteriorate rapidly, as we saw recently during the sub-prime mortgage market crisis in the summer-winter 2007. Thus it is fundamental to conduct a quantitative and qualitative analysis of the intermediaries' ability to manage risk, which can be done only through stress testing and on-site inspections on the supervised entity. For this reason, recent changes to FSA regulations require that banks use a series of risk management instruments, such as stress testing, to manage liquidity risk, as we will see later.

Regarding market-based indicators, they normally use real time information and, therefore, they reflect market expectations on the intermediary's future performance. They complement the backward-looking indicators described previously. Some of these indicators provide a direct estimate of the probability of financial distress, downgrading, or even default; others are constructed by combining balance sheets data with market-based infromation. Most of these indicators in effect do not represent the real probability of financial distress or default suffered by the intermediary, but rather the probability that can be inferred from the market for these events, on the basis of available information. Under specific assumptions, for the regulator, these indicators are anyway useful in that they make it possible to measure potential changes in market players' expectations.[27] While offering advantages, they still have some limitations.

Among the various market-based indicators, two are particularly useful: credit default swaps (CDS) spreads and the distance-to-default.[28] However, there are many other market-based indicators, based on the performance of bond spreads, equity indices, and implied market volatility, all widely used in macro-prudential analysis.

The CDS is a financial contract in which an investor (protection seller) assumes that payment is due to a counterparty (protection buyer) if a certain incident occurs (the so-called 'credit event', such as default, downgrade, etc.) to the reference entity (in our case a bank). In exchange for this contingent payment, the protection seller periodically receives a fee expressed in basis points over the relevant swap curve. Figure 5.1 shows the CDS spreads of some European banks and of two important British banks (HSBC and Barclays).

Another useful market-based indicator is the 'distance-to-default', or contingent claim (CC) indicator, that focuses on the determination of a firm's default probability by using information from its financial statements (balance-sheet data on liabilities) and the market price of its equities observable, for listed companies, in the stock exchange. Such indicator was formulated by using the Merton approach that considers the equity of a firm as a call option on the value of its assets struck at the maturity of its debt.[29] For a company, default is expected to occur if the assets value (i.e. the value of the firm) is not sufficient to cover the firm's liabilities. The reason is that equity holders are residual claimants on the firm's assets after all other obligations have been met. When the value of the firm's assets is less than the strike price (the so called 'default barrier'), the value of equity is zero. In other words, if the value of the assets is insufficient to meet the liabilities of the firm, then the shareholders (holders of the call option) will not exercise their option.[30] Bankruptcy is therefore viewed as an endogenous event resulting from the structure

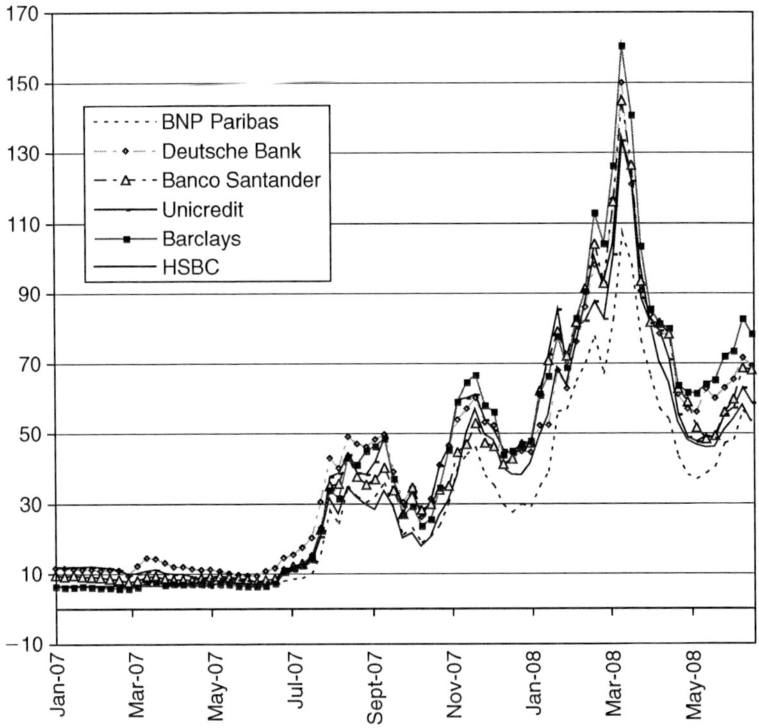

Source: based on data Thomson Financial Datastream.

Figure 5.1 Credit default swaps (CDS) spreads: large complex financial institutions

of the firm's capital, which is why this approach is also called 'structural' or 'contingent claim approach' (since liabilities are contingent claims on assets). This methodology encompasses a very important aspect of the traditional financial soundness indicators, namely considering the volatility component. In the traditional approach, firms (in our case, banks) with similar financial indicators would share the same probability of default; with the aforementioned methodology, however, firms with the same level of equity and debt, but with different volatility, would have a different default probability[31] In practice, it is important to stress two caveats surrounding the CC indicators: 1. they should not be interpreted as an absolute measure of strength but rather as relative over time, and 2. the volatility used in their calculation is a historic one-year volatility rather than implied volatility.

Source: DataStream and IMF (Monetary and Capital Markets Department), unpublished data. Banks included: Barclays, HBOS, HSBC, Lloyds TSB, Royal Bank of Scotland, Standard Chartered.

Figure 5.2 Major UK banks: contingent claim indicator

Figure 5.2 offers a representation of this indicator for the major UK banks.[32] It shows the worsening of the financial situation that took place between 2001 and 2003, after the bursting of the speculative bubble and the resulting erosion of intermediaries' profitability. The figure also shows the subsequent improvement, characterized by low volatility, higher capitalization and a low risk premium. Recently the situation has deteriorated again, in conjunction with the tensions in the sub-prime mortgage market in the United States.

The results have to be considered with caution and are purely indicative, for a number of reasons: liabilities are valued only on a semi-annual basis and not daily, as assets are; it is assumed that debt and equities have a fixed maturity for all firms and no rollover of debt; the residual value of the firm is not taken into account; the measure shown is risk-neutral and does not take into account risk preferences, which can change in times of difficulty; lastly, the indicator is not able to discriminate between idiosyncratic effect of single firm and a herding behaviour affecting simultaneously all the firms quoted on the market.[33] Even so, despite their limitations, this methodology if appropriately constructed and interpreted, can provide useful and timely information on the position of intermediaries and promote correcting actions.

A further tool for assessing the financial stability is the use of stress testing aimed at measuring the effects of different shocks on the financial system.[34] Both the Bank of England and the FSA use or promote stress-testing to assess the resilience of the financial sector under extreme but plausible scenarios. Stress testing is increasingly adopted by regulators as a fundamental tool to assess and, possibly, prevent financial instability. In the United Kingdom a major exercise was conducted in 2002, when the authorities performed the first stress testing in conjunction with the IMF assessment on the financial sector, the so called (FSAP).[35] The Bank of England published several papers on this topic and made use of the results in its Financial Stability Report. Before describing the Bank of England's approach to stress testing, it could be useful to outline some general features of stress testing that are normally performed by financial institutions.

Stress testing is a technique that can be employed to assess the vulnerability of the financial sector when dealing with exceptional but plausible events. It has been developed by dealers and risk managers to measure the effects of different types of risks (market risk, credit risk, liquidity risk, etc.). The main reason is that standard methodologies (for instance the Value at Risk, VaR[36]), aimed at measuring and mitigating the effect of stressed market conditions, are not adequate in case of unusually large shocks.

Stress testing can be used to analyse the impact (potential loss) of change in a single risk factor (sensitivity analysis) or the effect of a simultaneous movement in a group of risk factors (scenario analysis). The type of shock can entail changes in the level or volatility of individual variables or changes in the underlying correlation structure. Scenarios can be based historically or hypothetically.

Major financial institutions use 'internal models' to estimate the impact of exogenous shocks on the economic and regulatory capital. In the case of credit risk, the standard internal rating model includes a classification procedure with separate borrower grades. In order to make this classification, it is necessary to estimate the probability of default (PD) of borrowers falling in any specific grade, and the amount of loss in case of default ('loss-given default' or LGD), which depends in part upon institutional factors, such as the cost and timing of recovery rates. The product of PD, the LGD and the amount of the exposure at the moment of default (EAD) gives a measure of the expected loss (EL) which – as already stated – needs to be covered with adequate provisions. Credit risk stress testing is a requirement under the new Basel capital accord (the so called Basel II); such models are carefully approved by the regulator.[37]

In contrast with stress tests conducted independently by single institutions, system-wide stress testing applies a common set of scenarios to the whole banking sector. Each scenario, defined by the regulator, reflects a simultaneous variation of a set of risk factors (such as a shift in the term structure of interest rates as well as changes in credit rating, exchange rates, equity prices, and respective volatilities). A number of scenarios with different degree of severity are normally considered; the effect of the shocks on both the banking book and the trading book is assessed over a defined time horizon.

The design of the scenario is perhaps the most difficult part of the exercise. In its calibration it is advisable to produce an internally consistent set of shocks for key macroeconomic variables (for instance, we should expect some relationship between interest rate and exchange rate changes); in theory, economic consistency between variables should be maintained. However, this is particularly challenging, since the economic relationships estimated under normal market conditions cannot be any more reliable under extreme circumstances. A reasonable balance between scenarios based on historical events and correlations between variables and potentially new scenarios (or what we can call the 'think the unthinkable' scenarios) is therefore advisable.

There are two main approaches to simulate the effects of the scenarios on the banking system: the 'top-down' approach, where the impact is estimated directly by the regulator both at aggregate and disaggregate levels (using micro-data from regulatory returns, where available); the 'bottom-up' approach, where the impact of the same shock or set of shocks is estimated by the intermediaries under the direction of the regulator. The 'bottom-up' approach is usually performed by major systemically important banking groups using banks' 'internal models'.

The greater advantage of the 'top-down' stress test is the consistency between institutions, since it does not rely upon the internal models designed by banks (which can exhibit some methodological differences); it can also be performed on the whole universe of regulated entities using comparable data collected by the regulators. The main limitation of this approach is that it does not allow for simulating how banks would in practice react in order to prevent the negative effects of the shocks.

The FSA is working with firms to promote good practices in stress testing.[38]

A recent survey conducted by the FSA, in order to assess the 'state of the art' of stress testing among major institutions concluded that 'there was a general consensus that current stress testing (and risk management more generally) is risk specific, often failing to bring together the impact of stresses scenarios across different types of risk (market, credit, liquidity, operational, etc) and across business'. Therefore, 'stress testing aggregated risks remains a longer term objective'.[39]

In defining the good practice of stress testing, which should be seen as integral part of the ARROW Risk Mitigation Programme (see Chapter 8), the FSA underlines six aspects: 1. senior management should be able to identify an articulate firm's risk appetite and understand the implications of stress events within this context; 2. it should also take an active part in identifying potential stress scenarios; 3. output from stress testing should be communicated to the senior management in a comprehensible format; 4. the senior management should have an overview of firm-wide risks and a concept of total risk, even where precise aggregation is not possible; 5. it should consider formally the implications of stress testing for a firm's strategy or business profile; 6. and finally, the IT system, resources and procedures should allow the senior management to identify, quantify and manage efficiently the risks that affect a financial group.[40] Broadly speaking, the FSA found that most firms had practices that went some way to meeting the characteristics of the above mentioned comprehensive format.

The Bank of England is mainly involved in top-down simulations, which are a tool of assessing aggregate risks. This is consistent with its responsibilities for monitoring macro-prudential stability. The aim is to consider the effect of the shocks or scenarios on banks' profitability (after-tax profit) and capital adequacy.

The Bank of England stress testing is based on six steps. The first step is the selection of the shock or combination of shocks to use in the simulation. The subsequent steps are the estimation of the following aspect: the impact on the economic environment through functional relationships of the macroeconomic model; the effects of changes to the economic environment on the balance sheets of main economic sectors (households, corporate and financial institutions), arrears and asset prices; the effects of the increase of the arrears on loan portfolios, which also depends on the value of collateral after the shock; the effects of the changes in the economic environment on banking profitability; and, finally overall impact on banks' balance sheets.

Recently, the Bank of England has further refined its approach in order to better define the set of potential vulnerabilities, to consider stress scenarios that could identify these vulnerabilities, to estimate the potential impact on the system and, finally to promote possible actions aimed at mitigate such risks. Recent methodological improvements moved from the observation that in the traditional approach, either the number of potential risks is too high (all possible domestic and exogenous shock) or too narrow, aggregated in the usual categories such as credit risk, market risk, etc. More importantly, it is critical to integrate in a common framework various categories of risk.

Particular attention has been devoted to identifying shock propagation in the financial system and possible policy action. For instance, in 2006, six stress scenarios exposing the following vulnerabilities has been estimated: shift from the unusually low current risk premia; significant corrections of the global imbalances; rising global corporate indebtedness; excessive household indebtedness in the UK; adverse interactions among systemically important large corporate financial institutions; and, finally, problems in the area of market infrastructure. Where possible, the impact of these events has been quantified in relation to the following typology of risks: credit risk (foreign and domestic households and corporate), counterparty risks, market risks in the trading book, funding risks, and operational risks.

6
Markets and Market Infrastructures: Institutional and Prudential Aspects

In previous chapters we have seen how the configuration of financial intermediation changed, through further consolidation and the blurring between various segments of the industry. What emerges from this chapter is that, alongside the blurring between banking and other intermediaries, there is a similar phenomenon between exchanges and the OTC market.[1] In perspective, it is possible that an increasing number of transactions between financial intermediaries performed on a bilateral basis in the OTC market will be settled through clearing houses, thereby reducing (but not eliminating) the counterparty risk for a number of more standardized transactions, which is a typical feature of the regulated and organized markets. The development of financial engineering, both in products – especially derivatives – and in market infrastructure, such as integrated electronic platforms, underpins these market transformations but also introduces new regulatory challenges. These markets are interconnected through the activity of both domestic and large foreign complex financial institutions. These intermediaries are active in structured products where a large volume of transactions simultaneously involves organized markets and OTC markets, both on-shore and off-shore.[2]

Concerning the wholesale banking market, we discuss important structural changes in international flows, which shed light on the changing role of London as an international banking centre. In particular, we will note that the UK's market share of global international liabilities has increased. The nature of banking intermediation has, however, changed, with a shift from a purely interbank activity (inflows and outflows of assets and liabilities among banks) to intermediation between the banking sector and the non-banking sector, such as securities houses or hedge funds.

Particular attention has been devoted to the fact that, in the last few years, the 'major UK banks' have experienced a growing gap between 'customer funding' and 'customer lending', where 'customer' refers to all non-bank borrowers and depositors.[3] A significant part of the resulting 'customer funding gap' is funded in the wholesale market. Banks, therefore, appear to be exposed to unexpected changes in conditions in the domestic wholesale market, which – in turn – is strictly connected with the international environment.

A description of some important aspects of the credit risk transfer (CRT) market is also provided. It shows that, while CRT instruments have facilitated the management and diversification of risk, they have also posed some new challenges to regulators, particularly in the area of market incentives to monitor credit standards, transparency and liquidity of structured products. All these aspects offer a useful background to understanding the financial turmoil that started in August 2007 and its effects on the UK banking sector (Chapter 7).

A leading theme of this chapter is the relationship and – to some extent – the transformation, of credit risk into liquidity risk. The analysis also sheds light on three critical aspects of the recent financial turmoil: the mis-pricing due to over-complexity of some products, the counterparty risk, and the necessity to extend the role of a centralized clearing house system.

A description of the market infrastructures, of payment and settlement systems, as well of the reforms of the liquidity regime and of the money market arrangements allows us to interconnect all the components of such a complex environment, where banks have substantially changed their model of intermediation (from the originate-and-hold to the originate-and-distribute model), while, however, still maintaining their central role in the financial sector. Here, the focus is on the techniques of monitoring and managing both market and funding liquidity. As we will see in Chapter 7, the complex interaction between the market liquidity, related to an easy and prompt liquidation of hard-to-value structured products without altering their price and the funding liquidity, due to the maturity mismatching, plays a critical role in the global propagation of the sub-prime credit crisis.[4]

6.1 Stock exchanges and the OTC derivatives market

At the outset, it might be useful to provide some general information on both the organized exchanges and the OTC derivatives market. In the United Kingdom, the two most important exchange markets are the LSE and the Alternative Investment Market (AIM).[5] At the end of 2006, there were 3,256 companies listed in the LSE and 1,210 in AIM. The LSE is very open to foreign companies, which number 610 (versus 453 in the New York Stock Exchange [NYSE]). It has, however, a share of global equity-market capitalization of 7.5 per cent, much less than that of the Tokyo (18 per cent) or US (41 per cent) markets.

The LSE and AIM comprise about 41 per cent of the global turnover of foreign equities, almost double that of the NYSE (about 22 per cent) and Switzerland (18 per cent).[6] The LSE also accounted for 37 per cent of the European IPO market. For derivatives, the principal stock market is Euronext.liffe, which offers a single electronic market for products listed on its Amsterdam, Brussels, Lisbon and Paris exchanges. Euronext.liffe also serves as a clearing house for the international OTC market. The derivatives markets, supported by a single electronic platform (LIFFE CONNECT), are available to customers at over 680 locations in 29 countries worldwide.[7] The turnover of financial exchanges in derivatives is very concentrated at the global level: the Chicago Mercantile Exchange has 45 per cent of the notional value of global contracts, while Euronext.liffe accounts for about 27 per cent and Eurex for about 8 per cent.[8]

As to the volume of some types of derivatives transactions completed in the OTC market, it is necessary to look to the BIS survey conducted every three years, which examines a sample of the principal types of contracts.[9] According to BIS data, in 2004 the activity in OTC derivatives in the United Kingdom, based on the average daily turnover and booking location, was equal to 38 per cent of the global total (US$3.089 billion), with an increase over previous surveys in 2001 (33 per cent) and 1998 (35 per cent). This confirms the London market's leadership on these types of contracts. It is also interesting to note that in 2004, at the global level, average daily trading was predominantly among 'reporting dealers' (defined by the Bank for International Settlements as 'large commercial and investment banks and securities houses') and came to 51 per cent of the total, down from 62 per cent in 1998, while the average among 'other financial institutions' (hedge funds, mutual funds, insurance companies, pension funds, and smaller commercial and investment banks) grew from 22 per cent (1998) to about 37 per cent of the total; the share among non-financial clients remained modest (11 per cent, compared to 16 per cent in 1998).[10]

An important category of OTC derivatives is credit derivatives, for which, however, there exist no official statistics. Sample data from the BBA estimate that at the end of 2006 the global market for credit derivatives (excluding asset swaps) was equal to US$20.2 trillion, versus just US$3.5 trillion in 2003 and US$180 million in 1997.[11] The BBA survey estimates that, in 2006, in the credit derivatives market 59 per cent of credit protection was acquired by banks, 28 per cent by hedge funds and the remaining 13 per cent was bought in equal proportion by pension funds, reinsurances, insurances, mutual funds, and non-financial corporations. In the same year, 44 per cent of credit protection was sold by banks and 32 per cent by hedge funds. London holds about 40 per cent of the global market of credit derivatives. It therefore appears that banks are net acquirers and hedge funds net sellers of protection.

Regarding the development of securitizations in general, it is sufficient to note that the United Kingdom, as the country of origin, has a leading position in Europe, with a value of US$241 billion (or 41 per cent of total European securitizations). The United States has, however, a dominant role in the market with almost 80 per cent of the global market share of securitizations. Fifty-seven per cent of European securitization products are collateralized debt obligations (CDOs) and the remaining 43 per cent are loans, leases, credit cards receivables and others.[12]

In order to understand the ongoing blurring between the organized and OTC markets, it is necessary to clarify some essential differences between the two.

In addition to the well-known characteristics between organized and OTC markets, aimed at guaranteeing transparency, integrity and an efficient market price discovery, there are important differences between the two markets with regard to the problem of counterparty risk, a crucial aspect of the futures and derivatives markets. In particular, in an organized market the counterparty risk is greatly reduced by the following institutional arrangements: (1) there is a clearing house that centralizes all transactions and assumes the systematic role of central counterparty for each participant in the market. Since the exchange clearing house is the only counterpart to all short and long positions, counterparty risk is almost eliminated. Moreover, the clearing house deals only with clearing house members; (2) the position of the counterparts is re-assessed daily by the clearing house, and variations in these positions must be settled in cash or Treasury bonds; (3) traders deposit an initial margin, often a small amount compared to the value of the transaction, serving as collateral in the event of default;[13] (4) there is a daily mark-to-market on which margin calls are calculated;[14] and (5) position limits are imposed on individual brokers and on the institutional members of the clearing house.

In this respect it is worth noting that in the cash market a trade is done and confirmed, and within a few days money and securities change hands (the so-called 'settlement period'). On the contrary, in futures and options markets, the trade consists of taking positions in a given moment, while the settlement is finalized after a longer period, once the derivatives expire. This implies a counterparty risk.[15] The trade is therefore followed by depositing a small guarantee (the so-called 'initial margin').[16]

The clearing house, then, not only centralizes the risk but manages it as well, mainly through its margin policy and the assessment of counterparty risks. Furthermore, in the event of default by a counterpart the clearing house reserves the right to liquidate that counterpart's deposit margin. If, however, the losses should exceed this margin, the difference would be covered by the capital of the clearing house, including that held by non-defaulting members. If the losses were so severe as to deplete the capital, then members could be required to provide additional capital.[17]

With time, the OTC market has also assumed some of the characteristics of organized markets. Although many transactions are still not standardized, they are conducted by means of precise documentation, established by international standard setters like the International Securities Market Association (ISMA) or the International Swaps and Derivatives Association (ISDA).[18] In particular, the standardized documentation developed by ISDA through the Master Agreement fulfils an important role in defining standards for the netting of bilateral positions. Once the net risk of two counterparts has been established, the debtor party may be called upon to provide collateral in the form of cash or risk-free bonds to the creditor party through a mechanism comparable to that of margin calls in the organized market. The netting and collateral mechanism has, therefore, contributed to reduce counterparty risk in the OTC derivatives markets.[19]

The growing use of electronic trading in OTC derivatives has further transformed this market. Alongside the traditional method, based on telephone dealing arrangements, there is an even greater use of electronic platforms. This has facilitated access to the wholesale market for a greater number of participants, including hedge funds.[20] Increasingly, small to medium-sized transactions are conducted through the electronic system, while large trades are conducted by market-makers on a bilateral basis, by telephone and in an anonymous way.

In particular, the traditional bilateral negotiation between dealers has been complemented by two different types of electronic platforms: brokering platforms and dealing platforms.[21] Both are networking technologies creating a multilateral trading environment, similar to the fully regulated and organized exchanges; however, in the former the firm operating the platform does not take a position; in the latter, the platform is set up by the dealer, who acts as a counterpart to every trade, taking positions and, therefore, holding the credit risk. This situation changes if the platform adopts a clearing house, which, as we have already seen, assumes and manages the credit and counterparty risk. In developing this technology, large international investment banks, acting as dealers with their own electronic trading platforms, to some extent, 'internalizing' the market.

These developments are not without problems, however. As Kroszner observed: 'With regard to systemic risk, the key question about the clearing of OTC derivatives is whether the risk-management techniques that have proved so effective in clearing exchange-traded products will prove equally effective in clearing products that are not as standardized.'[22] However, as we will see more extensively in the following paragraphs and in the chapter on the sub-prime related crisis, there is the necessity to rethink the over-complexity of instruments traded in the OTC market, returning back to more simple and standardized products. This should allow to use more extensively a centralized clearing house, so reducing substantially the systemic risk. If this perspective proves correct, we should witness in the market a move toward a relevant simplification in securitization products, associated with the necessity of a more active management of the so-called basis risk. Such risk arises when it is not possible for the intermediary to hedge perfectly his positions due to the necessity to use standardized products.

By the end of the 1990s, while market practices for processing trades of standardized transactions in the OTC market were becoming increasingly automated, the parallel expansion of structured products required extensive manual interventions.[23] The effect was that a number of dealers had large backlogs of unsigned agreements and some reported a large number of outstanding confirmations, with delays of even 90 days or more.[24] In early 2005 a number of prudential supervisors, led by the Federal Reserve, began to express increasing concerns about the size and rapid growth of confirmation backlogs of credit derivatives. Such concerns were one of the factors that motivated market participants to form the Counterparty Risk Management Policy Group II (CRMPG II) and to adopt a new ISDA protocol. The last BIS assessment, published in March 2007, noticed substantial progress, with a total number of confirmations outstanding reduced by 70 per cent. However, the problem has not been resolved. Not only is it emphasized that the outstanding confirmations remain high (20–30 days for some types of derivatives), but the average total deal volume has increased dramatically (for instance, deal volume for credit derivatives has increased on average by more than six times since 2002).[25]

The Bank of England and the FSA were among the supporters of that initiative.[26] A recent report by the BIS on clearing and settlements arrangements for OTC derivatives showed that more should be done in this area. In particular, dealers might do more to mitigate risk associated with unconfirmed positions and to promote better reconciliation in cases of default.

Technology has, therefore, brought about important changes as well challenges, over the years in over-the-counter markets. As has been noted, 'the exchange and OTC markets are clearly becoming blurred, and are not as marked as they were before. The traditional activities of exchanges are getting broken down and parcelled off. The OTC markets are developing their own clearing facilities and are linking up with clearing houses. So, essentially, standards have to be set for both'.[27]

Concerning market regulation, we should at the outset note that, in the UK markets, exchanges and clearing houses are regulated by the FSA as Recognized Investment Exchanges (RIEs) and Recognized Clearing Houses (RCHs). Investment firms trading outside exchanges and regulated alternative trading systems are regulated as authorized firms, subject to rules that focus primarily on their 'fitness and properness', their financial resources, and their conduct of business with clients. OTC market participants are required to comply with the FSA's Code of Market Conduct and the Inter-Professional Code, which are part of the FSA's Handbook of Rules and Guidance.

The FSA's supervision on exchange markets reflects principles set by IOSCO. Such principles recognize that markets should be: 'fair' (free of unfair practices and abuses and such that all investors have a reasonable opportunity to trade at the best price available for their transaction size); 'efficient' (such that users can achieve optimum pricing based on adequate information, and that they can have maximum choice of methods for minimizing their exposure to risk); and 'safe' (in the sense that the infrastructure should be reliable and robust).

In this regard, it is also worth mentioning that in March 2000 the European Council endorsed the Financial Service and Action Plan (FSAP), to remove regulatory and market barriers that limit the cross-border provision of financial services in the EU area. The FSAP in mid-2004 was an important achievement, with relevant implications for the UK, too. In this context it is sufficient to say that the principal vehicle for designing and implementing the FSAP is the so-called Lamfalussy process.[28]

Among the principal initiatives of the FSAP in addition to the implementation of Basel II, is the Market in Financial Instruments Directive (MiFID), which provides securities firms with an updated EU passport, allowing them to offer a wider range of financial services across member states on a 'home-country control' basis.[29] MiFID is expected also to contribute to improving cross-border clearing and settlement efficiency, as it extends the rights of market intermediaries and regulated markets to access Central Counterparties and Securities Settlement Systems located in other member states under non-discriminatory conditions. It will not only affect investment banks, portfolio managers, stockbrokers and broker-dealers (investment banks), and other financial firms, but also retail banks and building societies when selling securities or investment products that contain securities.[30] In January 2007 the United Kingdom transposed Levels 1 and 2 of the MiFID and enforced it in November 2007.

Among other aspects, MiFID extends the scope of the passport to include personal recommendations for a core of investment services, credit and commodity derivatives, and other financial contracts. It also provides a passport to firms offering multilateral trading facilities (MTF)[31] and includes new pre-trade and post-trade transparency requirements for equity markets, and more extensive transaction reporting requirements for stock exchanges and MTF firms, as well as for the so called 'systematic internalizers' (firms that conduct OTC trading in an organized and systemic way). This has important implications for the OTC market in terms of efficiency and transparency: the 'systematic internalizers' should provide a quote of liquid assets prior to a transaction and those quotes, subject to certain waivers, must be binding for trades up to a certain threshold. The quote is published in the market, giving interested parties a chance to respond. Post-trade obligations meet the same transparency requirements that regulated markets do. MiFID will, therefore, allow shares to be traded without the involvement of the stock exchange, while requiring those transactions to be reported to the rest of the market. Moreover, anyone buying or selling shares will be entitled to the 'best execution' (best available price, subject to various conditions such as the time and size of the order).

It is difficult to say what the impact of MiFID will be on the European market and on the UK stock exchanges. It is however possible that a number of multilateral trading firms will, to some extent, threaten the current oligopolistic position of stock exchanges. MiFID will also facilitate cross-border trading, encourage the integration of the European capital market, and ensure stronger and more even-handed investor protection. It is also possible that, after some time and adjustment costs, London-based entities will, once again, take the lead, moving ahead on the efficiency frontier, transforming into an opportunity what at first glance may appear a challenge. Lastly, MiFID will further increase the blurring between banks or other intermediaries and markets, while reducing the role of stock exchanges and promoting the entry of a number of firms specialized in electronic trading services.

However, as recently noted by the FSA, there is the risk that fragmentation of trading as well as of trading data may result in a reduction in market transparency for both regulators and market participants. Moreover, most of UK recognized bodies are now part of a large multi-jurisdictional groups, creating a number of regulatory difficulties, such as the need to achieve a common set of rules across regulated entities and how to deal with non-regulated holding companies.[32]

6.2 Recent developments in the wholesale banking markets

It is well known that the United Kingdom is an important international centre for wholesale banking. A recent study by the BIS tries to quantify this role by measuring the relative weight of various international banking markets on the basis of the share of banking liabilities (primarily deposits) of those countries that report total 'international liabilities' to the BIS.[33] The main change observed between 1990 and 2006 is the great reduction in the percentage share of Japan – from 20 per cent to 4 per cent – and of the offshore Asian centres (Hong Kong and Singapore), from 10 per cent to 5 per cent. This 'market share' was gained mainly by the United Kingdom (from 21 per cent to 27 per cent) and by the euro area (from 16 per cent to 26 per cent). The shares of the United States, Switzerland, and Luxembourg (about 10 per cent, 5 per cent, and 2–3 per cent respectively), remained stable, while that of Caribbean offshore centres declined slightly (from 9 per cent to 6 per cent).[34]

If the share of 'international liabilities' of the United Kingdom banks increased, there was, however, a reduction in purely inter-banking intermediation; the 'inter-bank' recycling ratio – defined as the proportion of total interbank funds deposited with London banks and recycled into the interbank market – declined by 25 per cent since mid-2002, compared to the average long-term value. On average, between the end of the 1970s and the mid-1990s, between 66 and 75 cents of every dollar placed in London was recycled in the interbank market; afterward it declined by 25 per cent.[35] The interbank source of funding was increasingly used for credit activity towards non-bank clients.

Various explanations have been put forth. First of all, it has been noted that with the introduction of the euro, operations in the foreign-exchange market have declined, which has, in turn, reduced the need to complete transactions in the inter-bank market. This occurs because of the intimate link between the foreign exchange market and the inter-bank market: forward contracts are priced on the basis of interest differentials in the inter-bank market and are almost always hedged with deposits in that market.[36] Moreover, the consolidation in the banking sector and the growing use of the electronic brokering system have reduced inter-dealer business.[37]

Even more interesting is the fact that the growing financing of non-bank subjects like securities houses, hedge funds, and other non-bank financial institutions – particularly in the USA – which have relied on banks in London to leverage their capital in taking positions in fixed-income securities, contributed to reduce the 'inter-bank recycling ratio'. In fact, an increasing amount of funds deposited in London banks were committed to non-bank debtors. For example, it was calculated that, between the end of 1997 and the beginning of 2002, liabilities in dollars deposited with banks in the United Kingdom (equal to US$1.3 trillion) more than doubled, while inter-bank lending grew by only 60 per cent. This generated a net stock of dollars not re-deposited in the inter-bank market of US$368 billion, or an excess of dollars that would be used primarily to finance the borrowing of non-banks, mostly in the United States, particularly securities houses, hedge funds, and other non-bank financial entities.[38]

In the last few years, another important development of the banking activity in the United Kingdom has been the difference between the modest growth of customer funding and the strong dynamic of their customer lending. As a result, greater use of wholesale funding by banks has been observed. This strategy has somewhat increased the liquidity risk for some banks, as wholesale funding may be difficult and costly to roll over during times of company-specific or market-wide stress.

In particular, major UK banks' lending to 'customers' (i.e. all non-bank borrowers) exceeded the growth of deposits from this sector. This has created a 'customer funding gap' (the stock of lending to customers exceeds the stock of deposits).[39] This 'customer funding gap', equal to zero at the end of 2001, reached £564 billion at the end of June 2007, or 22 per cent of UK banks' 'customer lending' (£259 billion, or 10 per cent of 'customer lending' excluding securitization). This funding gap implies a growing use of wholesale funding. Such funding, which can take various forms, like borrowing in the inter-bank market or the issuing of debt securities – for instance commercial papers or certificates of deposit – has various macro-prudential implications, as we will discuss subsequently.

As noted by the Bank of England, with the exception of mortgage-backed securities and some other types of ABS, deposit collection in the wholesale market needs to be rolled over within a year, which makes cost and availability much more sensitive to market conditions.[40] Even before the August 2007 sub-prime credit and liquidity crisis, the Bank of England underlined that problems could arise if market conditions deteriorated to the point that UK banks found themselves unable to securitize existing assets and thereby free up funds for new business.[41]

A second implication concerns the management of liquidity in currency, namely, the risk arising from banks' reliance on continued liquidity in foreign exchange markets to meet their obligations in one currency with funds in another. Furthermore, to the extent that banks hedge foreign currency liabilities, they have to roll over the swap and, in so doing, are exposed to cash-flow implications of movements in the spot foreign exchange rate and in relative interest rates. This highlights the need for an all-currency approach to liquidity monitoring and control.[42]

6.3 The market for credit risk transfer

Before discussing the recent financial turmoil and its effect on the UK banking system (Chapter 7), it is necessary to describe, if only in broad terms, some technical aspects of the so-called market for CRT.[43]

Techniques of CRT, such as financial guarantees and credit insurance, have been used for decades in financial markets. Syndicated loans in the primary market, as well as standard securitizations, began in the 1970s, while the secondary market of bank loans developed in the 1980s. Nevertheless, it is only from the 1990s onward, with sophisticated forms of CRT based on financial engineering and on the use of credit derivatives, that we witness a true technological breakthrough with deep effects on the financial industry and new challenges for the regulator. Such new forms of CRT increased the linkages between banks and other intermediaries, transformed the incentive structures between borrowers and lenders, changed the nature of the banking products, making credit more homogeneous and easy to be traded in the secondary market.

In normal market conditions, CRT allows banks to diversify and better manage their own loan portfolios – including the possibility to sell pools of non-performing loans – to save regulatory capital and to reduce funding costs. CRT broadened the number of institutions interested in the purchase and management of credit risk (like, monoline insurers or 'financial guarantors', pension funds, hedge funds).[44] These institutions are characterized by different risk attitudes and time horizons. Hedge funds, for example, enter into this market mainly to take advantage of arbitrage opportunities and potential short-term profits. They increase the efficiency and liquidity of the market through a large volume of transactions that reflect high leverage. Institutional investors, on the other hand, are characterized by higher risk aversion and generally adhere to a buy-and-hold strategy.

As recently noted by a Working Group on Risk Assessment and Capital (Joint Forum of the Basel Committee on Banking Supervision), geographically, the risk in CRT is spread across the globe. 'It has been estimated that, in aggregate, US managers sell CRT into United States, Europe and Asia in roughly equal shares, while CRT from European managers splits 60–40 between Europes and Asia.'[45]

CRT instruments can be classified on the basis of two general characteristics: (1) whether the instrument transfers the risk associated with an individual borrower ('single name') or a number of borrowers ('portfolio'); and (2) whether the instrument is funded or unfunded. When the transaction is funded, the loan is sold in the secondary market after being transformed into a tradable security, the repayment of which is backed by the cash flows of the original loan; in the case of an unfunded transaction, a derivative contract is used, producing a 'synthetic securitization'. In this case the originator, while selling the risk of default, maintains the credit relationship with the borrower.[46] A typical single-name unfunded CRT instrument is the CDS, while a typical portfolio CRT instrument is an ABS.

The CDS is a bilateral financial contract in which the protection buyer pays a fixed fee for a contingent payment by the protection seller, triggered by a well-specified credit event on the reference asset.[47] It is important to underline that, while the risk of default is insured, the protection buyer retains a residual risk (the 'counterparty risk'), deriving from the inability or unwillingness of the protection seller to own up to its commitments.

ABS securitization involves the pooling of similar assets (for instance mortgages) into a special-purpose vehicle (SPV). The SPV issues securities with different classes of seniority (tranches) that represent claims on the assets. Such tranches reflect different levels of risk and returns: the 'senior', or less risky debt tranche (usually with a AAA rating); the 'mezzanine' tranche (usually from AA+ to BBB– rating); and the 'equity', more risky and usually unrated tranche. Losses are applied in reverse order of seniority and so junior tranches offer higher coupons to compensate higher default risk.

In practical terms, the sponsoring bank or financial institution sells the assets (usually held on its balance sheet but which may be purchased in the market) to a vehicle; an *ad hoc* structure often created and managed by the sponsor. The purpose of the vehicle is to hold the assets (the collateral) and to issue securities backed by them in the capital market (hence 'asset-backed securities'). All cash flows generated by the assets are collected by the sponsor, which then pass them on the investors by means of the vehicle.[48]

SPVs or similar structures are legal, 'bankruptcy remote', entities such as trusts, corporations or limited liability partnerships (LLPs).[49] Off-balance vehicles are created also to exploit regulatory capital and tax advantages. Such structured investment vehicles (SIVs) and conduits are usually highly leveraged and with significant maturity and liquidity risk. It is worth noting that in many regimes such vehicles are or were unconsolidated. In the UK, banks and building societies have increasingly used LLPs for funding and CRT purposes. Differently from other schemes of SPVs, 'in the LLPs, the bank themselves (rather than the SPVs) continue to hold the assets and issue the so-called covered bonds secured against them. The LLP effectively only comes into operation in the event that the issuing bank defaults, thereby providing an additional guarantee to investors in the bonds'.[50]

Another financial instrument worth mentioning here is the asset-backed commercial paper (ABCP) conduit, originally developed by banks to provide cost-efficient funding to non-financial corporations in the commercial paper market (short-term liabilities sold in the money market). In particular, the bank helps the corporation establish the SPV and provides credit and liquidity support to the vehicle. Subsequently, banks started building their own ABCP programme. The portfolio composition of such conduits was originally based on 'traditional' corporate assets such as trade receivables, mortgages, credit cards and auto loans, etc. More recently, the banks have been setting up 'credit arbitrage' conduits backed by other CRT instruments, such as ABS and CDOs. Also, they have created structured investment vehicles, which are very similar to ABCP conduits, but funding comes from a combination of short-term paper and longer-maturity notes.

The increasing demand for high rated high-yield securities by institutional investors, in a contest of low interest rates, has developed the market of more complex structured products such CDOs. CDOs are very similar to ABS, in that they are comprised of multiple tranches, with the main purpose of creating at least one class of securities whose rating is higher than the rating of the underlying collateral asset pool. This process is called internal credit enhancement. For instance, mezzanine structured finance CDOs use, as input, BBB-rated tranches of other ABS and CDOs to produce CDOs, about 60 per cent of which are comprised of senior AAA tranches, 15 per cent of junior AAA tranches and numerous other lower rated tranches. In recent years, more and more complicated instruments have been engineered, such as CDOs made with mezzanine tranches of other CDOs ('CDO-squared'), as well as synthetic CDOs (based on CDS). This financial development has further complicated the process of measuring the performance of the underlying collateral, to value the securities, and estimate their credit rating.[51]

Often, the senior tranches so generated have been sold by the originators to a broker–dealer, and then to other intermediaries, sometimes located in different countries (so-called the 'originate-to-distribute' model). The final risk takers were keen to increase the profitability of their portfolios buying senior tranches, assuming that the price of such assets would remain weakly correlated with lower quality tranches.

The economic structure of various securitization vehicles is critical for several reasons and depends by the degree of diversification, tradability of underlying assets, maturity mismatching and level of leverage. Most of such vehicles or conduits, while well diversified, have significant liquidity risks either because some assets are not highly tradable, or because of maturity mismatches between assets and liabilities. Therefore, they face delicate risk management problems: if the structure cannot rollover, it must find another source of short-term financing, or else dissolve itself and sell the underlying assets. However, since such assets are traded only in the OTC market, they can be illiquid. The price of such structured products are often inferred from prices of credit spread of similar rated comparable products for which quotations are available.

For these reasons, the 'sponsor' supports the vehicle with a stand-by credit facility that, in the event of an unforeseen liquidity crisis, should be able to refund the investor even if the quality of the underlying asset portfolio deteriorates. The sponsoring bank earns also a fee from the programme by providing back-up liquidity or contingent credit support to the vehicle.

A large amount of structured credit products was held in banks' trading book, where capital requirements reflect market risk. Basel II, as currently designed, explicitly captures only the default of risk that is in the banking book. As noted by the Financial Stability Forum (FSF): 'were market risk capital measures do not fully capture the credit risk of these products, there is a regulatory arbitrage incentive to reduce capital requirements by holding such exposures in the trading book'.[52]

Moreover, 'Basel I created perverse regulatory incentives to move exposure off the balance sheet and did not fully capture important elements of banks' exposures within the capital adequacy calculation. Basel II, by contrast, provides better support to sound risk management practices by much more closely aligning minimum capital requirements with risks banks face (Pillar 1), by strengthening supervisory review of banks practices (Pillar 2) and by encouraging improved market disclosure (Pillar 3).' In particular, 'Pillar 1 subjects on- and off-balance sheet exposure to regulatory capital requirements [...]. Its securitization framework aims to eliminate regulatory capital arbitrage incentives for moving exposures off the balance sheet or distributing them through the securitization process.'[53]

It is also worth noting that, under Basel I, the capital requirements on contingent liquidity lines to structured investment vehicles was – under certain circumstances – relatively low if compared to the capital requirements that sponsored banks had to pay if SIVs' assets were held on the bank's balance sheets.

On the basis of what we have said, it is easy to understand the opportunities offered by the CRT, but also its relevant challenges from the prudential point of view. The main implication from the prudential perspective is that, while the originator has transferred the credit risk, it still bears a residual risk related to the contingent liquidity line offered. When this happens, there appears to be a sort of transformation of some of the credit risk into liquidity risk. More generally, in case of market distress, contractual or non-contractual (reputational) considerations can require the sponsoring bank to provide funding to the unconsolidated vehicles or to reabsorb in the bank's balance sheet the assets kept in such structures. This could place strain on the bank's capital or liquidity position.

Many financial institutions and investors have delegated in an acritical way the measurement and monitoring of the credit risk to the credit rating agencies. In this regard, it is important to note that the rating is only an assessment of the probability of default or credit risk. It does not measure the likelihood of mark-to-market losses and other risks such as liquidity risk or operational risks. Estimating the probability of default of the underlining risk and the correlations of the individual components – at the base of the rating process – became increasingly difficult. Moreover, most of the CRT securities are rated by credit rating agencies in exchange for payment of a fee by the issuer, an arrangement that – according to several observers – has been a source of potential conflicts of interest. Furthermore, the issuer does not explicitly pay for post-issuance monitoring costs, except when the instrument is being prepared for sale. For all these reasons, regulators have underlined that market participants, in using ratings, need to be aware of their limitations.[54] Rating agencies are now responding to these challenges by restructuring themselves and designing new services aimed at reducing the above-mentioned problems.

Several regulators have in the last few years brought to light several critical aspects of the CRT. In particular: the necessity for the intermediaries to maintain adequate risk management procedures, the presence of potential regulatory arbitrage, the lack of transparency and poor disclosure, and the difficulty to determine where the final risk has been transferred. Complex accounting problems were also noted, concerning the perimeter of consolidation, the difficult pricing and the poor liquidity of complex products. The presence of distorted incentives or conflicts of interest on the part of various actors has been underlined as well.[55] In particular, since the credit risk is priced and transferred in a context of imperfect information, the incentive to perform a stringent screening and monitoring in order to assess the creditworthiness of the borrower is attenuated.

These issues were the subject also of a broad international debate by the Committee on the Global Financial System at the Bank of International Settlements, in which numerous regulators and central banks participate. Among various initiatives, in October 2004, the Joint Forum's Working Group on Risk Assessment and Capital, to which we refer for a more in-depth analysis, made numerous recommendations, in response to requests by the FSF, on some critical aspects of the CRT.[56] Further, more detailed and penetrating recommendations has been delivered by the FSF in April 2008.[57]

6.4 The payment system and the role of the settlement banks

The growing volume of wholesale transactions in the domestic interbank market and the great number of retail transactions via electronic instruments have made the role of an efficient and secure payment system crucial. It is estimated that the amount of payments carried out annually through the United Kingdom's payment system is about 140 times the country's GDP.[58]

A payment system is defined as any organized arrangement for the transfer of value between economic agents. In value terms, most of these transactions involve high-value transfers, typically between financial institutions, such as transfers of funds between banks in response to reciprocal lending or lending to customers, or settlements of transactions involving foreign exchange, equities, bonds, money market instruments and other financial assets. Others transactions are greater in number but smaller in value, reflecting transfers between individuals and/or companies (transfer orders, direct debits, cheques, credit card payments, etc.). Before continuing further, it might be useful to provide some definitions and to clarify some technical aspects of the payment system.

British intermediaries use the following payment systems: the Clearing House Automated Payment System (CHAPS), a real-time-gross settlement system (since 1996) for high-value interbank payment transactions in sterling and euro; CREST, a delivery-versus-payment for securities, specifically a real-time gross settlement system in central banking money[59] for gilts, equities, and money market instruments, including repos; and Continuous Linked Settlement (CLS), launched in 2002 and designed to eliminate principal risk in the settlement of foreign exchange transactions.[60] There are then the other systems for retail payments (BACS, Cheque & Credit Clearing, Visa, etc.). In September 2002, CREST merged with Euroclear to create a pan-European securities settlement system for equity and fixed-income transactions.[61]

Until recently, the structure of the British settlement system was very asymmetric: on the one hand, there was a very limited number of banks (about 12, accounting for 3–4 per cent of the total number of banks in 2004) that acted as first-tier banks in CHAPS, and settled directly with the central bank; on the other, there was a great number of banks (second-tier banks) that processed their payments through primary banks. This configuration dates back to the second half of the eighteenth century, when the 'country banks' banked with the 'London banks', which – in turn – banked with the Bank of England.[62]

Clearing involves transmitting, reconciling and in some cases confirming payment orders or security transfer instructions prior to settlement, possibly including the netting of instructions and the establishment of final positions for settlement. Sometimes the term is used (imprecisely) to include settlement.[63] As we have already seen, a clearing house is a central location or central processing mechanism through which financial institutions agree to exchange payment instructions or other financial obligations (e.g. securities). In order to reduce the settlement risk, the clearing house normally performs a comprehensive risk management that allows for the early identification of customers who might be unable to fulfil their obligations.[64]

It is worth mentioning that the principal clearing house of the United Kingdom is the London Clearing House (now LCH.Clearnet).[65] The LCH is now a central counterparty, serving major international exchanges and platforms, equity markets, exchange-traded derivatives markets, energy markets, the interbank interest rate swaps market and the majority of euro-denominated and sterling bond and repo markets. Since 1999, the LCH is the central clearing house for certain types of OTC derivatives contracts, thereby accentuating the blurring phenomenon mentioned earlier. It is also interesting to note that small new entrants and commercial bank providers are increasingly offering multicurrency clearing and settlements services. Moreover, while, historically, financial infrastructures has typically evolved along national lines, cross-border alliances allows now to trade securities in one country and to complete the settlement in another.[66] Therefore, differences between regulatory regimes for incumbent providers of infrastructures and those of either commercial banks or small new entrants not subject to oversight are creating a new challenging environment for regulators.

Although the old system proved in fact very robust for many years, it was less than optimal, since temporary difficulties under particular conditions could not be excluded. Exposure could arise to the extent that first-tier banks offer unsecured credit to the second-tier banks. As underscored by the IMF, too, in its assessment of the UK financial sector,[67] in periods of general market stress, the first-tier bank could in fact delay in making payments on behalf of clients of second-tier banks, preferring to make its own payments and/or reducing the intra-day credit lines extended to the customer of its second-tier banks, thereby exacerbating any liquidity pressures faced by the second-tier banks. Payments to and from indirect participants may result in settlement banks offering unsecured credit to indirect participants. These exposures could be large, especially in stressed market conditions. An additional risk in a tiered system is the concentration of activities in a limited number of key settlement banks.[68]

In part in response to the IMF's assessment, over the last few years the Bank of England has intensified payment system oversight and introduced important reforms in order to increase the number of first-tier banks. Moreover, in January 2005 the Bank of England published its first Payment System Oversight Report.[69] The report clarifies the role of the central bank in payment system surveillance and increases transparency in this area.[70] As we will see, after the reform of the monetary arrangements (described in the next paragraph), individual settlement banks operating in the real-time gross settlement system (RTGS), now have the choice of acquiring their reserves indirectly, via unsecured money markets, or directly, via one-market operation or intra-day repos with the Bank. The new system encouraged a larger number of banks to join the RTGS. The number of banks participating in the reserve scheme increased from 12 to 41, representing now almost 90 per cent of the UK bank's total assets.

6.5 The sterling money market and liquidity management

A well-functioning money market and good liquidity management by financial intermediaries are essential preconditions to ensuring that funds are allocated efficiently in the economy. Monetary policy and precautionary arrangements, aimed at maintaining the stability of the banking system and the reliability of the payment system, are two distinct but strictly interconnected issues. An overview of these aspects, at the core of the banking activity, is therefore crucial from a macro-prudential perspective.

The Bank of England's liquidity framework is based on three building blocks: the reserve-averaging scheme, standing facilities and open-market operations. Recently, the Bank of England promoted a number of reforms so as to enhance the distribution of daily liquidity to the market, and to minimize the probability and costs of potential systemic risks.[71] The resulting framework is particularly due to recent reform, implemented in May 2006. The FSA, for its part, has refined the prudential guidelines for an effective risk management by regulated firms and has recently proposed, in a discussion paper, further enhancements in this area.[72] Let us examine these two aspects in turn.

Regarding the Bank of England's liquidity framework, we should note that all deposit-taking members (banks and building societies) of the reserve-averaging scheme are allowed to hold reserve balances in central bank money at the Bank of England.[73] These banks agree to maintain, on average, a level of reserves at about the target they choose (within a +/− 1 per cent range). Banks are allowed to vary their reserve balance from day to day, and their monthly target from one Monetary Policy Committee (MPC) meeting to the next (the so-called 'maintenance period'). The Bank, however, sets a ceiling on individual institutions' reserve targets and has the right to limit changes to the target, should there be large fluctuations in aggregate target reserves. Such reserves are remunerated at the Bank Rate set by the MPC. Penalties are applied if, at the end of the maintenance period, a bank fails to meet the target.[74]

In order to meet their targets, eligible banks face the choice between trading in the market and using the deposit and collateralized lending facilities ('standing facilities'). For instance, if market rates are below the official Bank Rate, banks have an incentive to borrow in the market, and *vice versa*. This mechanism helps keep market rates toward the centre of the monetary policy corridor, close to the official Bank Rate.

For the first time in its history, the Bank has therefore begun to pay interest on balances held by the banks participating in the arrangements; banks now hold target balances with the Bank on average over a month, rather than having to 'square up' every day; deposit and collateralized lending facilities are widely available; and the Bank has moved open market operations from daily to weekly. With the current arrangements, if any individual bank misjudges its reserve target and needs additional liquidity, then it is supplied automatically against eligible collateral at a penalty rate.

The Bank of England undertakes a routine open market operation (OMO) on the final day of the maintenance period in order to be sure that reserve banks can collectively hold reserves close to their aggregate target, with balanced risks to the up-side and down-side. OMOs encompass short-term repos, long-term repos and the outright purchase of bonds.[75] In the event of money market or infrastructure disruptions, the Bank of England can increase the supply of central bank money through exceptional OMOs or widen the reserve target range.[76]

The Bank of England provides central bank money in its OMOs and standing lending facilities, against eligible collateral such as gilts, UK government foreign-currency debt securities, certain sterling- and euro-denominated securities issued by the central banks or major international institutions of the European Economic Area, and in exceptional circumstances US Treasury bonds as well.[77] Regarding the second aspect, that of liquidity management by banking intermediaries and the FSA guidelines, it is helpful to make some preliminary considerations as to the nature of the problem.[78]

An important element of banking is maturity transformation and provision of liquidity. However, in performing these duties, banks expose themselves to liquidity risk. This risk is twofold, and concerns the possibility that a bank, although technically solvent, cannot generate sufficient cash resources to meet its payment obligations at a certain moment in time (the so-called 'funding liquidity risk'). Moreover, in some circumstances, the bank can provide liquidity only at materially disadvantageous terms ('market liquidity risk'). As a consequence, in monitoring the liquidity of their portfolios, banks should consider the expected cost of liquidation at any point in time, the expected behavior of other market participants, and the extent to which the banks are able or willing to provide financing.

In order to maintain a precautionary liquidity buffer, a number of strategies are available to banks: holding a sufficient amount of immediately available cash or marketable assets; securing an appropriate matching of future cash flows from maturing assets and liabilities; and further borrowing.[79] Banks are reluctant to hold a large stock of immediately available cash or marketable assets, as these generate a low return. Therefore, they depend on future cash flows and their ability to raise funds in the market, as the need arises. What matters is not so much the contractual maturity (the date of maturity of a particular asset or liability), but rather the 'behavioural maturity', or the average expected maturity, for each asset and liability. This implies a much more sophisticated management of liquidity and a clear perception of current and future market conditions by the intermediaries.

In recent years, liquidity management has also become more complicated because of the increasing volume of securitization and, in general, OTC market transactions. Estimating the liquidity of OTC derivatives products is particularly difficult. OTC derivatives are often recorded at fair value, defined as the amount at which the instrument could be exchanged in current transactions between market participants. In practice, however, fair value may be estimated using a model of a present value of future cash flows. Therefore, for illiquid OTC derivatives positions, valuation may be imputed from analogous portfolios of more liquid derivatives. When models are used to mark positions, they need to be periodically checked against market quotations.[80]

The FSA's liquidity requirements for banks and building societies are based on both quantitative rules and high-level guidelines regarding the responsibilities and involvements of the bank's board and management, particularly in risk awareness and implementation of adequate liquidity stress tests.

Concerning quantitative rules, the current regime is based on the following three aspects:

1. The Sterling Stock regime, introduced in 1996, applies to most retail banks on a consolidated basis.[81] The objective of the regime is to ensure that the 'sterling stock bank' has enough highly liquid assets to meet its outflows for the first week of a liquidity crisis, without recourse to the market for renewed wholesale funding. The stock is limited to central-bank eligible assets and assets held at the central bank itself ('reserve balances'). Retail banks should maintain in their portfolios a stock of sterling liquidity assets sufficient to cover possible exceptional outflows over the following five business days;[82]
2. The Mismatch regime, which applies to all other types of banks (non-sterling-stock banks), aims to ensure an adequate balancing of maturities on both the debit and credit sides, according to a schedule articulated in different timeframes (maturity ladder). The FSA focuses its attention on very short-term maturities (one week, one month) verifying that in such timeframes banks do not generate significant misalignments with respect to total deposits;
3. The Building Societies regime sets a limit for the net liquidity needs of those banks in the short-term timeframe (up to 8 days), so that 3.5 per cent of bank liabilities are covered by activities that are readily able to be liquidated and of high quality. For overall liquidity requirements, the percentages are fixed directly by the building societies, under FSA supervision.

Regarding liquidity stress testing, the FSA has recently emphasized the importance of market-wide simulations to hypothesize the interruption, or even the closure, of one or more markets. The simulations should consider both short-term (a few days or weeks) and chronic liquidity shocks. In addition they should take into account potential difficulties in the movement of liquidity between countries, and thus from one currency to another and/or from one legal entity to another, and in the presence of the regulatory and time constraints of market operations. Furthermore, it should be taken into account that some financial instruments can become illiquid if a large number of banks simultaneously decide to withhold greater liquidity for precautionary reasons. The liquidity stress-tests must also duly consider the risks deriving from off-balance sheet exposures and from the use of liquidity contingency lines. The possibility for banks to refinance through the Central Bank has to be contemplated with respect to the possible repercussions in terms of loss of market reputation. Lastly, liquidity contingency plans should accurately verify the interdependencies within the banking system that could bear contagion risks.

In view of the recent financial turbulence (discussed in the next chapter), the FSA has also brought to light some limitations of the aforementioned regime and has suggested some changes. In addition to certain technical aspects regarding the Sterling Stock regime and the Mismatch regime, the FSA has suggested a unified regime for all types of intermediaries. Overall, the FSA reconfirmed the usefulness of the quantitative rules, noting that 'those countries which do rely solely upon qualitative requirements for liquidity risk normally do so in the context of a supervisory regime that includes extensive, detailed and sometimes burdensome on-site inspections. We are not convinced that in the context of the UK market this is the most cost-effective method of achieving our regulatory objectives'.[83]

7
The Sub-prime Mortgage Market Crisis and Its Effect on the UK Banking Sector

In August 2007, a serious credit, liquidity and confidence crisis started in the CRT market and spread, at the global level, into the inter-bank market. The deterioration in the American mortgage market was, however, only one component of the crisis. The search for yield, stimulated by years of low interest rates and high liquidity, had promoted the developments of increasingly complex products, which in turn brought serious mis-pricing of risk in a number of financial assets. Increasing and unexpected correlations among different classes of assets and markets emerged. This was particularly remarkable for assets linked to mortgage credit: with the increase in interest rates and decreasing house values, it is inevitable for borrowers to face difficulties. This situation was particularly worrying in the US, where the sub-prime mortgage market is wide, but the turmoil spread rapidly in other markets and countries as well.

According to the IMF, in 2007 the total outstanding in the US market of non-prime mortgages (sub-prime and Alt-A) was about US$2.3 trillion. It has estimated that, at global level, potential losses and writedowns generated by the crisis, based on market prices, should be around $945 billion (about half of which absorbed by US and other international banks).[1]

Compounding the problem – and making this turbulence a historically unique event – was the extended use of structured credit products, especially instruments of CRT. The complexity and opacity of the products, and the impossibility to pinpoint exactly where the risk was concentrated, paralysed the whole market. At the core was the increasing uncertainty of the valuation of structured products. The consequent loss of liquidity in these markets triggered serious funding problems for several banks, active in that market, and their sponsored vehicles, undermining the capacity of market participants to maintain the level of reciprocal confidence necessary to make the market operate normally.

This generated a liquidity crisis that turned into a systemic crisis, despite massive central banks' interventions.

Before the crisis, there were signs that the delinquencies in the sub-prime market were increasing rapidly. The cross-border dimension of financial markets, which manifests itself in the CRT instruments previously described, made it so that the worsening of creditworthiness in a sector of a given country (the United States) had an immediate impact on financial systems in other countries as well. But one should not forget that the root of the problem, the mis-pricing of assets due to the high complexity of the financial instruments, was widespread and not confined only to the United States.

In Britain, both the FSA and the Bank of England had flagged, on several occasions, an increasing trend in interest rates from the low level that had prevailed for years and, more generally, a worsening in the global credit conditions that could have repercussions in the mortgage market, and therefore on the banking system, in relation to the possible deterioration of the value of collateral in the event of a fall in housing prices. The second potential fragility, concerning the liquidity of the market, was also signalled. For instance, in January 2007, the FSA Financial Risk Outlook alerted firms of the need to consider how they would operate in an environment where liquidity was restricted and reminded firms of the need to incorporate stress testing in their business models.

Various international bodies perceived potential risks, although not in the form and intensity emerged in August 2007. In March 2007, the Financial Stability Forum noted that the problems in the US sub-prime mortgage market 'largely reflect a progressive weakening of credit standards in this market segment' and offered some insight into how sectoral credit problems could play out more generally in the new 'originate-and-distribute model' of credit intermediation.[2] It also underscored the importance of sound counterparty risk management practices by all financial intermediaries, including margining, collateral, and stress testing practices, and emphasized the importance of enhancing market discipline.

In April 2007, the *Financial Stability Report* of the Bank of England noted: 'financial institutions can become more dependent on sustained market liquidity both to allow them to distribute the risks they originate or securitize and to allow them to adjust their portfolio and hedges in the face of movements in market prices. If it becomes impossible or expensive to find counterparties, financial institutions could be left holding unplanned credit risk exposures in their "warehouses" awaiting distribution or find it difficult to close out positions, as was apparent in synthetic US sub-prime mortgage markets in February'.[3] An overview of the sequence of facts that preceded these dramatic events sheds light on some interesting aspects of the crisis and hints at some important prudential implications.[4]

Since the beginning of June 2007, the media reported that the US sub-prime mortgage-bond market had been hit by rapidly escalating defaults in the previous months and that some hedge funds had caught the attention of the ISDA for suspicion of possible market manipulations by certain banks.[5] In an already nervous market, around the middle of June, various rating agencies began downgrading some securities backed by US sub-prime mortgages and the associated CDOs. Some observers believed that these downgradings were too late and that it would have been opportune to review the rating methodologies to make them more forward-looking, inclusive of risks in general and not only of credit and making them more smooth so as to avoid a multiple-notch downgrading.

A few days later, two highly leveraged hedge funds managed by Bear Stearns, with gross assets of some US$20 billion appeared to be in serious difficulty to meet margin calls from lenders (some important investment banks), due to losses from trading mortgage-related securities. A few more days later, market analysts reported that Bear Stearns would provide liquidity of up to US$3.2 billion via a fully collateralized repurchase facility to one of the two hedge funds.[6] However, tension in the market began to increase and spread because it came out that the sale of the mezzanine tranches at very low prices was also reflected in the price of highly rated tranches, which were becoming more and more illiquid. Many analysts remained concerned about the possibility of a wider re-pricing in the ABS and CDOs markets, which could trigger margin calls for banks and other market participants. This derived from the fact that many securities in this market are traded very infrequently and so many funds may carry them on their books at unrealistic prices; forced sales would compel the funds to mark these securities to market.

The valuation problems in the market of structured products, such as CDOs of ABS, generate an environment of uncertainty where investors are not able to discriminate different classes of assets. In particular, in the sub-prime market, the assumptions about the probability of defaults and about recovery in case of defaults, as well as the correlations between various tranches or securities with different ratings, become unreliable.

At the end of July, the German bank IKB warned of losses related to the fallout in the US sub-prime mortgage market and, on 9 August,

BNP Paribas froze redemptions for three investment funds, citing an inability to appropriately value them in the face of market disruptions. This produced a sharp reappraisal of the risk by investors in the whole CRT market. Not only did the risk premim demanded by investors on all risky assets rise sharply, but also the volume of transactions in some markets virtually closed. Those days were also critical for the hedge fund market. In early August a number of quantitative hedge funds experienced huge and unprecedented losses. The speed with which the losses occurred and the impact on prices suggested that a sudden liquidation by multi-strategy hedge funds and proprietary-trading desks, possibly due to margin calls or risk reduction, triggered the reaction of the above-mentioned quantitative funds, with an amplifying effect in the market overall. These events are related to the increased interconnectivity between hedge funds and the progressive increase, in their leverage as a reaction to the declining profitability of these funds.[7]

On 9 August, the ECB made the first injection of liquidity in overnight markets through special auctions, followed by other major central banks. A few days later, on 16 August, Countrywide Financial, the largest mortgage lender and sub-prime originator in the United States, tapped a large bank credit line, containing an ongoing deposit run, and a day later another German-owned public bank (the KfW) exposed in the market of ABS backed by sub-prime mortgages, was also bailed-out.

During the month of August, spreads on securities backed by sub-prime mortgages widened substantially, while various vehicles started facing increasing difficulties as the demand in the ABCP market declined sharply. Illiquidity also arose in money markets, at first because of uncertainty about counterparty risk and, subsequently, because banks retained liquidity in anticipation of expanded balance sheets due to contingent liabilities related to ABCP. As soon as the demand for ABCP vanished, a number of institutions needed to fund loans that they had not expected to retain in their balance sheets; in other cases the funding mismatch materialized in the sponsored vehicles and the banks needed to buy the assets back in order to avoid the winding down of the vehicle (with resulting reputational costs for the sponsor), or to activate the contingent liquidity line. Many banks started increasing their precautionary liquidity buffers, reducing the liquidity supply in the money market.

Thus it was noted by various observers that there were potential fragilities; nevertheless, it was difficult to imagine the dimension and dynamics of the crisis: 'whilst we felt that a market correction was likely, we attached a very low probability to a tightening of the speed, duration and scale which we have just experienced', noted the FSA in its memorandum to the Treasury Committee of the House of Commons dated 9 October 2007.

It was this generalized crisis of confidence in the CRT and inter-bank markets that triggered the crisis of Northern Rock, a former building society demutualized in 1997 specialized in mortgage lending. The bank was struck by a deposit run, something that has not happened in the United Kingdom since the Victorian age.[8] The Bank had had a spectacular performance, increasing its consolidated assets from £15.8 billion to £101 billion in only nine years. In the same period, the retail deposit and funds, as a proportion of total liabilities and equities, had fallen from 62.7 per cent to 22.4 per cent, against, for example, 43 per cent of Alliance & Leicester and 49 per cent of Bradford & Bingley, that were previously building societies like Northern Rock.[9]

While solid on the asset side (arrears for the last 15 years had consistently been around half of the industry average), the bank had a complex funding policy, relying heavily on an off-shore entity (a master trust called Granite).[10] Roughly 50 per cent of Northern Rock's funding used this securitization vehicle. Moreover, 25 per cent of the bank's funding was on the wholesale market, half of which with less than one year duration, while 10 per cent was covered bonds. Overall, the securitization had an average life of three and a half years and was geographically diversified (Europe, Far East, and North America).

As noted in the Treasury Committee's report on the Northern Rock crisis, soon after inter-bank and other financial markets stalled on 9 August, it became evident that the bank would have faced severe problems if the market were to stay frozen for long. In the money markets, funding costs increased sharply and maturities shortened significantly.[11] Since the beginning of August, it became clear that Northern Rock was facing difficulties in refinancing its obligations as a result of the squeeze in funding markets, despite no direct exposure to the US sub-prime market, a good quality of mortgage books and a healthy capital position. In particular, the bank was unable to tap the securitization and covered bond markets and faced difficulties in securing new money market funding or in rolling over existing market borrowings. The main weakness was that, as the market appetite for securitization suddenly faltered, Northern Rock did not have in place alternative sources of funding to warehouse the increase in mortgage loans, given the structure of its liabilities that we have mentioned earlier.

Starting from 10 August, Northern Rock and the Tripartite authorities began discussing three options: the possibility for Northern Rock to resolve the liquidity crisis through its own actions in short-term money markets and securitizing its debt; a takeover by a major retail bank; and a support facility from the Bank of England guaranteed by the Government.[12]

On 5 September, the Bank of England announced that, if the secured overnight rate had not fallen from the higher than usual level above the Bank rate, the Bank would be prepared to offer additional reserves amounting to 25 per cent of the requested reserves target before the end of the 'maintenance period'. On 13 September, this criterion was met and additional reserves were provided.[13]

Just the day before, on 12 September, the Governor wrote a letter to the Chairman of the Treasury Committee pointing out that he did not agree with additional measures, such as lending at longer maturities, removing the penalty rate or increasing the range of collaterals. He underscored that the banking system as a whole was strong enough to withstand the impact of taking onto the balance sheet the assets of conduit and other vehicles and expressed the opinion that a gradual revaluation of the assets-backed securities would have improved the liquidity in the market. Most of all, in relaxing the criteria of liquidity provisions, there would have been the risk of moral hazard.[14]

On 14 September, a statement of the Tripartite authorities formally announced that the Bank, in its role of lender of last resort, stood ready to make available facilities both to Northern Rock and to other institutions that might face short-term liquidity problems for the duration of the market turbulence. Three days later the Chancellor of Exchequer announced that the Government, with the Bank, would put in place arrangements that would guarantee deposits held at Northern Rock.[15]

There are some aspects of the Northern Rock case that are worth mentioning. As it has been observed, the crisis was not caused by the use of short-term wholesale funding *per se*. The FSA noted: 'in terms of the net short-term wholesale funding to balance sheet asset ratio, it was not a significant outlier in relation to other banks. Rather its key dependency was its use of securitization; its securitization product was a simple one, based on high-quality assets'. Moreover, 'the market disruption did not affect Northern Rock's existing securitization, but the market of new securitization had largely closed. Neither did the market disruption lead to a cessation of Northern Rock's wholesale funding, but rather to a shortening of its duration and an increase in its price'.[16] It was therefore the combination of these circumstances that induced Northern Rock to ask liquidity assurance from the Bank of England.

The Bank of England found itself faced with a difficult dilemma, clearly expressed by Governor King in his paper submitted to the Treasury Committee: 'on the one hand, the provision of greater short-term liquidity against illiquid collateral might ease the process of taking the assets of vehicle back onto bank balance sheets and so reduce term market interest rates. But, on the other hand, the provision of such liquidity support undermines the efficient pricing of risk by providing ex post insurance for risky behaviour. That encourages excessive risk-taking, and sows the seeds of future financial crisis'.[17]

Moreover, according to the Governor, it would have been difficult to undertake support on the scale required by Northern Rock without drawing attention to the bank and therefore avoiding it becoming 'stigmatized' by the market. The only way to avoid that – observed King – would have been to offer to lend to all banks at a rate that many others, in addition to Northern Rock, found attractive to pay. This would have required a massive injection of cash into the banking system.[18]

At the end of 2007, despite the gravity of the crisis, the UK banking system appeared, in the opinion of the authorities, robust: stress testing performed by the Bank of England after the crisis showed that even under extreme circumstances, where major UK banks were not able to distribute any assets and were required to provide full liquidity support to all off-balance sheet vehicles for a relatively long period of time, the erosion of capital would be marginal.[19]

From a policy perspective, three lessons were identified by the Governor of the Bank of England from the Northern Rock crisis:[20] (1) regulators worldwide have paid insufficient attention to liquidity, focusing instead mainly on capital; (2) it is necessary to pass a special insolvency law for intervening pre-emptively when a bank is in trouble, in order to separate the retail deposit book (the insured deposits) from the rest of the bank's balance sheet; and (3) the traditional discretion of the central bank operating as a lender of last resort is at risk in an age of almost instant communication. Leaking of confidential information may indeed destabilize the illiquid bank (the so called 'stigma'): that discretion must be restored, the Governor noted. The Bank of England's Financial Stability Report stressed that the crisis highlighted the risks associated with high dependence on wholesale funding and the need to implement contingent plans and better stress testing. It also underscored that financial institutions should better recognize their liquidity needs including those associated with off-balance sheet commitments.[21] Finally, the adequacy of the deposit protection arrangement during the crisis has also been questioned, as discussed in Chapter 8.

In January 2008, the Treasury, the FSA and the Bank of England published a consultation document reviewing the current regulatory and supervisory regime.[22] The document set out a number of proposals and recommendations. Besides the review of the liquidity prudential guidelines and the reform of the deposit compensation arrangements, the report addressed a number of issues aimed at strengthening the financial stability and resilience of the banking sector. It suggested promoting initiatives in a number of areas, such as better risk management and stress testing practices in banks and other financial firms. Improving the valuation of complex and illiquid products in the securitization market is also recommended. However, the document underlined that it is not the case to rush into a regulatory action. It noted that consideration should be given to whether disclosure is adequate when model-base valuations use short run time series and when unexpected correlations between seemingly different assets across and within portfolios emerge. Regarding the role of credit rating agencies, the consultation document noted that the authorities are already pressing credit rating agencies to make proposals to address potential conflicts of interest and to enhance the informational content of the ratings (expected loss distributions of structured products, probability ranges for their scores on the risk of default, measurements for other than credit risk, etc.). It also observed that the UK authorities intend to work with their international partners to identify whether there remains under Basel II an incentive to minimize regulatory capital by holding SIVs or other funding vehicles.

In order to reduce the likelihood of banks failing, the report suggests requiring banks to be in a position to provide additional evidence to the FSA at short notice that they are meeting threshold conditions (inadequate resources, etc.) on an ongoing and forward-looking basis. The authorities, according to the report, are also proposing a legislation to ensure that there is no statutory impediment to the FSA sharing information with the Bank of England and the Treasury for purposes of financial stability. The document proposed to assign formal oversight of the payment system to the Bank of England (currently the Bank does not have statutory responsibilities in this area).

On the framework for provisions and disclosure of the Bank of England's liquidity assistance for banks facing temporary problems, the authorities set out proposals in order to clarify the circumstances in which disclosure of emergency liquidity assistance may be delayed. This includes removing the current requirement for the Bank of England to release a weekly publication of a summary balance sheet (according to the Bank Charter Act 1844). They also proposed a legislation granting the Bank of England statutory immunity from liabilities in damages arising from acts or omissions in carrying out its responsibilities in relation to its statutory functions. It is also suggested to remove current provisions which restrict building societies in the amount of funding they can borrow from the Bank of England and their ability to pledge collateral to the Bank if needed.

In order to resolve the crisis of a failing bank in a more orderly manner, the consultative document considered it important to introduce new arrangements, such as a 'special resolution regime'. This includes several options such as an accelerated method to transfer the bank's business to a healthy bank; a 'bridge bank'; the deployment of a restructuring officer, and other procedures similar to those implemented in other countries.

Finally, on the issue of the coordination between the Bank of England, the FSA and the Treasury, the three authorities reaffirmed the validity of the current framework, with some changes in the way the arrangements work in practice. In particular, a statutory basis for the Bank of England's stability role and better governance arrangements within the Bank to support the new statutory obligations are recommended. Strengthening the Memorandum of Understanding to clarify responsibilities within it, in order to achieve more effective cooperation particularly when emergency liquidity assistance is needed, is also proposed

The Bank of England should be informed about developments in individual institutions when they represent a risk to the stability for the financial system. Procedure for data sharing and development of thematic work on key issues such as stress testing are also recommended.

In conclusion, at the heart of the turmoil there were, therefore, problems of mismatching (very short-term and volatile liabilities against long-term assets), transparency (opacity and extreme complexity of financial instruments) and mis-pricing, accentuated by the mechanism of risk transfer. Credit risk transfer, also implemented through vehicles, conduits or other structures, having extended the chain of the final institutions holding the risk, increased the informative asymmetries and reduced the incentives for a stringent credit risk monitoring, which had been delegated to rating agencies. More in general, it is perhaps possible to say that little has changed since the old times when financial crises where causes by a real-estate boom followed by a deterioration of collateral in the mortgage market. What is new, though, is the fact that the repricing of risk associated with the valuation of the underling assets, because of the great transformations introduced by opaque financial products, happens very suddenly and in a disorderly manner, as is more typical in financial markets than in credit ones; its effects then reverberate simultaneously in various markets far from the country where said risk was originated, and the risk itself can blow up to be a generalized crisis of confidence not only among depositors but also among sophisticated market players. The smooth and relatively slow process of credit deterioration is replaced by a much more rapid market dynamic. In the new environment, when the risk is not properly priced, the whole incentive structure along with the distribution chain (from the originator to the final risk taker) is distorted. The effect is an insufficient screening and monitoring effort by the creditor. In the new environment, when risks (credit risk, liquidity risk, counterparty risk, etc.) are not properly priced, the whole incentive structure along with the distribution chain (from the originator to the final risk taker) is distorted. Under these circumstances, consumers' intertemporal plans are also altered. When the mis-pricing is a persistent phenomenon – perhaps also fuelled by an accommodative monetary policy – and not just a short-term deviation from the equilibrium, the quantity of credit supply could be excessive. Ultimately, the 'second round' effect, from the real economy to the financial market, may be severe, while the sharp repricing of risks needs a rapid recapitalization by the intermediaries.

Part II
The Legal and Regulatory Framework

8
The New Regulatory Framework: The Financial Services Authority

It is difficult to find a single, major cause for the creation of the new regulatory framework in the UK, but several factors have contributed to the reform, that have spanned a period of approximately four-years. The creation of complex financial intermediaries had caused the distinctions that had previously characterized the financial sector to become blurred. Banks did not appear to be 'special' anymore or at least not as special, as before, now being in competition, both on the provision and on the gathering of funds, with other financial institutions, and entering themselves into other fields of financial intermediation, while the regulatory structure remained fragmented, and still very much reliant on self-regulation.

The availability of financial products, which is sometimes difficult to understand for the retail customer, raised a problem of customer awareness and protection. This problem was compounded by the mis-selling of some products, particularly pension products, where inadequate supervision was found.

The stability of the banking system had remained largely intact, but some big failures: the cases of BCCI and Barings, raised questions about the effectiveness of the supervision of the central bank. The idea of a conflict of interest between the regulatory and supervisory function, and the monetary policy function, was strongly supported and pointed to a separation of the two functions, and the need for them to be allocated to different bodies.

The models of supervision available are numerous, as the experience of diverse countries demonstrates, but can be summarized under three headings: the single regulator; the twin peaks regulation, where supervision is split according to the purpose: prudential/stability on one side, transparency/conduct of business on the other; and regulation by sector (banks, securities firms, insurance, etc.). Variations may exist for each model, and their distinction is, in fact, not so clear-cut as theoretically possible. The role of the central bank may range in its extension, but it is never totally out of the supervision perimeter.

Britain's choice has been the single regulator, the FSA, and a role on macro-systemic oversight attributed to the Bank of England, that keeps anyway the lender-of-last resort responsibility. This choice is based on consideration of cost-effectiveness, economies of scale and scope, on the opportunity of a uniform approach to regulation, and on consumer protection and financial crime prevention. The stability issue is not damaged, in the legislator's view, by the division of responsibilities between the regulator and the central bank – that is between the micro-supervisor and the macro-oversighter: the linkage between the FSA and the Bank rests on a Memorandum of Understanding (that includes the Treasury) and is assured by a continuous contact between the two.

The objectives and principles to be followed by the FSA are determined by the FSMA 2000 and they are strictly derived from the above view. The Act also specifies the legal status, the governance, the accountability of the FSA, and delegates to the Treasury, and to the same FSA, secondary legislation powers, to be exercised in a very detailed way. The regulatory approach of the FSA is described as 'risk-based', that is proportional to the riskiness of the supervised institution, where the intensity of the risk is measured on the basis of probability that a problem occurs, and on the impact that the institution's problem may cause in the system. The other approach of the FSA is 'principle-based', an approach that seems still underway and that has to be reconciled with the detailed regulatory framework set up by the statutory legislation.

This chapter ends with an illustration of retail customer protection, where there is ample room for self-regulation (the Banking Code), and with the connected theme of crisis management. This issue is under review, particularly in connection with the turmoil of 2007; the crises of banks are, presently, not subject to special legislation as in other countries, and the deposit protection is structured in a way rather similar to the protection of other financial instruments, a consequence of the blurring, already mentioned, of the boundaries between financial intermediaries. However, an increase in the level of protection of bank deposits has been recently, and hastily, approved.

8.1 An overview

As seen in previous chapters, the pressure exerted by market forces had given rise to complex new intermediaries and financial products, thanks in part to the widespread application of data processing technology. A financial structure in which banks, building societies, securities firms and insurance companies belonged to almost completely separate sectors had given way to one in which these intermediaries were largely in competition with each other, both as fund-raisers and as finance providers.

The morphology of the banking and financial industry at the beginning of the 1990s was marked by characteristics very different from the models that were still prevalent at the end of the 1970s. The legislative framework had tended to encourage this process. However, despite the reforms enacted, all the various intermediaries were still subject to a plethora of different regulators.

The growing availability of sophisticated financial products that were nonetheless accessible to retail investors was another factor calling for a renewal of the system of supervision. Especially in banking, the relative simplicity and safety of the sector's typical product – the bank deposit – had not required a complex system for the protection of the consumer/investor and in fact the central bank – first the informal and then the statutory supervisor of banks – had not developed this aspect of supervision. This factor contributed to the establishment of a body that would also be charged with consumer protection, which meant that this supervision did not necessarily have to be entrusted to the central bank.

However, the move to the last stage, that of the single regulator, was beset with obstacles, right up to the time of its creation by the Labour Government in 1997. As already noted, with the Financial Services Act 1986 there remained a self-regulatory system, albeit under SIB, made up essentially of three principal SROs (see Chapter 1). While the SIB initially pursued a 'detailed and legalistic' regulatory approach,[1] subsequently, the prevalent trend appeared to make the SROs into bodies similar to the NYSE, with considerable regulatory and supervisory powers over its members as regards both prudential matters and the conduct of business. From 1990 onwards this appeared to be the new course, which saw the SROs continue to evolve from trade associations into regulators, even if the SIB always had responsibility for setting the standards SROs had to meet, and suggested that the new morphology of the banking and financial system might have been able to go hand in hand with traditional self-regulation.

Subsequent developments followed a different course, however, partly as a consequence of the mis-selling of pensions referred to in Chapter 3. This was connected, above all from the mid-1980s onwards, to the transfer of workers from public or company pension schemes to private pension plans; only limited or incorrect information was provided on the benefits of contracting out, with the result that many of the persons involved suffered large losses and there was a considerable social outcry. The mis-selling was widely considered to have been due to the inadequate surveillance of the SROs and contributed to the abandonment of self-regulation and to more intensive statutory regulation of the financial industry.

It is debatable whether safeguarding the stability of the banking system was a major factor in the reform of supervision, with an implicit criticism of the previous banking regulator, the Bank of England. As will be shown in the next section, it is a contentious issue, both in literature and in practice, whether to assign any responsibility for banking supervision to the central bank, in addition to monetary policy responsibility.[2] No definitive answer is readily available. In the absence of such an answer, it may be helpful to consider the practical experience of stability supervision by the central bank over a sufficiently long period to permit some conclusions to be drawn.

In this respect it has been seen in Chapter 1 that the high degree of self-regulation and the piecemeal nature of the legislation on bank supervision had limited the role of the Bank of England, if anything causing considerable reliance to be placed on moral suasion. It is worth noting, however, that despite the far-reaching changes in the morphology of the banking system, the ups and down of the economic cycle and some severe shocks, the stability of the system had been basically ensured while two laws, the Banking Acts 1979 and 1987, had better defined and formalized the responsibilities of the Bank of England. In the 1990s, however, the BCCI and Barings crises – even though they were neither on a systemic scale nor imposed a cost on the public purse – raised new questions, especially as regards the adequacy of the supervision of banks with a major international presence and – driven in part by public opinion – produced new pressure for a total reassessment of the structure of supervision that necessarily involved the body that had performed the function up to then, i.e. the central bank.

Lastly, another possible factor behind the reform may have been the intention to separate the performance of supervision from the conduct of monetary policy, once this had been entrusted to a central bank made fully independent by the Bank of England Act 1998. On a theoretical level the division of the two powers was defended on the ground of a possible conflict of interest arising from their simultaneous exercise; this argument was strengthened by stressing the excessive concentration of power that would have derived for the single authority, despite the reply that the creation of a single regulator would also have brought together a whole mass of powers in the same body.

All told, various important factors influenced the shape of the new reform: the tendency for the borders of the different intermediaries to blur; the persistent differences in the regulations they were subject to; the growing complexity of financial products, with the consequent risk of mis-selling and need to protect consumers; the alleged separateness of the functions of monetary policy and banking and financial supervision, in view of the potential conflict of interest between the two functions.

8.2 Different supervisory systems

The regulation and supervision of a banking and financial system can be structured in very different ways that go from the concentration of all the related activities in just one body, the single regulator, to their distribution among a number of specialist agencies.

In turn, this distribution can be organized on the basis of different principles, of which the most commonly adopted are the distribution by purpose and the distribution by function/sector. The first (also called the 'twin peaks' principle) refers to the two primary objectives of the regulator: prudential supervision, which is concerned with the financial soundness of the regulated institutions, and conduct-of-business supervision, which is concerned with the way in which their products are marketed and sold.[3] The second principle, regulation by function/sector, refers to the sectors of activity in which the regulated intermediary operates, mainly banking, insurance and securities. Complications can arise in these models of regulation and supervision owing to a variety of factors. For example, if a country has a federal structure, a central, i.e. federal, system of supervision may coexist with a local, i.e. state or provincial, system.

Another very important factor is the allocation of regulatory and supervisory functions to the central bank. In relatively recent times stress has been placed on the latter's responsibility for ensuring macroeconomic stability, especially where responsibility for stability at micro level has been allocated elsewhere.

The allocation of banking and financial regulatory powers is influenced by a number of relevant aspects, which include the country's legal tradition and hence the constitutional and institutional framework within which the matter is set; the reputation, independence and adequacy of the resources of the institutions involved in supervision; and the market's perception of these institutions.[4]

The more general reasons that lead to the centralization of responsibility for supervision are the potential, in a context of limited resources available to the regulator, for economies of scale and scope, with consequently lower costs for regulated institutions. The change in the functional and geographical boundaries between intermediaries, markets and financial instruments, both due to the emergence of large and complex financial institutions and because the historic distinctions between loans, on the one hand, and traded securities, on the other, are decreasingly relevant in a world of traded credit derivatives.[5]

On the other side there are reasons for decentralizing: the costs and risks inherent in the shift towards a centralized system; the technical specialization in the various types of prudential risk if it is agreed, for example, that banking risk is different from insurance risk or from the risk facing pension funds; to avoid the politicization of supervision, which is easier when regulatory power is more concentrated; the desirability of distinguishing between the fields of transparency, disclosure and correct behaviour, i.e. business conduct, where supervision consists basically in an almost judicial check on legitimacy and compliance with the rules; and that of the stability of intermediaries, where the scope for the supervisor to exercise discretion is inevitably increased and thus greater the need for independence in its decision-making.[6]

There appears to be a broad theoretical consensus that no one ideal model of supervision exists on which to converge and that an effective supervisor should reflect the structure of the regulated markets.[7]

Thus, for example, where the main financial products are relatively simple, the need to regulate business conduct will perhaps be felt less strongly; where financial intermediaries tend to resemble each other, the drive to establish a single regulator will be stronger; where the country's financial system is prevalently bank-based, the greater will be the involvement of the central bank and all the more so if stability supervision and monetary policy, rather than in conflict, are deemed to be complementary. This complementarity is considered to exist on at least three levels: that of experience and professionalism in monetary, banking and financial matters; that of the reciprocal flow of information; and, above all, that of the risks, of the individual intermediary or the financial system as a whole. Another argument in favour of the central bank having a role in banking supervision is that since the banks provide the channel for the transmission of interest rate changes to the economy as a whole, the central bank must ensure their stability as a precondition for the success of its monetary policy.

On the other hand, if supervision is entrusted to a body other than the central bank while the latter continues to act as the lender of last resort, this arrangement may better clarify the accountability of the two institutions, because last resort lending is not influenced by any responsibility for the continued supervision of the institution.[8]

It is therefore hardly surprising that countries have shown a propensity to adopt different solutions, although three are the prevailing models of supervision: the single regulator, 'twin-peaks' supervision, and supervision by function/sector. In view of what has been said, so strong are the structural and historical forces present in the various countries that even when one of the three models is adopted, it is never entirely exclusive but incorporates some characteristics of the others.

A rapid survey of the supervisory structures of the G7 countries and of the interesting cases of the Netherlands and Ireland (Table 8.1) shows that four countries are oriented towards the single regulator, two are purpose-based (i.e. oriented towards the 'twin-peaks' model), and three are function/sector based. However, even in the countries that have adopted the single regulator, there is still room for other bodies that perform supervisory functions; in the countries that have adopted the 'twin-peaks' purpose-based model, the supervisory bodies can be more than two; and the countries that have sector-based supervision incorporate aspects of the purpose-based model.

The position of the central bank differs considerably across the various institutional arrangements found. In some countries it remains fully responsible for prudential banking supervision (Italy, the Netherlands and the United States, although in the latter case it shares responsibility with other agencies); in others it maintains only responsibility for systemic stability (the United Kingdom and Canada); in Ireland,[9] a new supervisory authority has been created but set – albeit with a degree of autonomy – within the institutional framework of the central bank. In Germany the central bank is involved in ongoing supervision under a memorandum of understanding with the single regulator. In France and Japan the central bank is entrusted with tasks of banking supervision, albeit under an overarching authority. Lastly, the involvement of the central bank in the protection of consumers is generally modest or nil.

In no country is the central bank outside the perimeter of supervision, however. In the most restrictive cases (the United Kingdom and Canada), it continues to perform macrostability control functions, while at the other extreme (the Netherlands) its powers extend to non-bank intermediaries.

Table 8.1 Financial supervisory structure in selected countries

Canada: twin peaks

	Banks	*Securities firms/asset managers*	*Insurance companies*	*Pension funds*	*Markets*
Prudential:					
– *micro*	OSFI	Provinces	OSFI Provinces	OSFI Provinces	OSFI
– *macro*	BoC/OSFI/DF	BoC/OSFI/DF	BoC/OSFI/DF	BoC/OSFI/DF	BoC/OSFI/DF
Conduct of business/ consumer protection	FCAC	FCAC	FCAC Provinces	FCAC	FCAC

Notes: BoC: the central bank of Canada; OSFI: Office of the Superintendent of Financial Institutions; FCAC: Financial Consumer Agency of Canada; DF: Department of Finance.

France: by sector

	Banks	*Securities firms/asset managers*	*Insurance companies*	*Pension funds*	*Markets*
Prudential:					
– *micro*	CB/CECEI/BF	CB/CECEI/AMF	CEA/ACAM	ACAM	AMF
– *macro*	ME/ANF/BF	ME/ANF/BF	ME/ANF/BF	ME/ANF/BF	ME/ANF/BF
Conduct of business/ consumer protection	AMF/ME	AMF/ME	AMF/ME	AMF/ME	AMF/ME

Notes: CB, CECEI: Committees with responsibilities for banks and securities firms; CEA: a Committee with responsibility for insurance; AMF: Authority for the Financial Markets; ACAM: Authority for Insurance and Cooperatives; BF: the French central bank; ME: Ministry of the Economy.

Germany: single regulator

	Banks	*Securities firms/asset managers*	*Insurance companies*	*Pension funds*	*Markets*
Prudential:					
– *micro*	BaFin/BB	BaFin	BaFin/Lander	BaFin	BaFin
– *macro*	MF/BaFin/BB	MF/BaFin/BB	MF/BaFin/BB	MF/BaFin/BB	MF/BaFin/BB
Conduct of business/ consumer protection	BaFin	BaFin	BaFin/Lander	BaFin	BaFin/Lander

Notes: BB: the German central bank; BaFin: Federal Financial Supervisory Authority; MF: Ministry of Finance.

Table 8.1 Continued

Ireland: single regulator

	Banks	Securities firms/asset managers	Insurance companies	Pension funds	Markets
Prudential:					
– *micro*	FRI	FRI	FRI	PB	FRI
– *macro*	CB Irl	CB Irl	CB Irl	CB Irl	CB Irl
Conduct of business/ consumer protection	FRI	FRI	FRI		FRI

Notes: CB Irl: the central bank of Ireland; FRI: Financial Regulator Ireland (within the Central Bank and Financial Services Authority of Ireland); PB: Pensions Board.

Italy: by sector

	Banks	Securities firms/asset managers	Insurance companies	Pension funds	Markets
Prudential:					
– *micro*	BI	BI	ISVAP	COVIP	CONSOB/BI
– *macro*	ME/BI/ CONSOB	ME/BI/ CONSOB	ME/BI/ CONSOB	ME/BI/ CONSOB	ME/BI/ CONSOB
Conduct of business/ consumer protection	BI/CONSOB	CONSOB	ISVAP	COVIP	CONSOB

Notes: BI: the central bank of Italy; CONSOB: authority for market regulation; ME: Ministry of the Economy and Finance; ISVAP: Insurance regulatory agency; COVIP: Pension regulator

Japan: single regulator

	Banks	Securities firms/asset managers	Insurance companies	Pension funds	Markets
Prudential:					
– *micro*	FSA/BoJ	FSA	FSA	FSA	FSA
– *macro*	MF/FSA/BoJ	MF/FSA/BoJ	MF/FSA/BoJ	MF/FSA/BoJ	MF/FSA/BoJ
Conduct of business/ consumer protection	FSA	FSA	FSA	FSA	FSA

Notes: FSA: Financial Services Agency; BoJ: the central bank of Japan; MF: Ministry of Finance.

Table 8.1 Continued

Netherlands: twin peaks

	Banks	Securities firms/asset managers	Insurance companies	Pension funds	Markets
Prudential:					
– *micro*	DNB	DNB	DNB	DNB	DNB
– *macro*	DNB	DNB	DNB	DNB	DNB
Conduct of business/ consumer protection	AFM	AFM	AFM	AFM	AFM

Notes: DNB: The Dutch National Bank; AFM: Authority for the Financial Markets.

United Kingdom: single regulator

	Banks	Securities firms/asset managers	Insurance companies	Pension funds	Markets
Prudential:					
– *micro*	FSA	FSA	FSA	PR	FSA
– *macro*	BoE/FSA/T	BoE/FSA/T	BoE/FSA/T	BoE/FSA/T	BoE/FSA/T
Conduct of business/ consumer protection	FSA	FSA	FSA	FSA	FSA

Notes: BoE: the central bank of England; FSA: Financial Services Authority; PR: the Pensions Regulator; T: HM Treasury.

United States: by sector

	Banks	Securities firms/asset managers	Insurance companies	Pension funds	Markets
Prudential supervision:					
– *micro*	4 Federal agencies* States	SEC/Fed	State Insurance Commissioners	Dept of Labor	SEC (and SRO)
– *macro*	Fed/T/SEC	Fed/T/SEC	Fed/T/SEC	Fed/T/SEC	Fed/T/SEC
Conduct of business/ consumer protection	Fed	SEC	State Insurance Commissioners	Dept of Labor/T	SEC

Notes: * Federal Reserve, Federal Deposit Insurance Corp., Comptroller of the Currency (Treasury). Office of Thrift Supervision (Treasury). SEC: Securities and Exchange Commission; SRO: self-regulatory organizations; T: Treasury.
For all countries' macro-prudential supervision, the authorities listed are those participating in the Financial Stability Forum.

8.3 Financial reform (1997–2001): the FSA and the FSMA

In the light of the above, it cannot be said that the UK financial reform was triggered – as were the reforms in some other countries – by serious banking crises, although these were not lacking. Rather, it was the response of public policy to changes in the morphology of the banking and financial industry and in the range and complexity of the products offered. The driving force of the reform was probably more public awareness and consumer protection than the instability of the financial system. Parliament supported the changes and above all addressed the question of the protection of the user of financial services; it introduced far-reaching innovations in the structure of supervision, in the belief that it had found one that better responded to the interests to be protected and the evolution of the industry.

The law did not radically change the structure of the UK banking and financial industry (for example, to the same extent as the Italian banking act of the 1930s or, more recently, the US legislation that broke down the barriers of the Glass-Steagall Act); indeed the authorities are at pains to show how little that structure was influenced by the new legislation. By contrast it changed the structure of supervision and, by granting broad powers to enact secondary legislation, not only to the Treasury but also to the new supervisory body, it created the conditions for the enactment of detailed secondary legislation, as has indeed been the case.

The single regulator, the FSA, was also created on the assumption – as mentioned earlier – that monetary policy and supervision do not necessarily have to be performed by the same institution and that a regular and effective exchange of information between the two entities that separately perform the two functions is sufficient. In 1997 a Memorandum of Understanding for Financial Stability was signed between the FSA, the Bank of England and the Treasury, which specified the forms of co-operation between the three authorities. It is this Memorandum and not statutory legislation that makes the Bank of England responsible for the macrostability of the financial system. The main forum for co-operation is the Tripartite Standing Committee on Financial Stability, which meets once a month to discuss cases of potential systemic significance and the situation in terms of financial stability. According to a recent amendment agreed in 2006, ultimate responsibility for authorizing support operations in serious crises now lies with the Treasury.

As part of the institutional linkage between the FSA and the Bank of England, the Chairman of the FSA is a member of the Bank's Court of Directors and the Bank's Deputy Governor for Financial Stability is a member of the FSA's Board.

The FSA opposes the view that the potential increase in systemic risk, due to the creation of large financial conglomerates, must lead to supervision being placed in the hands of the central bank. Rather, it believes that conglomerates require a single regulator but also – as just noted – that an appropriate exchange of information between the regulator and the central bank is sufficient.[10]

The FSA considers that one of the benefits of the single regulator is to be found in the economies of scale that derive from a single centre of administrative support (through unification of IT services, property management and financial control, etc.) and from a single staff structure and a uniform approach to regulation, authorization, supervision and enforcement in general, consumer education and action against financial crime. With the new system, moreover, there is a single regime for the handling of complaints and a single system for the protection of investors and consumers, the Financial Services Compensation Scheme. Thus, according to the FSA, the single regulator is cost-effective, in the sense that it costs less than the sum of the costs of the individual agencies that preceded it.[11] Equally, economies of scope derive from tackling cross-sector issues more effectively, through an integrated approach.[12]

But, when addressing the reform of supervision, Parliament had to take account of another factor: the special nature of the City of London as one of the leading international financial centres, something that it would have been costly to lose in terms of the City's contribution to the national economy, financial policy strategies and national prestige, not least in view of the possible emergence of competing financial centres within the European Union. The international character of the City had become more pronounced in the 1970s. 'The explosive growth of the Euromarket within the "Square Mile" completely changed the character of most of the City's activity.'[13] There had been exponential growth in the number of branches and subsidiaries of foreign banks, above all American since the Glass-Steagall Act prohibited the mixing of commercial banking with investment banking exclusively in the US domestic market and led many of them over time to elect London as the centre of their investment banking, a strategy that was strengthened by the Second Banking Coordination Directive of 1989 and the adoption of London as the hub for their activity within the European Union (on this point, see also Chapter 1).

It was recognized as important to ensure that the new legislation on supervision, which was to replace self-regulation, did not spoil the benevolent and open attitude of the English authorities or at any rate the light regulatory touch that had always been one of the City's strengths.[14]

In this respect it is worth noting a constant underlying choice made by the UK authorities: to follow a regulatory and supervisory approach that would not limit the system's potential growth, and to provide a level playing field and balanced regulation,[15] with an open attitude towards foreign institutions, so as to maintain London's primacy as a financial centre.

The foregoing may help to throw light on the new legislation, the Financial Services and Market Act 2000 (FSMA 2000), and the *modus operandi* of the FSAs. The new structure of supervision was put in place gradually, the fruit of the pragmatism and reluctance to proceed schematically that are a characteristic feature of the United Kingdom. In May 1997 the Chancellor of the Exchequer announced the reform of financial services regulation and the creation of a new regulatory body. The reform involved the merger of banking supervision and investment services regulation. The SIB, which had been created with the Act of 1986, in October 1997 changed its name to FSA and in June 1998, within the framework of interim arrangements, the Bank of England transferred responsibility for banking supervision to the FSA. In turn the FSA entered into agreements with the former regulatory and self-regulatory bodies for the transfer of their staffs and the take-over of their functions (so-called contracting back). The FSMA, enacted in May 2000, came fully into force only on 1 December 2001, when the FSA completed the preparation of its Handbook (credit union sourcebook came, however, into effect in 2002) containing the relevant secondary legislation.

More specifically, the FSA replaced the Bank of England and the Building Societies Commission in the supervision of banks and building societies, the Treasury (Insurance Directorate) in the supervision of insurance companies, the SIB, of which it was the natural evolution, and the three main self-regulatory organizations that were linked to the SIB (SFA, IMRO and PIA) in the supervision of non-bank intermediaries. The FSA also replaced a series of recognized professional bodies (RPBs), trade associations with regulatory powers.

A peculiar regulatory situation was applied to the world of pension funds since those of an occupational nature came under their own supervisory body: initially OPRA, and then the Pensions Regulator (see Chapter 4), while those of a personal nature came under the FSA, even though it was the latter that regulated the asset managers of all the different kinds of pension fund.[16]

In general, the perimeter of those intermediaries subject to supervision did not change. However, in October 2004 the FSA took over the functions of regulating and supervising mortgage mediation and in January

2005 the general insurance sector as well. Moreover, in May 2000 the listing powers of the London Stock Exchange, the UK Listing Authority, had been transferred to the FSA. The listing powers had previously been part of the London Stock Exchange's self-regulatory powers, but it was considered inappropriate to leave them with the Exchange owing to the possibility of a conflict of interest following the demutualization of the Stock Exchange and its transformation into a commercial company.[17] The whole legislative structure is completed by the rule-making of the Treasury[18] and the FSA on the basis of mandates contained in the FSMA.

The scope of the FSMA and the technical nature of the rules, were in fact bound to lead to the use of secondary legislation on a major scale, with the allocation of legislative powers to the Treasury and the FSA, whose exercise has been highly proceduralized to counterbalance the absence of any form of control over the content, even by Parliament. Before the Act was passed comments were in fact made on the 'unusualness' of granting delegated rule-making powers to a body with the structure of a private-law company like the FSA (which in this respect resembled the body of which it was the 'natural' successor, the SIB).[19] The decision was nonetheless justified on the grounds of the FSA's closest understanding of the market conditions and its consequent greater facility in dealing with the issues involved.[20]

Accordingly, while the FSMA is a framework instrument integrated by the Treasury's secondary legislation, it must be added that, to understand the detailed, practical operation of the new regulatory system, one has to rely on the policies, rules and procedures adopted by the FSA in the exercise of its extensive powers.[21]

8.4 Objectives, principles and responsibilities of the FSA

The FSMA sets four objectives for the supervisory body (Sec. 2(2)) and establishes some principles that the FSA must comply with in its work. The objectives are:

- market confidence: this expression is normally interpreted as equivalent to maintaining the stability of the financial system.[22] However, the Bank of England continues to be the lender of last resort and – as mentioned earlier – a Memorandum of Understanding between the FSA, the Bank of England and the Treasury allocates the responsibilities, in the sense that the Bank of England remains responsible for financial stability at the macroeconomic level, while the FSA is more concerned with individual institutions. It was noted, when the FSMA entered into force, that the relationship between the FSA and the Bank continued to be 'ambiguous, at least in the abstract'.[23] The text is sometimes vague. The Memorandum, and the absence of specific provisions of statute law in this respect, probably reflect the traditional British reluctance to legislate in the continental style and the preference for the pragmatic criterion of proceeding on a case-by-case basis. According to the FSA, the pursuit of market confidence does not imply pursuit of a zero bankruptcy rate. In other words it must be compatible with competition and innovation. Otherwise, it would involve the imposition of regulatory costs that would exceed the benefits of absolute stability and be incompatible with the responsibilities of the firms subject to supervision and of consumers as well;

- public awareness (so-called *caveat emptor*); and
- consumer protection.

  The two latter objectives are closely related and in fact the FSA interprets them[24] in the sense that with the first it must promote public understanding of the financial system (financial literacy) and with the second it must protect consumers, in part through that very public awareness, from various risks: ranging from the prudential risk of the failure of intermediaries, to the risk of fraud, misrepresentation or mis-selling and to the risk of financial products being too complex or unsuited to consumers' needs. The FSA is not responsible, instead, for performance risk, the inherent risk that the investment does not deliver the expected return;
- financial crime reduction, with reference to money laundering, fraudulent activities and market manipulation, including insider dealing.

As for market abuse, this had already been provided for as a criminal offence in the pre-existing legislation. Part VIII of the FSMA covers a wider range of abuses related to the financial markets and includes a wider range of relevant penalties, giving to the FSA the power to impose them.[25]

In pursuing these objectives, the FSA must act in accordance with principles of good regulation (Sec. 2(3)). It must: use its resources in the most efficient and economic way; respect the management autonomy and responsibilities of firms subject to supervision and not interfere with them,[26] ensure its supervision is proportionate to the benefits that are expected to result from it; facilitate innovation; maintain the competitive position of the United Kingdom in the international field as regards financial services and markets; minimize the adverse effects of its activities on competition; and facilitate competition between the firms it regulates.

In regard to the UK financial competitiveness, the FSA underlines that it should not be confused with a role of promotion of London as an international financial centre, a role that does not pertain to them. Similarly, the FSA is inclined not to accept – or at least to qualify – the above mentioned expression 'light regulatory touch', preferring to speak of a risk-based and principle-based approach (accompanied by a cost-benefit analysis of the regulation), that does not necessarily reflect a lighter weight on the supervised person (on this point, see under 8.6).

It is worth noting that the promotion of competition was not included among the FSA's objectives, as the Cruickshank Committee[27] had instead suggested in an interim report, but only among the principles governing the operation of the FSA in order to achieve the four objectives referred to above. The relationship between supervision and the safeguarding of competition is in fact controversial. According to one view, competition is a necessary even if not sufficient condition of the soundness of the financial industry and consequently its promotion is an integral part of stability supervision.[28] According to another view, competition policy is based on consumer protection grounds. As such, it is peripheral to the primary responsibilities of the financial supervisor; therefore competition in the financial sector should be subject to the general rules on 'industrial' competition, and to the jurisdiction of the specific competition authority.[29]

Cruickshank's view, as expressed in the interim report, was different from the previous ones. He argued that only within the single regulator – the FSA – the optimum balance between prudential regulation, consumer protection and competition could be achieved, even if a mechanism should be envisaged to allow the competition authorities (the OFT and the Competition Commission) to review the FSA's decisions on this matter. The interim report observed, in particular, that to achieve the prudential and consumer protection objectives, some disapplication of general competition law would be required, and that only the FSA might have the competence of making the trade off between regulatory (prudential/consumer protection) and competition outcomes in financial services. Cruickshank took the view that 'any complex public interest outcome that is not enshrined in the primary statutory duties is very unlikely to be adequately delivered': hence, the recommendation of adding the competition to the FSA's primary objectives.[30]

As mentioned above, the UK legislator took a different position. Competition in financial services rests within the responsibility of the

OFT – the general competition authority. The Act provides for a significant external monitoring of the FSA insofar as the Office of Fair Trading, the Competition Commission and the Treasury are required to verify the impact of the FSA's regulations and conduct on competition (Secs. 159–164).[31] The FSA and the OFT works closely on specific plans where there is an overlapping supervision.[32]

The FSMA deals with the FSA's governance, accountability, complaint procedures in several sections.

The legal status of the FSA, important for an understanding of its responsibilities in pursuing the above-mentioned objectives and complying with the above-mentioned principles of good conduct, is that of a private-law entity (Sec. 1). 'In conferring regulatory powers on a body corporate, the Act departs from the practice adopted in the UK for the regulation of most industrial sectors'.[33] It does not operate on behalf of the Crown and its employees are not Crown servants.[34] Nonetheless, its Chairman and the other members of the Board are appointed and, if necessary, dismissed by the Treasury. The Board is entrusted with performing the FSA's regulatory functions: the issue of specific rules, directives and guidelines (Sch. 1.5(2)).

The Board currently consists of a Chairman, a Chief Executive Officer (originally, the two positions were held by the same person), three Managing Directors and nine non-executive directors. The non-executive members of the Board make up a committee charged with controlling that the operation of the FSA is efficient and economical and checking the operation of the internal audit system. The committee also determines the remuneration of the Chairman and the executive members of the Board (Sch. 1.4). Apart from the legislative powers, all the FSA's other powers can be delegated by the Board to committees, sub-committees and officials (Sec. 1 and Sch. 1.1–6).

Parliament sought to strike a balance between the independence and the accountability of the FSA; the model adopted is similar to that of the Bank of England, although – as mentioned earlier – the FSA is not a public corporation. According to the consolidated English constitution, corporations – even if they are public and all the more so if, like the FSA, they are private – cannot be directly accountable to Parliament. In both cases (the FSA and the Bank of England), primary accountability is to the Treasury, which has four main instruments for giving effect to the accountability of the FSA.

(a) as noted above, it appoints and dismisses the members of the Board, including the Chairman (Sch. 1.2(3)). Unlike the Governor of the

Bank of England, the appointment of the Chairman of the FSA is not for a fixed term, nor does the Chairman have to satisfy any particular requirements. The term of office is nonetheless specified in the Chairman's employment contract. As regards the Chairman's appointment, the standards of good conduct laid down by the Nolan Committee on Standards in Public Life, which provide for a degree of transparency in making public appointments, are deemed to apply.[35]

(b) at least three times a year it receives a report from the FSA on its activity, the achievement of its statutory objectives and its compliance with the principles of good regulation laid down by the FSMA (Sch. 1.10(1)). The report is accompanied by a report of the non-executive members of the Board (Sch. 1.10(2));

(c) where necessary, it may commission a review of the economy, efficiency and effectiveness of the FSA's discharge of its functions. The conduct of such reviews is entrusted to a person independent of the FSA (Sec. 12). The subsequent report is submitted to Parliament and published in the manner considered appropriate by the Treasury;

(d) it arranges independent inquiries in cases that pose a grave risk to the financial system, or caused or risked causing significant damage to the interests of consumers, or caused or could have caused significant damage to holders of listed securities, in the event of a serious failure of the regulatory system (Sec. 14). The results of such inquiries do not have to be submitted to Parliament. With this provision the FSMA formalizes a procedure that had already been adopted without a legislative basis (as in the BCCI case).

The FSA's accountability to the Treasury does not complete its accountability. It is also accountable to the public, certain stakeholders and, indirectly, Parliament itself.

In the first respect, the FSA must hold an annual meeting, similar to that of a public limited company, which any interested party may attend. The meeting has to be held not later than three months after the publication of the annual report and not later than one month after the meeting the FSA must publish a report of the proceedings (Sch. 1.11 e 1.12). In addition, the Treasury Select Committee of the House of Commons frequently questions senior representatives of the FSA.

As regards stakeholders, the FSMA gave legislative recognition on a consultative basis to two pre-existing Panels: the Consumer Panel and the Practitioner Panel (Secs 9 and 10); the opinions of the Panels must be considered, but they are not binding. However, the FSA must explain in writing why it disagrees with a representation of a Panel (Sec. 11). The members of the two Panels are appointed by the FSA itself, bearing in mind that they must represent the interests of respectively consumers, taken to include firms, and practitioners (authorized intermediaries, clearing houses and stock exchanges). In order to reduce the Panels' dependency on the FSA, the FSMA provides for the appointment and the dismissal of the chairman to be approved by the Treasury (Sec. 9 (3) and Sec. 10 (3)).

The FSA is not accountable to Parliament except indirectly, in the terms described above, although this aspect was debated during the passage of the FSMA through Parliament. Nor is it subject to scrutiny by the National Audit Office (NAO), since its resources come from the financial industry it supervises and not from the public purse.[36]

Lastly, from the standpoint of institutional accountability, it is necessary to consider the relationship between the FSA and the judicial authorities. The FSA is subject to scrutiny by the judicial authorities and in particular to the administrative law on the discharge of functions of a public nature. However, the FSMA provides for exemption from liability in damages for the FSA's members, officers and other employees in the discharge of their functions unless they acted in bad faith or in violation of the Human Rights Act 1998 (Sec. 102). The exemption was fiercely debated, not least in view of the breadth of the powers held by the FSA as sole regulator. Thus, though enacting the exemption, the FSMA provides for a complaints procedure against the FSA's decisions other than those of a legislative nature: an investigator, appointed by the FSA but approved by the Treasury, acts independently of the FSA and may recommend but not require it to make compensatory payments or to remedy the matter complained of when complaints are found to have been justified (so-called *ex gratia* payments) (Sch.1.7(1)(3), 8(5)). Here again, there has been strong criticism of the role of the investigator, asking how he can act independently if he is appointed by the FSA.[37]

Persons who consider they have been damaged by a decision of the FSA can always apply to the judicial authorities and the FSMA provides for cases to be heard by a special court, the Financial Services and Markets Tribunal (Sec. 132), whose decisions can be appealed – but only on a point of law – to the Court of Appeal and ultimately to the House of Lords (Sec. 137). The Tribunal comes under the Lord Chancellor, who appoints its members (some from the legal profession and some who are laymen), and is assisted by a staff and one or more experts if necessary (Sch. 13).

8.5 Scope of the FSA's powers and nature of its legislative function

The scope of the FSA's powers is clarified in the definition of the activities subject to supervision and of the persons who can perform them. Section 22 of the FSMA defines a regulated activity as an activity of a specific kind carried on by the way of business related to an investment of a specific kind, asset, right or interest.

It is thus necessary to clarify: what the specific activities are, what the specific investments or financial products are and the persons who can perform these activities in these instruments. The answers to these three questions are to be found in a complex set of primary and secondary legislation.

The activities are described in Schedule 2, Part I, of the FSMA and specified in detail in an Order issued by the Treasury under a mandate granted by Section 22 of the FSMA (the Regulated Activities Order – RAO).

This Order[38] includes mainly: accepting deposits, issuing electronic money, insurance, dealing in investments as principal and as agent, arranging deals in investments, managing and administering investments, collective investment schemes, sending dematerialized instructions relating to a security, stakeholder pension schemes, investment advise, funeral plan providers, Lloyd's related activities and mortgage lending.

As for the financial instruments by means of which to perform the above-mentioned activities, Schedule 2, Part II, of the FSMA includes mainly: deposits, shares, debt instruments, government and public securities, warrants, certificates representing securities, units in collective investment schemes, options, futures, contracts for differences, insurance contracts, participation in Lloyd's syndicates, regulated mortgage contracts, and generally any right or interest in an investment, defined as above.

As for the persons who can perform the above-mentioned activities in the above-mentioned instruments, according to Section 19 of the FSMA, they must be persons authorized by the FSA or expressly exempted from the authorization requirement. In turn authorized persons are listed in Section 31 of the Act, which provides for authorization to be granted: on the basis of certain requirements specified in Part IV of the Act to legal and natural persons who apply to the FSA; to persons who comply with European rules (EEA firms); and other persons otherwise authorized under specific provisions of the FSMA. Exemptions from authorization are granted directly by the FSMA to persons who operate under a mandate (appointed representatives) (Sec. 39) and to stock exchanges and clearing houses (Sec. 285) and by the Treasury in a special Order.[39]

Authorized persons include banks, but the FSMA does not contain a definition of banks nor does it include them in a separate category of authorized persons. For this it is necessary to refer to the FSA's Handbook and the Regulated Activities Order. According to which a bank is a firm that has been permitted by the FSA to gather deposits used to make loans to other persons; permission that entails being subject to the FSA's prudential rules.

As mentioned above, the FSA has developed a substantial body of regulation mandated by the FSMA, which, together with its actual operation, helps to define the 'style of supervision' or in other words the regulatory regime.

The Handbook of Rules and Guidance was published when the FSMA entered fully into force on 1 December 2001. It is divided into seven main parts, each of which is divided into manuals, first submitted to interested parties in the form of consultation papers. The complete shift to a heteronomous model and the adoption of a detailed regulation are remarkable in a country where self-regulation deriving from membership of trade associations had been the rule and seen as ensuring independence and non-interference. It is, however, true that the legislation of 1986 (the FSA) had already superimposed the SIB to the SROs, thus constraining their regulatory role, as we have seen above. This detailed regulation occurred despite declarations of principle and recommendations regarding the effectiveness and oneness of the responsibilities of corporate officers and of the principle of good regulation established in Section 2 of the FSMA concerning the FSA's non-interference with the management of persons subject to supervision. The FSA is now shifting to a more principle-oriented approach (see 8.6 below).

The regulatory function of the FSA is extremely proceduralized to ensure maximum administrative transparency. The FSMA specifies that it must be exercised by the Board of the FSA and mention the rule authorizing the exercise of this function. By contrast, all the other powers of the FSA may be delegated within the organization.[40]

A draft version of proposed rules must be made available to the public for consultation and participation in the definition of the content; it must contain a cost-benefit analysis in accordance with the principle of proportionality between restrictions and benefits and the reasons for the adoption of the restrictions and their compatibility with the more general objectives of the FSA's action. Lastly, the draft must indicate the time limit within which proposed amendments may be submitted.

Account must be taken of such proposals in preparing the final version and reasons given when they are not accepted in whole or in part.

The principle of the external assessment of the FSA from the point of view of safeguarding competition is implemented as follows: all the legislation it produces is scrutinized by the Office of Fair Trading, which, where it considers there exists a significantly adverse effect on competition, refers the case to the Competition Commission. If the latter confirms the existence of the adverse effect and does not consider this to be justified by the performance of the FSA's institutional activity, it indicates the steps the FSA should take and sends a report to the Treasury and the Authority itself. In turn the Treasury may request the FSA to take the action indicated by the Competition Commission if it has not already done so or establish, giving the reasons, that exceptional circumstances make compliance undesirable (Part XVIII, Chapter II).[41]

8.6 The FSA's supervisory style

The supervisory style of the FSA can be succinctly described with two expressions: risk-based and principles-based.

Taking the first expression, in the light of the four objectives that the FSMA set for the Authority in 2000 and the principles that the Act establishes to guide its action, the FSA plans all its activity in terms of the 'risk of not being able to achieve those objectives'. Its task, therefore, is to identify and mitigate the risks in the financial system, bearing in mind its own limited resources, informational uncertainty and the costs of its measures both for itself and for intermediaries.

The operational tool with which the Authority implements this approach is called ARROW (Advance, Risk-Responsive Operating frame-Work), which it revised in 2003 (ARROW II) and explained in a paper published in 2006.[42] The Authority takes several general factors into account in its supervisory action: (a) 'non-zero failure', for, as Callum McCarthy, FSA Chairman, observes, 'a zero failure regime would be incompatible with the risk taking that is necessary if there is to be a financial return, and would inhibit innovation';[43] (b) the great number of persons it supervises (more than 29,000 firms and 165,000 natural persons), making it necessary to differentiate the intensity of supervision; and (c) the need to harmonize supervisory instruments that before the creation of the single regulator were scattered among different authorities (for example, for capital adequacy in the life assurance industry the FSA has applied the same methods of analysis long adopted in banking supervision).

Thus, in principle, the FSA does not differentiate its approach by category of financial intermediary, banks in particular, but concentrates on the intermediary's risk. As we shall see later, the FSA pays more attention to large and complex banking groups than to other categories, but this is due more to their impact and potential risk than to the simple fact that they are banks.

The FSA needs to measure risk in order to calibrate its risk-based interventions accordingly. It does so using the following formula:

$$\text{Risk to FSMA objectives} = (\text{impact of the problem if it occurs}) \times (\text{probability of the problem occurring})$$

The impact of a risk and the probability of its occurring are thus the key factors in the FSA's analysis. Under impact, the Authority considers such elements as the seriousness of the problem, the intermediary's size and its perceived importance. Under probability, the FSA has identified two main risk factors (business risk and control risk), which it has broken down into 10 groups. Business risk comprises: environmental risks; customer, product and market risks; business process risks; and prudential risks. By contrast, control risk refers to: customers, products and markets; financial and operating controls; prudential risk control; control of management, governance and culture; control functions (compliance and audit); and capital and liquidity adequacy. Within each of these 10 groups the FSA has identified other risk elements in more detailed or granular fashion. For example, risks associated with legislation, the degree of competitiveness and the efficiency of the capital market are external to the firm and therefore classified under environmental risks; those associated with retail customers and retail financial products fall under customer, product and market risks; legal risk goes under business process risks; and credit, market, operational, liquidity and insurance underwriting risks are classified as prudential risks.

In assessing probability for the firm, the FSA considers each of the 10 risk groups separately and uses the ARROW model to obtain an overview of how they interact within the firm.

Combining the risk groups according to a grid, an FSA analyst arrives at an assessment of 'net probability'.

The resulting scoring is based on:

impact	probability crystallized (100 per cent probability)
high	high
medium-high	medium-high
medium-low	medium-low
low	low

The scoring will determine the FSA's overall approach and the intensity of its response. As at August 2006, of some 29,000 supervised persons, 94.9 per cent are small firms (below a minimum threshold) while only 0.3 per cent are 'large' firms (above the upper limit), but the impact of the latter in terms of market share is high, 64.2 per cent, whereas that of small firms is only 2.68 per cent.

FSA analysts apply this model on a cyclical basis with an 'adjustment' period of between one and four years between rounds of assessment. Although this may appear to be a rather long interval, it should be remembered that the FSA interacts frequently, even on a weekly basis, with high-impact firms in such forms as exchanges of information, requests for documents and sectoral meetings with corporate officers and managers. For large firms, that is financial conglomerates operating in different sectors, the analysis is conducted separately by business unit and then combined in a consolidated group-wide assessment. While the FSA assigns a relationship manager to each of the largest firms, it deals with those it classifies as 'small firms' through its Firm Contact Centre. Small firms are subject to occasional evaluation, mainly on specific issues that have been flagged as priority concerns on the basis of distance controls or information from the Financial Ombudsman Service and other sources. Small firms, however, are affected by the FSA's 'thematic work', that means setting up a specialist project team who would analyse a general theme (debt and affordability, for example), possibly coming from new or unexpected developments, also visiting a sample of small firms to gauge the size of the problem in the financial industry. By contrast, for the more complex firms validation of the results of analysis is performed by committees composed of FSA staff.

In view of the diversified set of firms that it supervises, the FSA has developed approaches of differing intensity in applying the Arrow II model:

1. 'Full-ARROW', a global evaluation of all business and control risks;
2. 'ARROW Light', covering only some areas or sectors deemed to be especially significant for the intermediary; and the
3. model for small firms, reserved to intermediaries judged to be 'low-impact'.

For example, in the field of authorization procedures the FSA has 'significantly automated its authorization process, so that detailed examination of firms seeking authorization is confined to a minority whose characteristics have required them to submit to a more detailed screening'.[44]

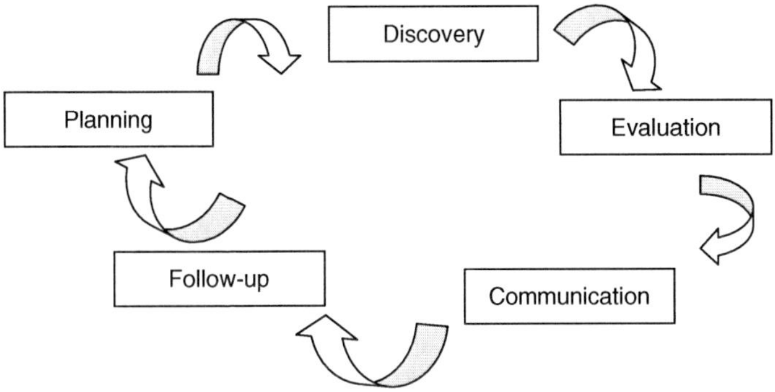

Figure 8.1 FSA assessment cycle

The supervisory assessment cycle is divided into the planning phase, discovery, evaluation, communication to firms and follow-up, after which a new round of assessment begins, as shown in Figure 8.1.

Turning to the FSA's other approach, principles-based regulation, the underlying idea is to focus on the outcome rather than focusing on compliance with the rules, which may concentrate on symptoms rather than causes of market problems.[45] Starting from a very detailed regulatory framework, this approach marks a significant development. The FSA has defined 11 general principles for businesses on the basis of the four objectives and the rule-making power assigned to it by the FSMA. The principles constitute 'a general statement of the fundamental obligations of firms under the regulatory system'.[46] It is important to note, however, that if the intermediary's regulated activity consists in accepting deposits (or issuing electronic money), violations of the principles are material only if they have implications for confidence in the financial system, the fitness of the firm or the adequacy of its financial resources.

The principle that has the greatest bearing on principles-based regulation in the field of conduct-of-business is the sixth, that of treating customers fairly. The Authority takes the approach that this principle should be implemented by means of regulation that is not overly detailed and intrusive, relying on the responsibilities of the intermediary's senior management, giving this more room for flexibility and innovation, and seeking a more interactive and positive relationship with the intermediary.

However, the FSA cautions intermediaries against a possible misunderstanding: this approach based on non-intrusive principles-based regulation is not intended as a sort of outsourcing of rule-making to trade associations, an anachronistic return to self-regulation, nor is there any possibility of the Authority's moving towards an exclusively principles-based regime. According to an opinion, however, the financial industry will move to fill the gaps, with an increased role for trade associations in providing guidance to infill around the principles.[47]

It is a question, rather, of striking a new balance between general principles and specific rules. This is not easy to achieve, not only given the constant stream of new rules from Brussels but also owing to what Callum McCarthy, FSA Chairman, calls intermediaries' 'surprising attachment to any rule'. In fact, within firms there is often disagreement between senior management, which is in favour of the approach, and lawyers and compliance officers, who lose the certainty of rules. One concern is that compliance officers – comfortable with detailed, prescriptive rules – may feel that their responsibilities are diminished or, rather, that the compliance officers might be worried about the responsibilities involved. The principles-based approach is likely to be the most effective instrument, as an alternative to highly prescriptive rules, to ensure a fair deal for the retail customer.

With the adoption of this approach, the length of the conduct-of-business Handbook is halved[48] and the burden of administrative costs that regulation places on firms is reduced. These costs were recently calculated at £600 million per year, or roughly 0.5 percent of the financial industry's turnover. The goal is to simplify rule-making by the end of 2008 for a vast set of activities that account for more than 80 per cent of the administrative costs borne by the industry, which thus stands to enjoy a 'regulatory dividend' from the implementation of the new approach.[49] The principles-based approach also involves a reduction in the Authority's staff, which currently numbers about 2,800 and is projected to fall by some 300 over the next three years.[50]

8.7 Crisis management tools: institutional aspects

At the outset of 2008, the UK does not have special legislation for the management of crises of banks and other financial intermediaries; the general provisions of the Insolvency Act for failures of companies apply. Nevertheless, considering the Authority's tasks of protecting the public interest, the FSMA (Part XXIV) gives it powers of intervention in insolvency proceedings: voluntary arrangements, administration orders, receiverships, and voluntary or court-ordered winding up procedures. The main provisions of the FSMA refer to the Authority's: power to challenge the voluntary arrangement in court if it is unfairly prejudicial

(Sec. 356); power to petition the court for an administration order (Sec. 359); right to be heard by the receiver and to the same statutory rights as unsecured creditors in receiverships (Sec. 363); right to be heard in court and be represented at creditors' meetings in voluntary winding up (Sec. 365); and power to petition the court for the winding up of an intermediary, which the court will grant if the intermediary is insolvent or if it is in any case just and equitable that the intermediary be wound up (Sec. 367).[51]

Completing the framework of crisis management is the FSCS, which the FSMA (Part XV) introduced as the sole compensation scheme for the entire financial industry, replacing seven previous schemes (such as the Deposit Protection Scheme for bank deposits). The single scheme is presently based on a simple tripartite division between bank deposits, insurance products and other financial products, further evidence of the response of UK legislation to the increasing blurring of the boundaries between the various types of financial intermediation. Mortgage advice and arranging, and insurance mediation have been added in 2004 and 2005.

Some of the principles underpinning the Financial Services Compensation Scheme can be gleaned from a joint document of the Treasury, the FSA and the Bank of England.[52] Guarantee schemes serve to compensate the customers of intermediaries in default, a need that must be kept separate from the regulator's objective of preserving financial stability; their role is, in fact, not to prevent an insolvency but to attenuate its effects. Further, although their resources come from member institutions, they are not charged with informing the markets on the intermediaries' risk, which must be drawn from other sources (for banks, from Basel II).[53] In other words, guarantee schemes should not attempt to replicate the supervisory regime. Lastly, guarantee schemes must minimize consumers' moral hazard while still giving them sufficient protection. This is reflected in the principle of setting a ceiling on compensation payments, thus making consumers (depositors in the case of banks) foot part of the cost of the intermediary's failure.

Part XV of the FSMA requires the Authority to constitute a body corporate to manage the FSCS (the scheme manager) (Sec. 212) and establish the system's operating rules. Like the FSA, the scheme manager does not exercise its functions on behalf of the Crown, nor are its officers Crown servants. The FSMA requires the FSCS to make payments only in the event that an intermediary is unable to discharge its obligations (Sec. 213 (1)).

The scheme manager is required to assess and pay compensation to the creditors of an insolvent intermediary and levy contributions on member institutions that serve to cover the Scheme's operating expenses and compensation payments (Sec. 213(3)). The Scheme announces the level of the levies at the beginning of its own financial years, although for the sake of convenience the FSA collects the levies along with its own fees.[54]

The FSA issued the rules (called COMP) regulating the FSCS in September 2001 as part of its own Handbook. Relations between the FSA and FSCS are governed by a Memorandum of understanding.

The following conditions must be satisfied for a claimant to qualify for compensation:

1. the claimant must be eligible. COMP (Sections 4.2 and 4.3) restricts eligibility to natural persons and 'small firms';[55] 'large firms' are generally excluded, albeit with some important exceptions;
2. the claim must qualify as a protected claim, of which there are three general categories (deposits, insurance contracts and other financial products). To qualify, claims must satisfy the requirements of COMP 5 of the FSA Handbook (companies established under English law, companies established under the law of a country outside the European Economic Area with branches in the United Kingdom, companies based in European countries that choose to add the UK scheme to their home-country scheme);
3. the claim must be in respect of an intermediary that participates in the fund (COMP 6.2.1 R);
4. the intermediary must be in default, which COMP 6.3 defines to cover both cases where a formal insolvency and winding up procedure is under way and those where the FSA deems that the intermediary is unlikely to satisfy the protected claims on it, even if formal winding up has not begun.

Limits are set on the amount of compensation payable for some categories of claim: for deposits, the level was £35,000, of which: the first £2,000 was fully covered, the rest covered at 90 per cent, for a total of 31,700 pounds. However, as of October 2007, it was brought to £35,000 at 100 per cent. The FSCS is financed by intermediaries (Handbook, Fees 6) through a pay-as-you-go system. The annual contribution to the fund may be waived if the fund's resources are deemed sufficient to cover any defaults that may occur during the year. The scheme is not, however, a pre-funded one (as, for instance, the FDIC in the United States), because, in the opinion of the UK authorities, this would unnecessarily tie-up resources that might be usefully invested elsewhere.

As mentioned, participation in the fund is divided into sub-schemes: accepting deposits, insurance business, investments, mortgage advice and arranging (from October 2004) and insurance mediation (from January 2005). Within the sub-schemes participants are divided into contribution groups according to the activity they perform. The contribution mechanism is designed to ensure that the amount of payments into the fund by a given contribution group reflects, as far as possible, the amount of claims for compensation in respect of that group, as provided by Section 213(5) of the FSMA. This arrangement also avoids cross-subsidies between groups. In the event of a sudden default by a large intermediary, each sub-scheme is permitted to borrow on the market or from other sub-schemes in order to meet its obligations.

The financial turmoil of 2007 has prompted the authorities to rethink the protection scheme and, beyond that, the whole framework for dealing with banks in distress. A Discussion paper has been jointly prepared by the three financial authorities – the Treasury, the FSA and the Bank of England – in October 2007. About deposit protection, the most immediate issues regarded the level of protection and the timeliness of repayments. As noted above, the urgency of the issue has brought to an increase in the level to 35,000 pounds, even before the publication of the Paper. About timeliness, in the current regime the administrator of the failed bank suspends payments to all creditors, including depositors: here, the issue is related to the fact that no special provisions are in force for failing banks (see 8.7 below), as in other countries. The Paper also raises the issue on whether some banking functions may be recognized as 'critical', so that they should be maintained for a certain period, even if the bank is in crisis (for example, the access to current accounts by retail consumers). The different levels of compensation according to specific financial products (see above) is also under review, because, the Paper argues, they may distort consumer behaviour.[56]

The Paper then proposed a deep revision of the sub-schemes into which the FSCS is divided. Almost immediately after, in November, the decision has been taken by the FSA: five new classes (rather than sub-schemes) have been established: deposit taking, investment, life and pensions, general insurance, home finance. Each class, with the exception of deposit taking, is divided into two sub-classes (rather than contribution groups). An explicit model of cross-subsidies between sub-classes, and classes, has been introduced: once each sub-class reaches its annual threshold,[57] the other sub-class will contribute to further compensation costs. A final layer of cross-subsidy is then available from the general retail pool: the other classes will come in support. These changes will take effect in April 2008.[58]

8.8 Retail banking: the residual role of self-regulation, the Consumer Credit Act and the Financial Ombudsman Service

It was remarked earlier that there is still self-regulation in the retail banking sector, but even there its scope has narrowed. Up to October 2004 the Banking Code and the Mortgage Code coexisted. Subsequently the important sector of mortgage advice, arranging and sales, overseen by the Mortgage Code Compliance Board, the self-regulatory body that had issued the Mortgage Code, passed into the domain of the FSA, which assumed responsibility for regulating and supervising the set of activities called mortgage mediation. The new regime, which is consistent with the FSA's statutory objectives of consumer protection and awareness, has produced a voluminous corpus of rules regarding the capital requirements and disclosure obligations of mortgage intermediaries. According to the Treasury, whose position reflected the recommendations of the DeAnne Julius Review Group,[59] a public regulatory regime entrusted to a single regulator would offer consumers better protection, reduce compliance costs for the industry and, by increasing transparency in the selling of mortgages, was likely to reduce informational asymmetries and thus enhance competition in the markets.

The Banking Code, instead, is a voluntary code of conduct issued by the British Bankers' Association with the collaboration of the Building Societies Association and the Association for Payment Clearing Services. Instituted in 1991 and periodically updated, it provides a regulatory foundation for the protection of the weaker contractual party, establishing principles that promote fair practices by banks in dealing with retail customers.[60] The Code also covers the information that banks are to give customers in offering a series of products, including current accounts, basic accounts, savings accounts, payment services, cards, lending and overdrafts. It lays down guidelines for product description, transparency of interest rates, individual transaction costs, advertising and, in general, contractual terms and conditions.

The Banking Code Standard Board, composed of independent members and representatives of the banks and building societies, was established in 1999 to monitor compliance with the Banking Code by participating banks, interpret the Code and promote its updating. Participating banks must complete a self-certification questionnaire and an annual statement of compliance and are inspected by a Board compliance team.

In general, the Code prescribes that banks must act fairly and reasonably towards customers, give clear information about how an account or service works, and deal quickly and sympathetically with things that go wrong. Customers must be notified in a timely manner of changes in interest rates, fees and contractual terms and conditions.

However, the framework of consumer protection in the field of financial services includes, alongside the self-regulatory Banking Code, two important pieces of legislation governing contractual relations between financial intermediaries and customers: the Unfair Contract Terms Act of 1997 and the Consumer Credit Act of 2006.

The Unfair Contract Terms Act is general in scope, covering contracts where one of the parties is a consumer. The implementing regulations to ensure that firms abstain from unfair terms in their standardized contracts are issued by the Office of Fair Trading except in specific sectors, where this responsibility is assigned to so-called qualifying bodies. Financial services are one such sector and the qualifying body is the FSA, which accordingly oversees standardized contracts in the field of investments, pensions, insurance, mortgages and banking products.

By contrast, the application of the Consumer Credit Act continues to be entrusted to the Office of Fair Trading, not the FSA. The Act establishes the licensing regime for consumer credit – the licence is issued by the OFT – and concerns, among other matters, the form and content of consumer credit contracts, the method of calculating the total charge of credit, insolvency procedures and extortionate credit bargains. In 2006 the limit on the contract amount to which the Act applied was eliminated (it had been £25,000), so that all consumer contracts, with few exceptions, fall within the scope of the Act regardless of amount. It is worth noting that Parliament chose not to incorporate the notion of usurious interest into the revised version of the Act. The question was considered in a 2003 White Paper of the Department of Trade and Industry (DTI) that addressed the problem of updating the Consumer Credit Act.[61] The DTI concluded that the highly diversified nature of the consumer credit market in the United Kingdom would make it difficult to introduce a cap appropriate to different types of product; that the total cost of credit could increase in other ways, thereby eluding the maximum statutory rate; that interest rates could end up by gravitating upwards towards the permitted ceiling; and that a number of lenders might exit the market, reducing the volume of credit available and thus forcing many consumers to turn to illegal lenders.

In the event of a dispute between a consumer and a bank, for example over unfair terms, the consumer can seek remedy on the basis of a direct agreement with the bank, a decision of the Financial Ombudsman Service or through the courts. If the consumer turns to the courts, he can cite the bank both on the basis of the contract and for tort (negligent advice, for example).

The FOS was created by the FSMA (Part XVI) to replace eight heterogeneous bodies. It can order the payment of compensation and make all decisions that are appropriate to the case at hand. The Consumer Credit Act of 2006 extended its powers to the consumer credit sector, where the only protection previously available had been that of the courts.[62] The FOS is administered by a Board appointed by the FSA; the appointment of the Chairman has to be approved by the Treasury. It acts independently in establishing its operating procedures and, obviously, in making decisions, but its independence is limited by the fact that the FSA is responsible for its structure and budget.

The FOS has two separate jurisdictions. The scope of its authority becomes clearer if one bears in mind the distinction between regulated and unregulated activities and between authorized and non-authorized persons (see 8.5 above). Three classes of activity have been defined in this regard:

- class A: regulated wholesale activities (e.g. corporate finance and reinsurance) carried out by authorized persons;
- class B: regulated and unregulated (e.g. issuing credit cards) retail activities carried out by authorized persons;
- class C: unregulated activities carried out by non-authorized persons (e.g. credit cards issued by a non-bank).

Class A and C activities do not fall within the FOS's compulsory jurisdiction, in the first case because they do not refer to retail customers, in the second because, although they are retail activities, they are unregulated and performed by non-authorized persons. Class B, which includes the typical retail activities of authorized persons, falls within the Service's compulsory jurisdiction.

9
The Combined Code of Corporate Governance

This chapter offers a short overview of the Combined Code of Corporate Governance. It is not intended to be an exhaustive survey of the corporate governance of the United Kingdom, but rather it outlines the main features by describing this prominent example of self regulation. This approach – used often in common-law countries – adapts itself especially well to a sector such as the financial one, which is constantly evolving. It provides for a form of flexible regulation, based more on principles than on rules and therefore can be updated more easily than statute legislation.

The UK has a long standing tradition of committees on corporate governance, starting with the Gladstone Committee (1844).[1] In modern times, the need to review corporate governance emerged at the beginning of the 1990s, mainly under the pressure from institutional investors, following some serious corporate crises caused by improper behaviour of management. The LSE, together with various entities representing the auditing profession, undertook this task and set up a committee, chaired by the industrialist Adrian Cadbury, that produced a series of recommendations manly regarding the role of board members and the establishment of audit committees.[2]

These recommendations were broadly shared by the promoters of the initiative, producing, in 1992, a code of self-regulation (the Cadbury Code). In 1995, the Greenbury Committee, aimed at creating more transparent rules concerning the remuneration of directors, was set up. This was necessary as in different companies, especially those recently privatized, conflicts of interests emerged between shareholders and directors and managers, who freely set their own remuneration. At the end of the same year, the Hampel committee promoted a consolidation of the rules of corporate governance into a single code: the so-called Combined Code (1998).

In 1999, a working group on internal control, chaired by Mr. Turnbull was established. The working group recommended in its report that internal control should be viewed by managers as integral to the wider management of risk; directors should see internal control as an ongoing process, embedded within an organization's operations, and responsive to changing risks within and outside the company.

Subsequently, the government decided to launch two independent working groups on the review of the Combined Code: the first, coordinated by D. Higgs, on the role of non-executive directors;[3] the second, coordinated by Sir R. Smith, on the role of audit committees.[4] Both contributed to the formation of the current version of the Combined Code, introduced in 2003.

The LSE Listing Rule 12.43A (b), approved by the FSA, under the FSMA (2000), requires listed companies to observe the Combined Code. In particular, public companies, including banks and financial institutions listed on the London Stock Exchange and other regulated exchanges, are required to state in their Annual Reports whether they comply with the Code or not, and if not, they must provide an explanation (the so-called 'comply or explain' principle). The Code is approved by the Financial Reporting Council (FRC), an independent regulator responsible for promoting confidence in corporate reporting and governance.

The principal changes introduced in 2003 concerned the corporate duties of the chairman and the directors, the reinforcement of the role of non-executive directors, and the introduction of an efficient channel of communication between shareholders and the board of directors. Some further changes were enacted after the recommendations of the Smith committee on the role of the audit committee.[5] It was established that the three non-executive directors (two for smaller firms) who make up the audit committee must be 'independent', and at least one of them must have a 'recent and relevant financial experience'.[6] Moreover, the role of the audit committee was better clarified. In effect, the Code was strengthened to reflect the problems that emerged from the Enron case.[7] Specifically, in its new version, the Code reinforces the role of the audit committee in monitoring the integrity of corporate accounting declarations, supervising systems of control and of risk management, making recommendations to the board as to the selection of external auditors, adopting policies of assignation of consultant contracts, and, lastly, evaluating the effectiveness, objectivity and independence of external auditors.[8] The entire matter of the structure of corporate accounting surveillance and of external auditors was broadly revised.[9]

At this point it is helpful to present a rather detailed summary of the Code, as published by the Financial Reporting Council in June 2006.

The Code is made up of two sections: the first concerns companies; the second, institutional investors. The first section is subdivided into four parts that address respectively: (a) directors; (b) their remuneration; (c) accountability and audits; and (d) relations with shareholders.

At the outset, the Code states that every company should be headed by an effective board, which is collectively responsible for the success of the company. The Board should provide entrepreneurial leadership of the company within a framework of prudent and effective controls that enable risk to be assessed and managed (Sec. 1, A.1).

The Code then devotes an extensive section to the role of the non-executive directors. It underscores that non-executive directors should constructively challenge and help develop proposals on strategy. Non-executive directors should also scrutinize the performance of management in meeting agreed goals and objectives and monitor the reporting of performance. They should verify the integrity of financial information and that financial controls and systems of risk management are robust and defensible. They are responsible for determining appropriate levels of remuneration of executive directors and have a prime role in appointing, and where necessary removing, executive directors, and in succession planning (Sec. A.1). This allows the non-executive directors to have a full understanding of the life of the company, which is a fundamental condition to perform a stringent and effective scrutiny of potential irregularities. The Code recommends that the chairman holds meetings with the non-executive directors without the executives directors present, while the senior independent non-executive directors should meet with other non-executive directors without the chairman present at least annually to appraise the chairman's performance (Sec. A.1.3).

A clear division of responsibilities at the head of the company between the running of the board and the executive responsibility for the running of the company's business is highly recommended (Sec. A. 2). Therefore, the roles of chairman and chief executive should not be exercised by the same individual, and the division of responsibilities between the chairman and chief executive should be clearly established, set out in writing and agreed by the board.

The Code underscores that the board should include a balance of executive and non-executive directors (and in particular independent non-executive directors) such that no individual or small group of individuals can dominate the board's decision-making (Sec. A.3). In particular, to ensure that power and information are not concentrated in one or two individuals, there should be a strong presence on the board of both executive and non-executive directors. The international experience indeed shows that several corporate crises are determined by misbehaviours related to an excessive concentration of power in the board.

The board should identify in the annual report each non-executive director it considers to be independent and should determine whether the director is independent in character and judgement and whether there are relationships or circumstances that are likely to affect, or could appear to affect, the director's judgement. (Sec. A.3.1). Except for smaller companies, at least half of the board, excluding the chairman, should be comprised of non-executive directors determined by the board to be independent. A smaller company should have at least two independent non-executive directors (Sec. A.3.2). Another important suggestion is that the senior independent director should be available to shareholders, if the latter have concerns that contact through the normal channels of the chairman, chief executive or finance director has failed to resolve, or if they believe such contact is inappropriate (Sec. A.3.3).

In appointing the board, there should be a formal, rigorous and transparent procedure (Sec. A.4) led by the nomination committee, whose majority of members should be independent non-executive directors (Sec. A.4.1). Moreover, the board should receive information in a timely manner, and in a form and of a quality appropriate to enable it to discharge its duties (Sec. A.5), and it should undertake a formal and rigorous annual evaluation of its own performance and that of its committees and individual directors (Sec. A.6).

As regards the remuneration policies, part B of the Code requires the board to establish a remuneration committee of at least three, or in the case of smaller companies two, members, who should all be independent non-executive directors (Sec. B.2.1). At a minimum, the committee should judge where to position the company relative to other companies (Sec. B.1) and have delegated responsibility for setting remuneration for all executive directors, the chairman and the company secretary. Moreover it should ensure that the performance-related elements of remuneration form a significant proportion of the total remuneration package of executive directors and are designed to align their interests with those of shareholders (Sec. B.1.1). On the contrary, remuneration for non-executive directors should not include share options unless in exceptional circumstances and provided that shareholders approval is granted in advance and the shares acquired by exercise of the options are held until one year after the non-executive director leaves the board (Sec. B.1.3).

On financial reporting (part C), the Code recommends that the board should present a balanced and understandable assessment of the company's position and prospects (Sec. C.1) and maintain a sound system of internal control to safeguard shareholders' investment and the company's assets (Sec. C.2). Moreover, it should establish an audit committee of at least three, or in the case of smaller companies two, members, who should all be independent non-executive directors. The board should satisfy itself that at least one member of the audit committee has recent and relevant financial experience (Sec. C.3.1). Among the responsibilities of the audit committee, there is the need to review and monitor the external auditor's independence, objectivity and the effectiveness of the audit process. It should also develop and implement policy on the engagement of the external auditor to supply non-audit services, taking into account relevant ethical guidance regarding the provision of non-audit services by the external audit firm (Sec. C.3.2). The audit committee should have primary responsibility for making a recommendation on the appointment, reappointment and removal of the external auditors (Sec. C.3.6). It is interesting to note that the Code does not provide guidance on the widely discussed issue of the rotation of the auditors and of the audit company, which is occasionally perceived as a device to increase the independence of the auditors, although at cost of some discontinuity in the auditing process.

In part D, the Code states that the chairman (and the senior independent director and other directors as appropriate) should maintain sufficient contact with major shareholders to understand their issues and concerns (Sec. D.1), It also underscores that non-executive directors should be offered the opportunity to attend meetings with major shareholders. The senior independent director should attend sufficient meetings with a range of major shareholders to listen to their views in order to help develop a balanced understanding of the issues and concerns of major shareholders (Sec. D.1.1).

Finally, in the part on the institutional shareholders (Sec. 2, part E), the Code underlines that they should enter into a dialogue with companies based on the mutual understanding of objectives (Sec. E.1). It recommends that institutional shareholders should consider carefully explanations given for departure from this Code and make reasoned judgements in each case. They should give an explanation to the company and be prepared to enter a dialogue if they do not accept the company's position. They should also avoid a box-ticking approach to assessing a company's corporate governance and bear in mind in particular the size and complexity of the company and the nature of the risks and challenges it faces (Sec. E.2).

10
The Competition Act (1998) and Related Regulatory Framework

Among the institutional and legislative reforms of the Labour government, there is the question of the protection of competition. As in other fields, the aim was to provide the country with a system for governing the economy based on independent, transparent and accountable entities with broad enforcement powers. As already noted in Chapter 4, in this field specific legislation does not exist for the banking sector, which is considered on a par with any other productive sector, apart from one important exception concerning agreements and abuses of dominant position, as will be shown below.

10.1 The regime proceeding the reform

In order to strengthen the protection of competition, two laws were passed completely revising the relevant legislation: the Competition Act 1998 and the Enterprise Act 2002. However, to understand the various aspects of the reform and grasp its scope, it is necessary to make a brief examination of the evolution of the law in this field. In the period from immediately after the Second World War to today, competition law in the UK has developed in a haphazard way. The system grew more and more complex because, since 1948, there have been several statutes extending the scope and adding new layers of legislation. Part of the law was judge-made in the form of common law doctrine. In the most recent period, moreover, Community law has exercised a powerful influence, in the same way as in the banking and financial sector, both through the adoption of new legislation and through judgments of the European Court of Justice.[1]

There was a shift from a dirigiste approach, relatively little market-orientated to one based on entities that were independent and more competition-oriented, from the priority assigned to the defence of a generic 'public interest' to the importance given to objective parameters for assessing the degree of competition and consumer protection; and, more generally, from a high degree of discretion and flexibility to a series of objective criteria established by precise guidelines.

In what follows mention is made of some key parts of the many laws passed since the end of the Second World War, so as to permit a better understanding of the present regime.

In the United Kingdom the modern legislation on competition begins with the Monopolies and Restrictive Practices (Inquiry and Control) Act 1948. This gave the Board of Trade (subsequently renamed the Department of Trade and Industry – DTI) the right to request an inquiry by the authority competent at the time, the Monopolies and Restrictive Practices Commission, when at least one third of the supply of a good was concentrated in a single entity or in entities that acted jointly, so as to reduce competition. However, it was not obligatory for the Board of Trade to refer cases to the Commission or to comply with its conclusions. Moreover, the Act did not specify any anticompetitive practices but simply referred to the concept of 'public interest' without mentioning the word 'competition'. The reference to 'public interest' is nonetheless important. It survived in the laws that followed and, as we shall see, is still used in certain circumstances.

In 1973 with the approval of the Fair Trading Act (FTA), the position of Director General of Fair Trading (DGFT) was established, the powers of the Monopolies and Restrictive Practices Commission were extended and it was renamed the Monopolies and Mergers Commission (MMC).[2]

The DGFT was appointed by the Secretary of State for Trade and Industry. He was authorized to hire the staff needed to perform the related functions. In this way a structure was created, the Office of Fair Trading, that would become the lynchpin of the United Kingdom's antitrust entity, although remaining on a non-statutory basis for several years. The Secretary of State also appointed the members of the MMC, up to 50, including a full-time Chairman and three part-time Deputy Chairmen. Investigations were carried out by panels, whose members could be just three for any single panel. Specialist panels were provided for specific industries.

The FTA introduced the concept of 'monopoly situation'. Basically, it exists, according to the Act, where a firm or firms control one quarter of the class of goods or services in question. The law refers to two main cases: the first ('scale monopoly') occurs when at least one quarter of the good/service is supplied by (or to) one person or a member of one group of interconnected bodies corporate. The second ('complex or behavioural monopoly') occurs when two or more persons, not being a group of interconnected bodies, voluntarily or not, by agreement or not, supplying at least one quarter of a certain good or service, conduct their affairs in a similar way to prevent, restrict or distort competition (Sec. 6(1)). One of the most controversial aspects of this provision was the method of calculating marker share.[3]

A similar case occurs when a certain good or service is prevented from being supplied in the UK (Sec. 6(2)).

When a monopoly as defined above was found by the DGFT, it was reported by this body or by the Secretary of State for Trade and Industry to the MMC. The Commission would carry out its investigation to verify whether the monopoly existed and, if so, whether it was contrary to the public interest.

An important feature of the FTA 1973 was in fact the concept – already seen in the earlier legislation – of 'public interest'. In considering harm to the public interest, the FTA listed several factors, to be taken into consideration by the MMC, such as maintaining and promoting effective competition, promoting consumers' interests (from the point of view of the prices, quality and variety of goods and services offered), promoting cost reductions and the use of new techniques and products, facilitating the entry of new competitors into the markets and promoting the balanced distribution of industry and employment as well as competitiveness abroad (Sec. 84). The elasticity of this concept allowed the antitrust powers to be used to pursue the various policy objectives considered of greatest importance in different periods.

If the MMC concluded its investigation stating that there were public interest detriments, then the Secretary of State had the power to take a large range of actions to remedy the position, making orders or, preferably, trying to reach agreement informally by negotiations between the firms in question and the DGFT.[4]

The MMC had the right to carry out investigations, make evaluations and issue recommendations concerning monopoly policy, anticompetitive practices, the efficiency of public bodies and, as we shall see, mergers. However, it was a 'passive' body insofar as it could operate only at the request of the Secretary of State or the DGFT, and its recommendations were not binding on the former. The FTA endowed the MMC with independent status: its members 'shall not be regarded as servants or agents of the Crown' (Sec. 1) and the government could not take action against a monopoly unless the MMC had decided it was contrary to the public interest. The role of the Secretary of State nonetheless remained important since he had the power to appoint the members of the Commission, to block recourse to the same and to choose the measures to be adopted on the basis of the Commission's conclusions. An example of the balance of powers typical of the Anglo-Saxon legal systems.

The British and European approaches differed in several ways. While the European system identified a dominant position without referring to a particular market share, the British system referred to 25 per cent as corresponding to a scale monopoly. On the other hand, that threshold was counterbalanced by the extremely flexible notion of public interest. 'The most striking difference between the European definition and those found in UK policy is that the meaning of dominant position is expressed in purely effect-based terms, without market shares being prescribed. Indeed there are no predetermined indexes of monopoly in the EEC law.'[5]

The FTA regulated mergers in a similar way. The initiative in this field was entrusted to the DGFT, which assessed the competitive impact and, where appropriate, reported to the Secretary of State, so that it could charge the MMC with an investigation based on a cost-benefit analysis account taken also of the public interest.[6] The MMC submitted its recommendations to the Secretary of State, who was not obliged to comply with them, however. According to the law, consideration was given only to mergers leading to a market share of 25 per cent or more and to those in which the assets of the firms involved exceeded a given threshold (Sec 64(1)).

At the end of the 1970s there was widespread dissatisfaction not only among regulators but also in the business world with the existing legislation. It appeared ineffective in countering cartels owing to the smallness of the related sanctions and the weakness of the DGFT's powers in collecting information; moreover, taken together the legislation was enormously complex, with the result that it often intercepted innocuous agreements but failed to catch those that were truly anticompetitive and the control over the conduct of firms with significant market power was modest. The Commission's reports in the 1970s called attention to competitive problems in services and consumer products. The UK economy was found to be dominated by large firms, oligopolistic markets and extensive monopolizing practices.[7]

This dissatisfaction led the Conservative government of the time to promote a series of green papers that would suggest reforms. Basically, however, there was an attitude marked by a degree of benevolence towards monopolies that was reflected in the Competition Act 1980. This did not bring the desired reform but rather supplemented the FTA 1973. Compared with the preceding legislation, the Competition Act 1980 mainly provided a way to investigate particular companies or productive practices rather than the market as a whole. The legislative stratification that had taken place over the years made a complete revision of the field necessary. In the meantime, issues of market competition were brought to light by the radical programme of privatization of state-owned monopolies, market deregulations and the introduction of competition sector by sector. New independent sector regulators were being created, modelled on the OFT.[8]

10.2 The Competition Act 1998 and the Enterprise Act 2002

The Competition Act reorganized the entire legislative framework and eliminated earlier legislation, notably large part of the Competition Act 1980. In addition, it brought UK law in the competition field into line with European law.

The CA broadened the powers of the DGFT to gather information and gave it the power to inflict penalties; the MMC has been reformed by the Act, taking the name of CC, the competition matters are to be dealt in a manner consistent with the European law.

The Commission's historic role had principally been to study and recommend, although its finding that a merger or monopoly did not threaten the public interest was in effect a final decision.[9]

The members of the Commission are appointed by the Secretary of State for Trade and Industry (now, the Secretary of State for Business, Enterprise and Regulatory Reform). The composition of the CC has evolved. At present it consists of a Chairman and three Deputy Chairmen. With two non-executive directors, they form the CC Council, a strategic management board. Around 50 members form the reporting panel, which carries out the CC's general functions, then there are specialized panels performing functions on the basis of other legislation concerning specific industry sectors (water, electricity, telecoms). Another panel, the Appeal Tribunals panel, which had competence for appeals against decisions by the DGFT or the sectoral regulator, disappeared with the enactment of the Enterprise Act (see below).

Bearing in mind the three matters generally addressed by competition law – agreements (horizontal or vertical), abuse of dominant position, mergers – we shall now look at how they are dealt by the CA. The first two are the object of two prohibitions: Chapter I prohibitions (banning agreements that restrict competition (Sec. 2(1)) and Chapter II prohibitions (banning abuse of dominant position for the first time in the United Kingdom (Sec. 18(1)). One innovation is the introduction of prohibitions, according to an approach different from the earlier legislation but in line with Community competition law. In fact these prohibitions are in parallel with Articles 81 and 82 of the EC Treaty, which refer to agreements and abuses which may affect trade between member states and harm competition within the common market. Chapters I and II mirror these two Articles.

Although, as already mentioned, the law on the protection of competition applies to the banking and financial sector there is an important derogation from the provisions of Chapters I and II. Section 164 of the Financial Services and Markets Act, which states that Chapters I and II prohibitions do not apply to agreements, practices, conducts, when the parties involved include persons authorized by the FSA, or otherwise subject to FSA regulations, if these agreements, practices, conducts are encouraged by the regulating provisions of the FSA. FSA legislation is nonetheless subject, as mentioned in Chapter 10, to scrutiny by the OFT. The FSA is responsible for ensuring that its legislation does not conflict with the principles of market competitiveness. In particular, the OFT reports to the CC on provisions and practices adopted by the FSA having a significant adverse effect on competition. Where the Commission's further investigation and report are adverse, the Treasury may, but is not bound to, give directions.[10]

Regarding mergers, much of the merger review was analogous to the treatment under the FTA. This means that the assessment was made according to the general principle of the 'public interest' test. Structured thresholds continued to determine whether a merger was to be investigated: these are related to market share (25 per cent) or to the acquired assets (£70 million in value).[11]

The reform begun by the CA 1998 was completed with the passage of the Enterprise Act 2002 (EA). This is a wide-ranging piece of legislation that reformed not only the protection of competition but also bankruptcy law and consumer protection law.

The Act eliminated the position of the DGFT and recognized a statutory basis to the Office of Fair Trading (Sec. 1). It also created a new Competition Appeal Tribunal (CAT) to replace the Competition Commission Appeal Tribunals that had been established as part of the CC by the Competition Act 1998 (Part 2). The CAT is responsible for appeals against the decisions of the OFT and other sector regulators and reviews decisions made by the Secretary of State and the CC (Sec 120 and 179, regarding respectively mergers and market investigations). Impositions of a penalty by the CC may also be appealed to the CAT (Sec. 114). The CAT's decisions may in turn be appealed, with the CAT's consent, either in point of law or in penalty cases to the Court of Appeal (in England and Wales).[12]

The Commission remains however a 'Phase 2 Authority', because all cases are referred by another body: the CC has no original jurisdiction. On mergers, the referring body is the OFT; on markets, it can be, in addition to the OFT, another economic regulator.

We have just seen that mergers were investigated under the CA in ways very similar to those laid down by the FTA. By contrast the new Enterprise Act 2002 brought major changes: it abolished the position of Secretary of State for Trade and Industry, which had played a decisive role in the previous regime and entrusted the whole procedure – decision to intervene, investigation and any measures – to the OFT and the CC. It gave the OFT the power to activate the CC and the latter the power to establish remedies. These are imposed after a phase of consultation with the parties involved in the investigation.[13] The criterion on which the investigation of mergers still rests however on the two thresholds of market share and minimum turnover. A relevant merger situation occurs when the turnover test (£70 million) and the share of supply test (one-quarter) are passed.

In addition, the Act replaced the public interest criterion and the monopolistic situation with a 'substantial lessening of competition test'.[14] The 'public interest criterion' may nonetheless still be used in exceptional cases indicated by the Secretary of State (Sec. 42).[15]

The OFT, being closely connected with the markets' conditions, performs 'market studies' within its general functions of monitoring the economy (Sec. 5). The study either stops at the OFT itself, which will remedy the restriction of competition by using the Competition Act 1998 or Articles 81 and 82 of the EC Treaty, or will be referred to the Commission for a market investigation (Sec. 131).

The Enterprise Act (Part 4) contains a market investigation regime (MIR) that the CC has to follow. The MIR replaces the complex monopoly investigations. It relies on the concept of 'adverse effect on competition', that has a wider scope than Chapters I and II of the CA 1998 (or Articles 81 and 82 of the Treaty) and can arise from specific features of the market: market structure; conduct of suppliers and acquirers of goods or services; customers' conduct. These features are considered from the point of view of possibly causing prevention, restriction or distortion of competition (Sec. 134(1)(2)). The market share of 25 per cent has disappeared. The MIR may last up to two years and will possibly result in remedies, which may include recommendations for action by others and changes to existing legislation. These remedies can be appealed only by judicial review.

As mentioned earlier, the MIR is wider in scope than Articles 81 and 82: while prohibition systems – like these Articles – are tough on consequences of agreements and practices, market inquiries are designed to identify and eliminate the underlying causes.[16]

The role of the bodies for the protection of consumers has been strengthened. They can request the intervention of the OFT if there are market situations that have a significant effect on consumers. The OFT is charged with setting up a system for the approval of codes of practice for the protection of consumers.

As already noted, the importance of European law has gradually grown. We have mentioned Articles 81 and 82. In addition, it is necessary to consider the importance of the European Modernisation Regulation 1/2003, which has four features: parallel application of Articles 81 and 82 at European Union and national competition authority levels, concerning, as we have seen, agreements and abuses of dominant position on a cross border basis; national authorities cannot prohibit, on the basis of national laws, agreements which are permitted under Article 81; but can adopt stricter national measures against unilateral conduct prohibitions under Article 82; national authorities are not obliged to apply EC competition law as part of their national control of mergers.[17]

Recital 15 of the Regulation also envisages a network of public national authorities working in close cooperation – the European Competition Network – in order to assure parallel application and parallel results in the field of Articles 81 and 82.

Regarding operational aspects, they are defined by the guidelines of the Competition Commission. The main points are: (1) market definition; (2) the analysis of the structural or behavioural situations that substantially reduce competitiveness; and (3) intervention policies.[18]

Concerning market definition, the criterion of substitutability of the good or service is used. Said substitutability is verified using the so-called 'small but significant non-transitory increase in price test' (or the SSNIP test, also known as the 'hypothetical monopolist test'). In essence, it estimates whether a price increase of a good (or a group of very similar goods) might lead to a reduction in profitability. This would happen because of a decrease in demand deriving from the movement of clients toward other similar products, or because of a reaction by competitors. The latter would be in the form of an increase of supply by firms already present in the market or the entrance of new competitors. Once ascertained that an increase in the price of a group of goods bears a decrease in profitability, the same procedure is repeated on a broader group of less-similar goods. If the profitability increases (as if the clients were 'captured' by a monopolist), that means that the basket of goods thus identified describes the market area. SSNIP test is also considered when defining the geographic market over which the merging firms operate. The geographic market may be international, national, regional or limited to certain localities.

Analysis of the market and of its competitive tenor takes place through a multi-stage approach: it deals with intra-market rivalry before considering the possible effects of horizontal mergers. The structure of the market and its characteristics (concentration, switching costs, presence of network economies and information asymmetries, etc.) are also included. Both price and non-price factors are also considered. The interdependence between firms that might lead to 'implicit collusion' and bring about 'substantial reductions in competitiveness' is then studied.[19] The guidelines pay particular attention to the aspects concerning conditions for entrance, exit, and freedom of expansion in the market. In fact, the presence of entrance barriers (even strategic ones, such as higher-than-necessary expenditures for investment) and, in general, the existence of sunk costs,tend to discourage potential entrants, making the market less contestable.

Finally, the guidelines indicate various types of remedies, both 'structural' and 'behavioural': structural remedies could, for example in the case of mergers, impose the restoration of the *status quo* or the dismissal of certain production activities; the 'behavioural' ones aim to increase competitiveness by favoring the entrance of new firms or by removing those factors that could lead to a relevant market power. From the guidelines emerges a preference for remedies that are structural in nature, as the behavioural ones, in addition to sometimes having undesirable side effects, require continuous monitoring by the regulator.

11
Conclusions

We have tried to assess the financial sustainability and the configuration of two sectors of the UK economy – households and businesses – which appear crucial for understanding the features of the financial industry. We have also added a third sector, the foreign component, which is particularly relevant for Britain, given the high openness of the economy and the relevant amount of cross-border transactions by banking and financial intermediaries.

Over an extended period of time, up to 2005 and even later, the financial sustainability of households and non-financial firms was characterized by an increase in their debt position. This appears particularly noticeable in the case of households: at the end of the observed period, household debt stood at 160 percent of their disposable income, and their liquidity position had deteriorated beyond the already high level of the early 1990s. The mortgage market registered the highest share of this debt, the latter being strictly interrelated with the house-price boom. On the asset side, a marked shift from bank deposits to assets placed with non-bank institutional investors occurred, at least partly motivated by the relatively low levels of the state pension provisions.

These developments have had important implications for the regulator, both prudential and related to consumer protection: from the first standpoint, for the possible stress they may create on the banks' balance-sheet and, too, for the innovative techniques of credit risk transfer extensively used by banks (to which we will return later); regarding consumer protection, for the excessive risk-taking in borrowing from banks, which might have given rise to an increase in personal insolvencies, and for making households aware of the risk involved in the retail distribution of financial products, either because of their complexity or in relation to mis-selling practices.

A sounder balance-sheet seems to characterize the business sector. A remarkable development that occurred in the observed period has been a shift from bank loans to bonds on the liabilities side: a further confirmation of a market-oriented system, as we began to notice in the preface of this book. High levels of equity capital and profitability have not been matched, however, by corresponding performance in terms of investments: firms have followed a prudent investment policy. What is also relevant, in more recent years, is an increase in their capital gearing, which may have been the signal of an increased buy-out activity; this would be connected with the 'explosion' of private equity funds. It remains to be seen whether there is a highly cyclical component in this regard, or rather a permanent change in the firm's capital structure.

The observation of the foreign sector of the economy is a confirmation of the relevance of the financial industry. Its net earnings partly rebalance the current account of the UK's balance of payments, which would otherwise be deeply 'in the red'. The current account deficit is financed by an inflow of bank deposits, direct investments and portfolio investments, an activity strongly enhanced by the banking industry (this happens, however, at the cost of an unbalanced international investment position).

Turning to the banking system, which links the two key sectors of the economy and works as an essential hinge between the domestic and the international components, we can determine three main features of paramount importance in the observed period (1990–2005) and beyond:

- the openness and competitiveness of the UK banking market ('the City'), that increasingly defies the primacy of New York in several segments of the market. The most visible evidence is in the fact that foreign institutions account for more than 50 per cent of the total assets of the banking system;
- the distinction, within the banking system, between two sectors – the retail sector and the wholesale sector – that takes the place of the traditional distinction between commercial banking (lending to households and business) and investment banking (operating as securities intermediators). The wholesale sector is in fact a 'corporate finance' provider, dealing at the same time as a commercial and an investment banker. This tendency has contributed to the blurring of the boundaries between different categories of intermediaries and to the 'new' approach to regulation;
- the evolution of markets and their infrastructures. The transformation of banking from the 'originate and hold' model into a 'credit

risk distribution' model, through the extensive use of new financial techniques, influences the structure of the credit market, its development and its potential fragilities. Here both markets and products innovations are critical: the developments of CRT markets and of OTC platforms for derivatives transactions, as well as the evolution of risk management and the structure of the clearing and settlements systems are all greatly inter-connected. The nature of the market has changed, with a progressive blurring between types of products (credit and securities), between the activities of the various intermediaries, and between regulated and non-regulated electronic platforms, where non-standardized products are traded. In this context, however, the role of the bank as deposit-taker, accessing the central bank's liquidity still remains crucial. In this new financial environment, it may sound like a paradox that the early form of the credit transfer technique, or the securitization process, started in what might appear as the most traditional way of banking, i.e. in the retail – mortgage – market, and perhaps the most frequent source of financial instability.

Of these three features, the first is certainly the oldest, as we have seen since the introductory historical chapter of this book; the second is so well-established that it is difficult to see any reversal, or the adoption of alternative models, even if the 'speciality' of banks as truly separate institutions is sometimes discussed in the current difficult environment; the third is under severe test. In particular intermediaries, after a long cycle of securitization of their assets, are now engaged in a process of re-intermediation and re-pricing of the credit risk in part transferred: it would be imprudent and premature to advance any hypothesis as to the nature and entity of the phenomenon under way.

The use of innovative and complex financial products and vehicles has been an important factor of credit creation in recent years and has been exploited to fill the gap opened between the huge volume of bank loans, particularly mortgages, and the gathering of deposits from the public. Recourse to the money market, or short-term paper, through these instruments helped to fill the 'funding gap' of parts of the retail sector, at the cost however of a mismatching of long-term assets and short-term liabilities (it is observed, though, that the maturities transformation is an essential part of the banking activity and that new techniques of risk management, if properly implemented, should prevent serious problems from occurring).

The Northern Rock episode may have several readings, but certainly the crisis emerged when the amount of funding available suddenly fell. Here the interdependence of the markets, sectorally and geographically, has illustrated the particular fragility of this business model.

All of the above-mentioned changes have been accompanied, but not induced or altered, by the 'new' regulatory framework. Rather, this framework – namely, the FSMA and the FSA – is the result of efforts to attain a regulatory and supervisory structure as coherent as possible with the underlying, evolving banking and financial structure. The objectives and instruments of the regulator have been formally defined, and further developed through other pieces of regulation, guidelines, and principles of self-discipline. At the same time, some questions remain:

- Is the UK banking and financial industry really moving from a largely self-regulated market place towards a statutory and highly detailed regulatory framework? The reliance on 'principles', on market discipline, and explicitly on self-regulation in some segments of the financial industry, like hedge funds or private equity funds, leaves us uncertain about the answer. The view authoritatively expressed by Calomiris, that 'in most countries, the level of regulatory intervention in banking has increased dramatically relative to that in other sectors since the Great Depression' is correct on a comparative basis. Yet the banking sector has experienced in the past few decades a large 'deregulation' in most countries, the UK included, where regulation has been traditionally light and is trying to find the right balance between the drive to regulate and regulation in a manner uniform with that of the rest of Europe, at the same time keeping the features of an open and accommodative environment and adjusting to the innovative pressures coming from the market.
- How do we strike a balance between what has been called a 'public' and a 'private interest' view of financial industry regulation? The first view holds that governments regulate banks to facilitate their efficient functioning by correcting market failures (by merely admitting that market failures do not exist, the government role would be passive; but under this view the conviction is that market failures are many and to the extreme, this view sees banks as public utilities). In the other view, regulation is the result of the interaction of various suppliers and demanders, government itself, intermediaries, and consumers; a view that, to make this interaction more fair for all the interest groups involved, relies on market discipline, disclosure, self-regulation, and a 'light hand' of the regulator (according to this view, the interest of

the intermediaries, being more concentrated, is often on the winning side *vis-à-vis* the too widespread interests of consumers).

– Is the supervisory structure of the UK the most conducive to the regulatory objectives? We have tried to describe, almost synoptically, the different models of supervision, even though none has ever been adopted in its most schematic way by any country. Rather, there has always been overlapping of elements belonging to alternative models. We also expressed the opinion that no model is intrinsically superior, and that the supervisory structure should reflect the structure of the underlying industry. The adoption of the 'single' regulator has been considered coherent with the British financial structure and preferred to alternative models (the 'twin peak system', or the supervision by sector/product).

There are no unequivocal answers to these questions, in a world characterized by constant tension between the needs of the financial markets and economic agents and those of the regulators. The former are often driven by innovation and incentive for short-run profit, the latter must internalize long-term general interests and seek a possible cooperative solution at national and international level.

Notes

1 The Structure of the Banking System Between the 1960s and 1980s

1. See for example: R. Sayers, *Modern Banking*, Oxford University Press, 1967; J. Revell, *The British Financial System*, Macmillan, 1973; and J. Cooper, *The Management and Regulation of Banks*, Macmillan, 1984.
2. D.T. Llewellyn, *The Evolution of the British Financial System*, The Institute of Bankers, 1985, p. 10.
3. P. Cottrell, 'The Financial System of the United Kingdom in the Twentieth Century', in L. De Rosa (ed.); *International Banking and Financial Systems*, Ashgate, 2003, pp. 52–56.
4. J. Grady and M. Weale, *British Banking, 1960–85*, Macmillan, 1986, p. 202; R. Sayers, *Modern Banking*, p. 8; M. Collins, *Banks and Industrial Finance in Britain, 1800–1939*, Cambridge University Press, 1991, p. 86; F. Capie and M. Collins, *Have the Banks Failed the British Industry?*, IEA, 1992; E. Nevin and E.W. Davis, *The London Clearing Banks*, Elek Books, 1970, p. 134; D. Ross, 'Bank Advances and Industrial Production in the UK During the Interwar Years: a Red Herring?', in P. Cottrell, H. Lindgren, A. Teichova (eds), *European Industry and Banking between the Wars*, Leicester University Press, 1992, p. 199.
5. R. Sayers, *Modern Banking*, p. 103.
6. M. Collins, *Money and Banking in the UK: A History*, Croom Helm, 1988, p. 369.
7. J. Reid, *The Role of the Merchant Banks Today*, The Institute of Bankers, 1963.
8. M. Collins, *Money and Banking.*, p. 367.
9. Ibid., pp. 365–6.
10. The category of credit unions is not included in the Table 1.1. Credit unions are co-operative credit institutions with strong roots in local communities. Their total size, in terms of assets, is negligible.
11. Figures taken from Grady and Weale, *British Banking*, and Collins, *Money and Banking*.
12. M. Collins, *Money and Banking*, pp. 412–15.
13. Cited in Collins, *Money and Banking*, p. 389.
14. That is the case, for example, of Sayer and of Revell himself.
15. M. Collins, *Money and Banking*, pp. 380–1.
16. R. Sayers: *The Bank of England 1891–1944*, Cambridge University Press, 1976, vol. 1, p. 235.
17. Regarding the 'paternalistic' approach of the Bank of England, the following excerpt of the Radcliffe Report is telling: 'Like a good parent, the Bank does its best to help its children in maintaining the position that they have established, while reserving the right to keep the children in order.' See *Committee on the Working of the Monetary System Radcliffe Report*, HM Stationery Office, 1959, pp. 122–123.
18. J. Revell, *The British Financial System*, p. 340.
19. Ibid., p. 367.

20. Ibid., p. 356.
21. M.J.B. Hall, 'Secondary banking crisis', in P. Newman, M. Milgate, J. Eatwell (eds), *The New Palgrave Dictionary of Money and Finance*, Macmillan, 1992, p. 408.
22. See Bank of England, *Quarterly Bulletin*, 1971, no. 4, pp. 189–94.
23. Quantitative limits in the form of deposits with the central bank were reintroduced in 1973 under the Supplementary Special Deposit Scheme, known as the 'corset', which provided, however, for the various banking entities to receive equal treatment. The 'corset' was not abandoned until 1980. See M.S. Artis and M.K. Lewis, *Monetary Control in the United Kingdom*, Philip Allan Publishers, 1981, pp. 1–10.
24. J. Revell, *The British Financial System*, pp. 128–9.
25. The prudential principle of avoiding maturity mismatching 'was strictly respected by only a few [secondary banks]'. Moreover, 'this established principle of banking was new in the UK banking system'. In fact, neither deposit banks nor building societies addressed the problem of matching, which was actually implicit in their respective areas of operations (short term and long term). J. Revell, *The British Financial System*, pp. 245–6. On these aspects see: M.J.B. Hall, Secondary banking crisis, pp. 408–10.
26. See M. Clarke, *Regulating the City: Competition, Scandal and Reform*, Open University Press, 1986, p. 36.
27. See M.J.B. Hall, Secondary Banking Crisis, p. 409.
28. M. Reid, *The Secondary Banking Crisis, 1973–75. Its Causes and Course*, Macmillan, 1982, p. 190.
29. Ibid., p. 190.
30. P. Cottrell, 'The Financial System', p. 57.
31. P. Cottrell, 'A prime characteristic of the UK financial system from 1890 until 1973 was stability. It was affected by the 1931 crisis, but only lightly when compared with the experiences of other industrial countries', 'The Financial System', p. 64.
32. M. Taylor: *The Policy Background*, in: M. Blair (ed.), *Blackstone's Guide to the Financial Services & Markets Act 2000*, Blackstone's Press, 2001, p. 3.
33. In that episode, '[the banks] had lent on the basis of insufficient information on the systemic risk, in other words on the vulnerability of loans in a normal economic cycle....[they] had also concentrated the risks [excessively], without adequate capital and relying on an unstable source of financing such as the wholesale market' in E. P. Davis: *An Industrial Approach to Financial Instability*, Bank of England, Discussion Paper no. 50, 1990, pp. 26–7.
34. I. Morison, P. Tillett and J. Welch, *Banking Act 1979*, Butterworths, 1979, p. 17.
35. J. Grady and M. Weale, *British Banking*, pp. 139–40.
36. Ibid., pp. 171–3.
37. HM Treasury, *Report to the Committee Set Up To Consider the System of Banking Supervision*, HMSO, 1985, p. 4.
38. A great deal was written about the situation before and after Big Bang on the occasion of its 20th anniversary. For a useful summary, see A. Yarrow, 'The Challenges Facing Investment Banking in the UK', in *Big Bang 20 years on*, City of London, 2006.
39. R. Roberts and D. Kynaston, *City State*, Profile Books, 2002, pp. 93–5.

40. D.T. Llewellyn, 'Competition and Structural Change in the British Financial System', in E.P.M. Gardener (ed.), *The Future of Financial Systems and Services*, Macmillan, 1990, p. 18.
41. L.C.B. Gower, *Review of Investor Protection: Report*, part 2, 1985.
42. A. Alcock: *The FSMA 2000. A Guide to the New Law*, Jordan, 2000, pp. 6–7.

2 The UK's Financial Structure and Economic Sectors

1. An important clarification is necessary concerning the way in which the data on the assets and liabilities of the financial sector are aggregated in the National Statistics (NS). In particular, if a banking group does business in different sectors (such as banking, insurance and securities) with separate subsidiaries, these activities are included in the NS by sector and not shown together in the table on banks. This means that these tables, taken separately, do not provide a complete statistical representation of the role of financial groups as a whole.
2. Other financial institutions consist mainly of securities dealers, investment firms, unit trusts and leasing companies.
3. Clearly the evolution of stocks also depends on the capital gains and losses on the stock of financial assets and liabilities.
4. On the phenomenon of corporate saving in different countries, see: IMF, *World Economic Outlook*, April 2006, ch. IV.
5. Disposable income is defined as the amount of money available for spending after tax and other deductions. It should be observed that the National Statistics data on household saving include the Non-Profit Institutions Serving Households, such as academic bodies and charities. Private pension funds are also classified as a form of saving, while mandatory saving in the form of social insurance contributions is not.
6. See, for example: A. Daeton, *Understanding Consumption*, Oxford University Press, Clarendon Press, 1992; J. Muellbauer, 'The assessment: consumption', *Oxford Review of Economic Policy*, vol. 10, no. 2, 1994. See also: J. Muellbauer and A. Murphy, 'Is the UK Balance of Payment Sustainable?', *Economic Policy*, October, 1990 and Mervyn King's article in the same issue of that review.
7. In 2005 household debt as a percentage of disposable income was 38 per cent in the poorest percentile of the population (less than 20 per cent of income); 30 per cent in the 20–40 per cent bracket; 113 per cent in the 40–60 per cent bracket; 264 per cent in the 60–80 per cent bracket; 263 per cent in the 80–90 per cent category and 780 per cent in the richest percentile of the population. Source: Organisation for Economic Co-Operation and Development, *Economic Outlook*, 2006, ch. 3, p. 218. For an international analysis of households' accounts, see also: IMF, *Global Financial Stability Report*, April 2005, ch. 3.
8. OECD, *Economic Outlook*, p. 218.
9. S. Nickell, 'Two current monetary policy issues', Speech at a Market News International Seminar, Bank of England, September 2003, p. 11.
10. Between 1993 and 2000 the number of credit cards rose by 85 per cent. Between 2000 and 2005 there was a further increase of 26 per cent with an

increase of 62 per cent in the value of transactions. Source: British Bankers' Association, *Banking Business. The Annual Abstract of Banking Statistics*, 2006.

11. Over 40 companies were privatized in those years, including: British Petroleum (1979); British Aerospace, Cable & Wireless (1981); Britoil (1982); Jaguar, British Telecom (1984); British Gas (1986); British Airways, Rolls-Royce, BAA (1987); British Steel (1988); Regional water companies (1989). Subsequently, it was turn of the electricity distribution companies (1990), British Rail (1995), Nuclear Electric (1996). See S. Mahajan, 'Concentration Ratios for Business by Industry', *Economic Trends*, National Statistics, no. 635, 2006, p. 37.
12. See, J. Banks and S. Smith, *UK Households Portfolios*, The Institute for Fiscal Studies, W.P. 00/14, April 2000, p. 25.
13. Data from the Department for Work and Pensions.
14. Uniform data are not available on mutual funds, which, however, as seen above, account for a smaller proportion of household investment.
15. On the methodology used to produce this data: I. Hill, 'Ownership of United Kingdom quoted companies at the end of 1997', *Economic Trends*, no. 543, Office of National Statistics, February 1999. See also: National Statistics, *Share Ownership: A Report on Ownership of Shares as at 31st December 2004*.
16. M. King, *Public Policy and the Corporation*, Cambridge University Press, 1977.
17. For the sake of brevity, we consider private firms, which in any event are by far the most common.
18. DTI, *Small and Medium-sized Enterprise Statistics for the UK*, 2000.
19. On these issues see: M. Pagano, *et al.*, 'Why Do Companies Go Public? An Empirical Analysis', *Journal of Finance*, Vol. LIII, no. 1. February 1998.
20. For an exploration of the main reforms on this see: A. Cadbury, *Corporate Governance and Chairmanship: A Personal View*, Oxford University Press, 2002. We will deal with these questions in more detail in ch.9 on the Combined code of corporate governance.
21. See M. Becht and C. Mayer, *Introduction*, in F. Barca and M. Becht (eds), *The Control of Corporate Europe*, Oxford University Press, 2001, p. 19.
22. See: P. Garofalo and A. Roselli, 'Ownership Structure and Firm Performance in Italy', London School of Economics-FMG Working Paper, forthcoming.
23. See M. Becht and C. Mayer, *Introduction*, p. 30.
24. F. Lavington, *The English Capital Market*, Augustus M. Kelley Publishers, New York, 1968, Reprint of Economic Classics, first edition 1921, p. 202.
25. It cannot be ruled out that the high propensity in favour of equity capital was also due to the need, faced with an increasingly concentrated banking market, to diversify the sources of finance. In fact, in those years there was 'a strong movement of concentration among banks [. . .] several of whom have more than 500 branches'. 'This movement, due largely to the advantage of compounding risks and the needs of large scale industry, has reduced the number of banks to about eight private banks and some forty-four joint-stock companies, and has left the English system (in 1914) a small group of specialized and highly centralized institutions with most of its power lodged in the hands of ten or a dozen of its most powerful members'. See: F. Lavington, *The English Capital Market*, p. 127 and ch. 2.

26. London Stock Exchange and Oxera, *The Cost of Capital: An International Comparison*, City of London, 2006.
27. Capital gearing is normally calculated as the percentage ratio between the net debt of non-financial institutions and their market valuation.
28. See P. Bunn and G. Young, 'Corporate capital structure in the United Kingdom: determinants and adjustment', Working Paper, no. 226, Bank of England, 2004.
29. Ibid.
30. Ibid.
31. Some evidence supporting these theories for the United Kingdom and other countries has been found by P. Gibbard and I. Stevens, 'Corporate debt and financial balance sheet adjustment: a comparison of the United States, the United Kingdom, France and Germany', Working Paper, no. 317, Bank of England, 2006.
32. M. Burnett, 'Financial stability and the United Kingdom's external balance sheet', *Quarterly Bulletin*, Bank of England, Winter 2003.
33. Source: IMF, *International Financial Statistics*, December 2007, country table. International Investment Position: difference between total assets and total liabilities. For an interesting discussion on the IIP, see P.R. Lane and G.M. Milesi-Ferretti, 'A Global Perspective on External Positions', Working Paper, International Monetary Fund, 2005.
34. The 'valuation effect' is approximated by the difference between the change in the value of the stocks with respect to the previous period and the corresponding flow. The approximation is due to errors and omissions. We focus only on portfolio investments because direct investments are not valued at market prices.
35. For example, assuming that all assets are in foreign currency and all liabilities are in sterling (which is not necessarily the case), since both assets and liabilities are about four times GDP, a 2 per cent appreciation of sterling would worsen the net asset position by 8 per cent of GDP. See: S. Nickell, *The UK Current Account Deficit and All That*, Bank of England, 25 April 2006.
36. M. Obstfeld, 'External Adjustment', *Review of World Economics*, vol. 140 (4), 2004, p. 541.

3 The Development of Private Pension Schemes and the Pension Reform

1. Occupational schemes are pension schemes run by employers; a personal scheme is a pension that an individual buys from a pension provider, such as a bank, a life assurance company or a building society.
2. H. Pemberton, 'Politics and pensions in post-war Britain', in H. Pemberton, *et al.* (eds), *Britain's Pensions Crisis: History and Policy*, The British Academy – Oxford University Press, 2006, p. 41.
3. R. Disney, *et al.*, *Pension Reform and Economic Performance in Britain in the 1980s and 1990s*, Institute for Fiscal Studies, 2001, mimeo.
4. Based on National Statistics data (*The Blue Book*) for the United Kingdom.
5. S. Sass, 'Anglo-Saxon occupational pensions in international perspective', in Pemberton, *et al.* (eds), *Britain's Pension Crisis*, pp. 200–04.

6. The Pensions Commission, *Pensions: Challenges and Choices: The First Report*, HMSO, 2004, p. X.
7. The law is currently (2007) under review (the 'Thornton Review of Pensions Institutions'), to consider merging TPR and the PPF, bringing TPR under the FSA, and merging the Pensions Ombudsman and the Financial Ombudsman.
8. The Commission produced three reports: *Pensions: Challenges and Choices: The First Report*, HMSO, 2004; *A New Pension Settlement for the Twenty-First Century*; HMSO, 2005; *Implementing an Integrated Package of Pension Reforms: Final Report*, HMSO, 2006.
9. The Pensions Commission, *A New Pension Settlement*, p. 17.
10. Department for Works and Pensions, *Security in Retirement: Towards a New Pensions System*, TSO, 2006; *Personal Accounts: a New Way to Save*, TSO, 2006.

4 The Configuration of the Banking System in the Last 15 Years

1. On the modalities of conversion of building societies, see: K. Ryan, 'Building Society Conversions', *Financial Stability Review*, Bank of England, Autumn 1996, pp. 16–18. On the process of consolidation, see: S. Mahajan, 'Concentration ratios for business'.
2. Currently, with the exception of Nationwide (which has about a third of this market segment), there remain about sixty building societies that maintain their local, mutualistic function.
3. Other examples of consolidation, from the investment banking sector however, are: the acquisition by the Deutsche Bank of the Morgan Grenfell Group (1989) and of SG Warburg plc by the UBS/SBC (1995). For more on this, see: A. Monks and M. Stringa, 'Inter-industry linkages between UK life insurers and UK banks: an event study', *Financial Stability Review*, Bank of England, 2005.
4. In a perfectly contestable market it is possible to obtain the desirable Pareto-efficiency conditions of perfect competition even with two competitors, provided that 'entry is absolutely free, and exit absolutely costless' (W. Baumol, 'Contestable Markets: An Uprising in the Theory of Industry Structure', *American Economic Review*, no. 72, 1982, p. 4).
5. See: S. Mahajan, 'Concentration ratios for business'.
6. The data cited here regard the principal banking groups of the United Kingdom (called by the BBA 'Major British Banking Groups'). The data however refer to the consolidated world-wide group business, both banking and non-banking, of the aforementioned banking groups. See BBA, *Banking Business, The Annual Abstract of Banking Statistics* (various years).
7. The comparison is only indicative, based on the hypothesis that credit worthiness (and therefore the risk premium) in the domestic and foreign market is the same for the four principal banks in the UK.
8. BBA, *Banking Business*, 2005, table 3.07.
9. On regulatory and institutional aspects, see Chapter 10.
10. D. Cruickshank, *Competition in UK Banking: A Report to the Chancellor of the Exchequer*, The Stationery Office, London, 2000.
11. D. Cruickshank, *Competition in UK Banking*, p. VIII.
12. Ibid., p. XVI.

13. Concentration in the consumer credit sector, measured according to the HHI, was deemed to be 'low' (HHI = 0.071) thanks to the presence of numerous small banks (credit unions) operating in specific areas; in the sector of interest-bearing bank current accounts concentration appears to be 'just above the safety levels' (HHI = 0.091 per cent), while in all other market segments it was high. It was in fact deemed 'rather high' in the sector of credit cards and mortgages (respectively HHI = 0.19 and 0.11), and 'high' in the checking-account sector (HHI = 0.133). D. Cruickshank, *Competition in UK Banking*, pp. 106–20.
14. CC, *The Supply of Banking Services by Clearing Banks to Small and Medium-sized Enterprises: A Report to the Chancellor of the Exchequer*, The Stationery Office, London, 2002.
15. The clearing banks were selected by using the following criteria: 'banks that, directly or through subsidiaries, are members of the Cheque and Credit Clearing Company Limited'.
16. These are: deposits, loans (including home mortgages, factoring, commercial credit, etc.), leasing, payment-transmission services (including transactions in foreign currency), issuance of payment means (credit cards, checks, etc.), collateral, other administrative services.
17. These are: (1) the market for liquidity management services (business current accounts, short-term deposits, overdrafts); (2) the market for general purpose business loans; (3) the market for 'other types of loans' (invoice discounts, factoring, leasing, etc.); and (4) the market for 'other business deposits' held by SMEs.
18. CC, *The Supply of Banking Services*, p. 116.
19. On the definition of 'scale monopoly' and 'complex monopoly', see Chapter 10.
20. The first 'complex monopoly' is in favor of the following banks: Abbey National, AIB Group, Alliance & Leicester, Barclays, Bank of Ireland, Bank of Scotland, The Co-operative Group, HSBC, Lloyds-TSB, National Australia Bank, and the Royal Bank of Scotland. The second is in favor of the same banks, minus the AIB Group and the Bank of Ireland, and with the addition of the Nationwide Building Society.
21. On the definition of 'public interest', see Chapter 10.
22. For a definition of 'behavioural' and 'structural' remedies, see Chapter 10.
23. CC, *The Supply of Banking services*, p. 149.
24. Ibidem., p. 149.
25. Office of Fair Trading, *Banking Services to Small and Medium-sized Enterprises*, London, 2002.
26. D. Cruickshank, 'How bank reform was sabotaged', *The Financial Times*, 22 February 2005.
27. OFT, *Calculating Fair Default Charges in Credit Cards Contracts*, April 2006.
28. According to the classification of the British Bankers' Association, the Major British Banking Groups (MBBG) account for 80 per cent of the deposits of UK residents. They are: Abbey National, Alliance & Leicester, Barclays, Bradford & Bingley, HBOS, HSBC Bank, Lloyds TSB, Northern Rock, Royal Bank of Scotland. The data therefore cover the biggest part of the banking system, but not its totality. Furthermore, they refer to banks with headquarters in the United Kingdom, but not to the foreign subsidiaries. The latter is significant for the HSBC (which has large foreign subsidiaries): the gross profits of the

British bank were £3.796 m in 2006, out of £11.993 m of the entire group, including the foreign subsidiaries.
29. See OFT, *Calculating Fair Default Charges*, and various press releases.
30. The FSA is in fact one of the Qualifying Bodies having 'enforcement powers' granted by the aforementioned Regulations. According to a Concordat between the OFT and the FSA, the responsibilities of the FSA regard contracts stipulated by subjects who exercise the 'regulated activities' established by the FSMA 2000 (Regulated activities) Order 2001.
31. The FSA noted, however, that existing regulations do not give her the power to require lenders to pay compensation to customers in case of unfair terms. They should refer the complaint to the Financial Ombudsman Service. See FSA, *Fairness of terms in consumer contracts. Statement of good practice on mortgage exit administration fees*, January 2007.
32. For an analysis of the role of Marshall districts as a competitive factor see: P. Krugman, *Geography and Trade*, The Massachusetts Institute of Technology Press, 1991; the rediscovery of the Marshall school of thought as it refers to the district economy is attributable above all to Giacomo Becattini. See, for instance: F. Pyke, G. Becattini and W. Sengenberger, *Industrial Districts and Inter-firm Co-operation in Italy*, International Institute for Labour Studies, Geneva, 1990.
33. The analogy of the City of London and the economic district was also recently made by Sir John Gieve, Deputy Governor of the Bank of England: J. Gieve, 'The City's Growth: The Crest of the Wave or Swimming with the Stream', *Speech to the London Society of Chartered Accountants*, March 2007.
34. Lombard Street Associates, 'The importance to the UK Economy of a Successful Financial Sector', *A report prepared for the British Bankers' Association*, 2006, p. 51.
35. The Banker, November 1991, p. 60.
36. See, for example, The Banker, November 1996, p. 35.
37. IFSL, *City Business Series*, March 2006.
38. IFSL, 'Banking', *City Business Series*, March 2006, p. 11.
39. IFSL, 'Banking', p. 9.
40. IFSL, 'Fund management', *City Business Series*, August 2006.
41. FSA, 'Hedge funds and the FSA', Discussion Paper, n. 16, August 2002; R. Ferguson and D. Laster, 'Hedge funds and systemic risk', *Financial Stability Review, Special Issue on Hedge Funds*, Banque de France, April 2007.
42. IFSL, 'Hedge funds', *City Business Series*, April 2007.
43. FSA, 'Funds of alternative Investments Funds', Consultation Paper 07/6, March 2007.
44. FSA, 'Hedge funds: a discussion of risk and regulatory engagement', Discussion Paper 05/4, June 2005.
45. C. McCarthy, 'Transparency requirements and hedge funds', *Financial Stability Review, Special Issue on Hedge Funds*, Banque de France, April 2007, p. 80.
46. Ibid., p. 80.
47. Ibid., p. 82.
48. Ibid., p. 82.
49. A consultation document has been published by the Working Group in October 2007.

50. D. Walker, *Guidelines for Disclosure and Transparency in Private Equity*, Final Report of the Working Goup, November 2007.
51. EVCA/Thomson Venture Economics/PriceWaterhouseCoopers.
52. 'Equity' is the capital actually invested to purchase the 'target' company. It is generally smaller than the 'committed' capital by the partners. 'Leverage' is the external debt used to acquire the target company. The deal's value is the sum of equity plus leverage.
53. FSA, 'Private equity: a discussion of risk and regulatory engagements', Discussion Paper 06/6, November 2006.
54. At end-2007, a parallel investigation on private equity is underway at the Treasury Select Committee of the House of Commons.
55. See note 50.

5 The Stability of the British Banking Sector

1. R. Sayers, *Modern Banking*, p. 24.
2. Ibid., ch. 8. On the subject of stability, see also P. Cottrell, 'The Financial System of the United Kingdom in the Twentieth Century', pp. 64–5.
3. P. Cottrell, op. cit., p. 65; A. Bowen, *et al.*, *The Recent Evolution of the UK Banking Industry and Some Implications for Financial Stability*, Bank for International Settlements, 1999, pp. 286–7; T. Latter, 'Causes and management of banking crises', Bank of England, 1997, p. 32.
4. Bank of England, *Report and Accounts*, 1975, 1976 and 1977. In the balance sheet of the Bank for 1977, a further £10.2m was added to this provision, but it is not specified whether it was for the same crisis.
5. On the costs of this crisis in terms of loss of output, see G. Hoggart and V. Saporta, 'Cost of Banking System Instability', in Bank of England, *Financial Stability Review*, 10, 2001.
6. See Chapter 1.
7. Bank of England, *Report and Accounts*, 1985, 1986 and 1987. On this episode, see also under 2.3.
8. A. Bowen, *et al.*, *The Recent Evolution*, p. 287.
9. P. Jackson, 'Deposit Protection and Bank Failures in the United Kingdom', *Financial Stability Review*, Issue 1, Bank of England, 1996, p. 40.
10. Lovells, *Three Rivers District Council and Others, BCCI SA vs The Governor and Company of the Bank of England. New Particulars of Claims Served Pursuant to the Order of the House of Lords dated 22 March 2001*, folio 1309.
11. Source: FSCS.
12. T. Latter, 'Causes and Management', pp. 33–4. As part of the recovery of BCCI assets, in 1993 the liquidators, Deloitte & Touche, brought an action for liability against the Bank of England. After proceedings at several levels, the case ended only in November 2005 with the complete vindication of the Bank of England when the action before the Royal Courts of Justice was dropped.
13. T. Latter, 'Causes and Management', pp. 34–5; Bank of England, *Banking Act Report for 1994–95*.
14. Bank of England, *Report of the Board of Banking Supervision Inquiry into the Circumstances of the Collapse of Barings*, Stationery Office, 1995, pp. 251, 257–63.
15. T. Latter, 'Causes and Management', p. 32.

16. In reference to the credit unions, they became regulated in 2002. Since then, 15 were declared in default (source: FSCS).
17. Requirements under the Basel II and Capital Requirements Directive (Article 144 of Directive 2006/48/EC). See: FSA website: International & EU, Capital Requirement Directives/Basel2/Statistical Data.
18. OECD, *Bank Profitability: Financial Statements of Banks*, Paris; European Central Bank, *EU Banking Sector Stability*. Also, European Central Bank, *EU Banking Structures*. For a description of the data processed by the IMF, see: *Financial Soundness Indicators: Compilation Guide*, 2006.
19. For example, there exist no homogeneous cross-country data on non-performing loans. For a description of the methodologies adopted in various countries, see: A. Laurin and G. Majnoni, 'Bank Loan Classification and Provisioning Practices in Selected Developed and Emerging Countries', Working Paper, no. 1, The World Bank, 2003.
20. Contrary to the Generally Accepted Accounting Principles (GAAP), the International Financial Reporting Standards (IFRS), adopted in 2005, securitized assets are on the balance sheet.
21. FSA, *Financial Risk Outlook 2008*, p. 40. The largest five UK banks had at the end of 2007 a median tier 1 capital ratio of 7.7 per cent (5.7 per cent excluding all non-equity components – core tier 1 capital ratio).
22. IMF, *United Kingdom – Staff Report for the 2006 Article IV Consultation*, February 2007.
23. Insolvency Service website.
24. Bank of England, *Financial Stability Report*, July 2006, p. 29.
25. In order to monitor the group of the most active international banks, the Bank of England has identified the following set of intermediaries, called large complex financial institutions (LCFI): ABN Amro, Bank of America, Barclays, BNP Paribas, Citi (formerly Citigroup), Credit Suisse, Deutsche Bank, Goldman Sachs, HSBC, JPMorgan Chase & Co., Lehman Brothers, Merrill Lynch, Morgan Stanley, RBS, Société Générale and UBS.
26. FSA regulatory reporting.
27. For a recent comparison of certain market-based indicators (credit default swaps, bond spreads and stock prices) and the changes in agency ratings for a number of international banks, see: A. Di Cesare, 'Do Market-based Indicators Anticipate Rating Agencies? Evidence for International Banks', *Temi di Discussione del Servizio Studi*, no. 593, Banca d'Italia, May, 2006.
28. Bank of England, *Financial Stability Review*, June 2005, p. 72. The method of distance-to-default has also been used by the Bank of England to estimate financial stability of firms. See: M. Tudela and G. Young, 'Predicting default among UK companies: a Merton approach', *Financial Stability Review*, June 2003.
29. More specifically, the Merton model, or asset value model, considers a firm financed through a single debt and a single equity issue. Therefore the total market value of assets at any time is equal to the market value of the claims on the assets (equity and risky debt, with a given maturity date). The assets value is unobservable and is assumed to follow a stochastic process (a geometric Brownian motion, in the simplest case); in the future it may decline below the point where debt payments cannot be made. The risky debt is equivalent in value to the default-free debt minus a guarantee against default. The

equity can therefore be modelled and calculated as an implicit call option on the assets, following the Black-Scholes approach. See: R. C. Merton, 'On the Pricing of Corporate Debt: The Risk Structure of Interest Rates', *Journal of Finance*, no. 29, 1974.

30. Under the model assumptions, both the assets value and its volatility cannot be observed; however, they can be inferred by the equity value and its volatility, solving a system of nonlinear equations in order to calculate the distance-to-default. This is a metric indicating how many standard deviations the equity holders call option is in-the-money. The smaller the distance to default, the more likely a default is to occur. The probability of default is precisely the probability of the call option expiring out-of-the-money and it can be computed directly from the distance-to-default, if the probability distribution of the assets is known, or, equivalently, if the default rate for a given level of distance-to-default is known. See, for instance, M. Vassalou, Y. Xing, 'Default Risk in Equity Returns', *The Journal of Finance*, vol. LIX, no. 2, April 2004.
31. An interesting application of the Merton model or contingent claim approach to the economy-wide balance sheets (corporate, household, financial and foreign sovereign sectors) has been developed by Gray, Merton and Bodie. See: D. Gray *et al. A New Framework for Analyzing and Managing Macrofinancial Risk of an Economy*, NBER working paper no. 12637, October 2006.
32. For a practical description of the distant-to-default indicator see: G. Löffler and P. N. Posch, *Credit risk modeling Using Excel and VBA*, John Wiley, 2007.
33. Some authors have tried to construct synthetic indices for all the banks in the system, so as to capture the 'portfolio' effect and contagion, or the joint probability of bankruptcy by more than one bank. The primary difficulty lies in the fact that default is such a rare event that the distribution of probability is not normal. In these circumstances, the indices of correlation are invalid, as they measure the relationship between central measures of probability distribution and are not invariable to non-linear transformations. In this context it is necessary to use more sophisticated methodologies that make use of non-normal distributions. See: C. Goodhart and M.A. Segoviano Basurto, 'Banking Stability Index', Working paper, International Monetary Fund, mimeo, 2007.
34. M. Čihák, 'Introduction to Applied Stress Testing', Working Paper, International Monetary Fund, March 2007.
35. The Financial Sector Assessment Program (FSAP) is a program introduced by the IMF in May 1999. The aim is to analyze the stability of the financial system as well as the capacity of the regulator to prevent and cope with real or financial shocks, involving, on voluntary bases, countries identified as vulnerable or 'systemically important'. The FSAP program consists of three parts: i) the assessments of compliance with internationally accepted standards and codes; ii) a macro-prudential analysis; and iii) a series of stress tests and scenario analysis. During the program, several documents are produced: the Financial System Stability Assessment (FSSA), which includes reports of the results of the program and a summary of the 'Detailed Assessments' of the observance of standards, produced by the Fund. The British authorities allowed the publication of both the FSSA and the 'Detailed Assessments', available on the IMF web site on the page for the United Kingdom.
36. Under the Value-at-Risk framework (VaR), the risk measure is an estimate of the maximum expected amount that could be lost on a set of positions due

to general market movements over a given holding period at specified confidence level. The VaR methodology is also used to define the Capital-at-Risk (CaR), which is the capital required to absorb potential (unexpected) losses at a given tolerance level. The CaR of a portfolio is commonly defined as the difference between the mean of the portfolio Profit & Loss distribution (expected loss) and a small quintile of this distribution (VaR, that represents the unexpected loss). Therefore, expected losses (i.e. losses which occur on average) are covered through provisions, while 'unexpected' losses, estimated by VaR, need to be covered by capital (CaR). Exceptional losses (greater than the tolerance level established by VaR) not absorbed by the economic capital, imply technically a 'default'.

37. For a description of Basel II, see: Bank for International Settlements, 'International Convergence of Capital Measurement and Capital Standards'. A Revised Framework, Comprehensive version, June 2006.
38. FSA, 'Stress testing', FSA Discussion Paper, 05/2, May 2005.
39. FSA, 'Stress testing', p. 15.
40. FSA, *Stress testing thematic review*, October 2006, p. 5.

6 Markets and Market Infrastructures: Institutional and Prudential Aspects

1. An OTC market is a market for securities where trading is not conducted through an organized exchange but through bilateral negotiations. Often these markets are intermediated by brokers and/or dealers. OTC contracts are less standardized than exchange-traded contacts, and therefore they help to 'complete' the market. Examples of OTC derivatives transactions include currency swaps, interest rate swaps, foreign exchange forward, and credit default swaps. Recently, trading arrangements have become more formalized in a few segments of OTC derivatives markets. For an interesting description of the OTC market and its potential fragilities, see: G.J. Schinasi, *Safeguarding Financial Stability: Theory and Practice*, IMF, 2006 (ch. 9).
2. The main difference between an on-shore market (both a formal exchange and an over-the-counter) and an off-shore (or eurodollar, euro-equity, euro-commercial paper, euro medium-term note, etc.) is that the latter is outside the formal control of regulators and central banks (reserve requirements, registration process, tax requirements, etc.). The term euro does not refer to the location of the intermediaries (it could be between two banks in London or in New York), nor does it refer to the euro as a currency.
3. Membership in the 'major UK banks' group is based on the provision of customer services in the United Kingdom, regardless of the country of ownership (Bank of England definition). The group includes the following banks: Alliance & Leicester, Banco Santander, Barclays, Bradford & Bingley, HBOS, HSBC, Lloyds TSB, Nationwide, Northern Rock, and RBS.
4. On the sub-prime credit crisis, see: IMF, *Global Financial Stability Report*, October 2007 and, April 2008.
5. The Alternative Investment Market (AIM) is a component of the LSE. From October 2004, AIM ceased to be classed as a 'regulated market' under EU Law and became an 'exchange regulated market'. This change was driven

by changes in EU Law (under the Prospectus Directive and Transparency Directive) which affect AIM's regulatory environment. AIM's change of status enabled the preservation of the existing admissions process and regulatory structure, allowing AIM to continue to offer the flexibility that smaller growing companies need, while retaining high standards of regulation. Euronext launched a new 'organized' but unregulated market (Alternext), accessible to equity issues with limited requirements, but still offering investors more guarantees than the so-called 'free market'.

6. International Financial Services London, 'International Financial Markets in the UK', *City Business Series*, November, 2006, p. 8.
7. International Financial Services London, 'Derivatives', *City Business Series*, p. 5.
8. Eurex is one of the world's leading derivatives exchanges and is jointly operated by Deutsche Börse AG and SWX Swiss Exchange. See: International Financial Services London, 'International Financial Markets', p. 4.
9. Bank for International Settlements, *Triennial Central Bank Survey: Foreign Exchange and Derivatives Market Activity in 2004*, Basel, March 2005, p. 19.
10. Ibid., p. 15.
11. British Bankers' Association, *BBA Credit Derivatives Report 2006*, London, 2006.
12. International Financial Services London, 'Securitisation', *City Business Series*, March 2007, p. 1. On ABS and CDOs, see paragraph 6.3 on credit risk transfer.
13. R. Bruyère *et al.*, *Credit Derivatives and Structured Credit: A Guide for Investors*. John Wiley, Chichester, England, 2006. p. 27.
14. Mark-to-market means a position or portfolio valued at the most recent price at which a financial instrument can be bought or sold in normal conditions.
15. The counterparty risk is the possibility that a protection seller is unable to fulfil his contractual obligation.
16. The margin is the amount of cash or eligible collateral an investor must deposit with a counterpart or intermediary when conducting a transaction. For example, when buying or selling a futures contract, it is the amount that must be deposited with a broker or clearing house. If the futures price moves adversely, the investor might receive a 'margin call' – that is, a demand for additional funds or collateral to offset position losses in the margin account.
17. For an interesting and synthetic description of the historical evolution of clearing house operations, from the simple activity of market arrangement to reduce transaction costs, to an effective central counterpart to reduce systemic risk, see: R.S. Kroszner, 'Central Counterparty Clearing: History, Innovation, and Regulation', Speech at the Conference on Issues Related to Central Counterparty Clearing, European Central Bank, Frankfurt, April 2006.
18. The International Securities Market Association (ISMA) is a professional body that, among other activities, after negotiations with relevant parties homogenizes contracts for OTC transactions. ISDA is the International Swaps and Derivatives Association.
19. R. Bruyère *et al.*, *Credit Derivatives*, p. 27–8.
20. Hedge funds often employ a prime broker, usually an investment bank, that handles financing, custody recordkeeping and clearing activities. In some cases the prime broker sets up a separate company to offer post-trade operations associated with the derivatives.

21. A useful description of these aspects of the OTC derivatives markets is: R. Dodd, 'The Structure of OTC Derivatives Markets', *The Financier*, vol. 9, nos. 1–4, 2003.
22. R.S. Kroszner, 'Central Counterparty Clearning', p. 5.
23. Bank for International Settlements, 'OTC Derivatives: Settlements Procedures and Counterparty Risk Management', Report by the Committee on the Payment and Settlement Systems and the Euro-Currency, Standing Committee of the Central Banks of the Group of Ten Countries, Basel, September 1998.
24. The practice in the OTC market of executing transactions before signing the master agreement may jeopardize a dealer's ability to close out and net outstanding transactions in the event of its counterpart's default. Once the transaction executed by telephone is concluded, a written confirmation is needed. If this occurs with a relevant delay, both parties are exposed to legal, market or credit risks. As noted in 1998 by a BIS report on the OTC markets, such market inefficiencies have relevant implications: the failure to confirm a transaction may jeopardize its enforceability or ability to net it against other transactions. Unconfirmed trades may also allow for errors compromising the monitoring and management of credit risk. This, in turn, could lead to inaccurate margin policy and other problems, which – if they are on a large scale – could create a potential systemic risk. While the use of collaterals and of a central counterparty clearing house has the potential to mitigate counterparty risks, in stressful circumstances the liquidity risk remains high, since a number of derivative contracts are inherently less standardized and more difficult to value. See: Bank for International Settlements, 'OTC Derivatives', p. 20.
25. Bank for International Settlements, 'New Developments in Clearing Settlement Arrangements for OTC Derivatives', Committee on Payment and Settlement System, March 2007, pp. 17–18.
26. A few years ago, a report expressed concern about the feasibility of close-out procedures in the event of default of a large market participant in stressed market conditions (see: Counterpart Risk Management Policy Group II, *Toward Greater Financial Stability: A Private Sector Perspective*, New York, 2005). For recent developments pertaining to these aspects, see: Bank of England, *Financial Stability Report*, April 2007, p. 54.
27. A. Murfin, *Regulating the OTC Market in London*, The LBMA Indian Bullion Market Forum, New Delhi, January 2003.
28. Initially limited to securities markets, the Lamfalussy process was extended in 2003 to banks and insurance companies, pension funds and mutual funds. It is based on four levels: Level 1 consists of core principles mainly in the form of Directives or Regulations, to be decided by normal EU legislative procedures; Level 2 arranges for the implementation of detailed measures following Level 1, in consultation with various committees composed of high-level representatives from Member States (namely, the European Banking Committee, the European Insurance and Occupational Pension Committee, and the European Securities Committee); Level 3 consists in enhanced cooperation and networking among EU supervisors to ensure consistent and equivalent transpositions of Level 1 and 2 legislation. The Level 3 activities also aim at addressing the supervisory challenges stemming from the increasingly integrated financial markets; not only does regulatory convergence need to be complemented by supervisory convergence, but the cooperation

and exchange of information among authorities is also needed in order to implement an effective supervision of cross-border financial institutions. The development of Level 3 activities has been entrusted to three supervisory committees composed of representatives from national supervisory authorities (the Committee of European Banking Supervisors, based in London; the Committee of European Securities Regulators, based in Paris; the Committee of European Insurance and Occupational Pension Supervisors, based in Frankfurt). Finally, Level 4 consists in strengthening enforcement, notably with action by the Commission to enforce Community law, underpinned by enhanced cooperation between Member States, their regulatory bodies and the private sector (See: European Central Bank, 'Developments in the EU Framework for Financial Regulation, Supervision and Stability', *Monthly Bulletin*, November 2004). For an assessment of integration of European markets, see: IMF, 'Euro Area Policies: Selected Issues', *Country Report*, no. 05/266, August 2005. See also: European Commission, 'Green paper on Financial Services Policy (2005-2010)', *COM*, 2005, no. 177.

29. The harmonization process foresees other different aspects as well, such as: the *Prospectus* (single prospectus approved by the regulatory authorities of the issuer's country); *market abuse* (harmonized rules on the prevention of insider dealing and market manipulation on regulated and unregulated markets); *cross-border mergers* (rules governing take-over bids and protection of minority shareholders); *status of collateral* (improvement of the legal certainty regarding the validity and enforceability of collateral arrangements backing cross-border transactions); *transparency* (financial reporting and dissemination of information about securities issues); financial market instruments (regulation of the authorization, behavior and conduct of business of securities firms and exchanges); decision on whether and how to implement the IFRS *accounting standards*; and *financial conglomerates* (identification of 'significant financial groups' and designation of a supervisory co-coordinator for each conglomerate). Other very important directives concern the payment system and the insurance sector (Solvency II; the equivalent of Basel II for the insurance sector).
30. In particular, the MiFID Level 2 measures cover three areas (the first two are in the form of directives, the last is in the form of regulations). They are: 1) organizational requirements (internal controls, record-keeping, conflict of interest, etc.); 2) conduct of business (client classification, information about the services, client agreements, best execution, etc); and 3) markets and transparency (post-trade transparency, multilateral trading facilities, etc.).
31. The term 'trading facility' refers to a person or group of persons or firms that constitutes, maintains, or provides electronic facilities or platforms in which multiple participants have the ability to execute or trade agreements, contracts or transactions. On these aspects see: R. Dodd, 'The Structure of OTC', *The Financier*, vol. 9. A 'data aggregator' is a firm that collects and sells to the public trading information.
32. FSA, Financial Risk Outlook, April 2008, p. 53.
33. 'International liabilities' comprise cross-border liabilities in all currencies and liabilities to residents in foreign currencies. See: P. McGuire and N. Tarashev, 'Tracking International Bank Flows', *Bank for International Settlements Quarterly Review*, December 2006.

34. Euro-denominated cross-border bilateral flows within the euro area are excluded.
35. See: P. McGuire, 'A Shift in London's Eurodollar Market', *BIS Quarterly Review*, September 2004.
36. Ibid., p. 72.
37. Lombard Street Associates, 'The Importance to the UK Economy of a Successful Financial Sector', p. 35.
38. P. McGuire *et al.*, 'Tracking', p. 76.
39. The 'customer funding gap' is defined as 'customer lending' minus 'customer funding', where 'customer' refers to all non-bank borrowers and depositors. 'Customer deposits' at the end of 2006 were equal to 41 per cent of the liabilities of 'major UK banks', while lending to domestic clients, corporate and households, was equal to 27 per cent of bank assets. A relevant share of assets (41 per cent) is in favour of non-residents. See: Bank of England, *Financial Stability Report*, April, 2007, p. 26. On this issue see also: G. Speight and S. Parkinson, 'Large UK-Owned Banks' Funding Patterns: Recent Changes and Implications', *Financial Stability Review*, Bank of England, December, 2003.
40. G. Speight and S. Parkinson, 'Large UK-Owned Banks', p. 140.
41. Bank of England, *Financial Stability Report*, April 2007, p. 29.
42. G. Speight and S. Parkinson, 'Large UK-Owned Banks', p. 142.
43. On CRT see: D. Rule, 'Risk Transfer Between Banks, Insurance Companies and Capital Markets: An Overview', *Financial Stability Review*, Bank of England, December 2001; Financial Services Authority, 'Cross-sector Risk Transfers', Discussion Paper, May 2002; Bank for International Settlements, 'Credit Risk Transfer', Report submitted by a Working Group established by the Committee on the Global Financial System, January 2003; Bank for International Settlements, 'Credit Risk Transfer', The Joint Forum. Basel Committee on Banking Supervision, October 2004; IMF, *Global Financial Stability Report*, October 2007, IMF, *Global Financial Stability Report*, April 2008.
44. Financial guarantors (such as AMBAC, MBIA or FGIC) have expanded their traditional business of insuring bonds issued by U.S. municipalities to include structured credit products (ABS, CDOs, etc.). A downgrading of a monoline insurance implies an immediate downgrade of the bond issued by the protection buyer (for instance a bank) and therefore an increase of its funding costs.
45. Bank for International Settlements, *Credit Risk Transfer. Developments from 2005 to 2007*, The Joint Forum, Basel Committee on Banking Supervision, April 2008. p. 10.
46. Bank for International Settlements, *Credit Risk Transfer*, p. 5.
47. Credit events are defined as failure to pay on the part of the reference entity (corporations, banks, sovereigns); bankruptcy of the borrower or of the reference entity; failure to pay, after any applicable grace period; and restructuring.
48. R. Bruyere *et al.*, *Credit Derivatives*, p. 107.
49. On these aspects, see: D. Marston, *et al.*, 'The Conduit Phenomenon: Do banks achieve lasting risk transfer?'*mimeo, IMF*, September 2007 and B. David, S. Simon, 'Accounting Treatment: Where Are We?', *International Financial Law Review*, vol. 25, July 2006, Supplement, pp. 10–13.
50. See: House of Commons Treasury Committee, *The Run on the Rock*, Fifth Report of Session 2007–08, Volume I, p. 13.
51. See: IMF, Global Financial Stability Report, April 2008, ch. 2,

52. Financial Stability Forum, *Report of the Financial Stability Forum on Enhancing Market and Institutional Resilience*, April 2008, p. 14.
53. Ibid., p. 13.
54. Bank for International Settlements, 'The Role of Ratings in Structured Finance: Issues and Implications', *Report submitted by the Working Group established by the Committee on the Global Financial System*, January 2005.
55. See, note 41 above.
56. The FSF underscored the necessity, on the part of market participants, to involve senior management in the responsibilities related to the CTR, to reinforce credit-risk models and to understand the nature and scope of external ratings (and their limitations). It was noted that market players should pay extra attention to counterparty, legal and documentation risks. They should also execute confirmations promptly, avoiding significant backlogs of unsigned documentation, and, in general, contain settlement and operational risks. The Joint Forum also recommended the reduction of market liquidity risks, particularly in the CDOs and other structured products. Specifically, it noted that firms should periodically consider how their positions in CRT instruments would behave under stressed liquidity conditions and incorporate the results in their risk management models. Finally, the Joint Forum noted that in the disclosure of information there is room for improvement as well as in the information sharing among regulators. For an overview of the activity of the Financial Stability Forum, and related initiatives, see: M. Draghi, 'Hedge Funds and Financial Stability', *Financial Stability Review*, special issue on hedge funds, Banque de France, April 2007.
57. See: Financial Stability Forum, *Report*, April 2008.
58. Bank of England, *Payment System Oversight Report*, January 2005, p. 5.
59. Central banking money is the ultimate means of discharging obligations between parties (primary banks) through central bank settlement accounts. In the delivery-versus-payment system, the final transfer of one asset occurs only if the final transfer of another asset (monetary assets, foreign exchanges, securities, etc.) occurs.
60. The CLS system helps reducing foreign exchange settlement risk between system users, by settling their transactions on a payment-versus-payment basis. Since 2002, the volume of foreign exchange transactions settled through CLS has increased dramatically; however, many foreign exchange transactions are still settled outside CLS.
61. The three main operational clearing companies (CHAPS Clearing Company; BACS Ltd; and Cheque and Credit Clearing Company Ltd) fall under the umbrella of a private sector body called the Association for Payment Clearing Services (APACS). Set up in 1985, APACS is a non-statutory association providing a forum for the major banks and building societies to discuss non-competitive issues relating to money transmission.
62. P.M.W. Tucker, 'Managing the Central Bank's Balance Sheet: where Monetary Policy Meets Financial Stability', Lecture to mark the fifteenth anniversary of Lombard Street Research, Bank of England, 28 July 2004, p. 4.
63. Bank for International Settlements, *A Glossary of Terms Used in Payment and Settlement Systems*, Committee on Payment and Settlement Systems, Basel, March 2003. See also: Bank for International Settlements, 'Payment System

in the United Kingdom', Committee on Payment and Settlement Systems Red Book, Basel, 2003.

64. Settlement risk is the possibility that settlement will not take place. In a net settlement system, the final settlement or transfer instructions occur only on a net basis at one or more discrete, specified times during the processing day. The failure of one participant to meet its obligations will cause other participants to be unable to meet theirs, thereby generating a systemic risk. For these reasons, a real-time gross settlement system has been developed, since it prevents a similar systemic chain reaction. Therefore, while in the pre-electronic era the settlement of only the residual net difference among parties was the most efficient way to proceed, now the vast majority of settlement platforms are performed through gross real-time systems, where the settlement of funds or securities takes the form of individual transfers, on an order-by-order basis (without netting), at any given moment.
65. Founded in 1888 to clear sugar and coffee trades in London and originally known as the London Produce Clearing House, the LCH becomes only later a proper clearing house, with the functions described above. During the late 1990's LCH's business expanded rapidly to introduce clearing for cash bonds, repos, inter-bank interest rate swaps, and energy (gas and electricity). In December 2003, the LCH merged with Clearnet to create LCH.Clearnet. Banque Centrale de Compensation, which traded previously as Clearnet and now as LCH.Clearnet, was formed in 1969 to clear contracts traded in Paris commodity markets. In March 2000, ParisBourse, the Amsterdam Exchanges, and the Brussels Exchanges announced their agreement to merge the Belgian, Dutch and French exchanges to create Euronext. See the LCH.Clearnet web site.
66. Jenkinson, N. 'New markets and new demands: challenges for central banks in the wholesale market infrastructure'. Bank of England, Central Bank Conference on Payment and Monetary and Financial Stability, November 2007.
67. IMF, *Financial System Stability Assessment – United Kingdom,* February 2003.
68. Bank of England, *Payment System Oversight Report 2004*, January 2005, p. 24.
69. There was however an earlier report on the topic in 2000, though not an annual report.
70. The Bank of England does not have statutory power over the payment system. However, under the Financial Markets and Insolvency (Settlement Finality) Regulations (1999), the Bank has statutory power to 'designate' UK payment systems, so that their relevant rules are protected from challenge, should a participant become insolvent. See Bank of England, *Payment System*, p. 12.
71. Our description of the money market arrangements is based on: Bank of England, *The Bank of England's Operations in the Sterling Money Markets*, February 2007 (also called 'Red Book'). See also: G. Chaplin, A. Emblow and I. Michael, 'Banking system liquidity: developments and issues', *Financial Stability Review*, Bank of England, December 2000, and P.M.W. Tucker, 'Managing the Central Bank's Balance Sheet'.
72. See: FSA, 'Review of the Liquidity Requirements for Banks and Building Societies', Discussion paper, 07/7, December 2007.

73. All UK banks and building societies that are required to hold a Cash Ratio Deposit (CRD) at the Bank are eligible to join the reserve-averaging scheme and have access to the standing facilities. Participation in the scheme is voluntary, apart from CHAPS sterling and CREST sterling settlement banks, which joined the scheme automatically.
74. On the final day of the maintenance period, the rate on the standing deposit facility is 25 basis points below the official Bank Rate and the rate on the standing lending facility is 25 basis points above it. During the rest of the maintenance period, the rates are set at +/– 100 basis points since they offer liquidity for insurance purposes. Moreover, settlement banks also pay a penalty if their reserve account is overdrawn at the end of the day, in the event they are unable to repay intraday credit from the Bank.
75. A repurchase agreement (repo) is an agreement between two parties whereby one party sells the other a security at a specified price with a commitment to buy the security back at a usually pre-agreed later date, for a specified price. In its repo operations, the Bank purchases eligible securities from its counterparts and agrees to sell back equivalent securities at a pre-determined future date.
76. It is worth noting that, since June 2001, the Bank has supplemented its daily open market operations with a collateralized overnight deposit facility (i.e. an overnight reverse repo facility). This facility enhances the means available to the Bank for intermediating between firms with liquidity shortages and surpluses in the rare circumstances where market mechanisms are impaired (e.g. because of infrastructure or confidence problems).
77. Since it was vital to assure that larger banks had better access to liquidity in stressed market conditions, the Bank of England introduced several improvements. In particular, in March 1997, the Bank widened the instruments used in its operations, including the gilt as a base for repo transactions. In 1998, the Bank further extended the range of eligible collateral, to include a wide range of central government/bank securities denominated in euro.
78. For a useful discussion of these aspects, see: Institute of International Finance, *Principles of Liquidity Risk Management*, March 2007.
79. Financial Services Authority, 'Interim Prudential Sourcebook: Banks', *FSA Handbook*.
80. G.J. Schinasi *et al.*, 'Modern Banking and OTC Derivatives Markets: The Transformation of Global Finance and its Implications for Systemic Risk', IMF, Occasional Paper, no. 203, 2000, p. 22. This paper offers a description of the OTC derivative markets and their implications from the point of view of market stability.
81. Previously, these banks were subject to the Mismatch regime. Subsequently, in light of the fact that this type of bank was considered to have a stable funding structure, a simplified regime was decided on. Recent events, following the sub-prime crisis, have made the FSA re-think this decision.
82. More precisely: the stock of sterling liquid assets should be at least equal to wholesale sterling net outflow for the following 5 business days (less allowable certificates of deposit) plus 5 per cent of sterling retail deposits contractually withdrawable over the following 5 business days.
83. See: FSA, *Review of the Liquidity Requirements*, p. 41.

7 The Sub-prime Mortgage Market Crisis and Its Effect on the UK Banking Sector

1. See: IMF, *Global Financial Stability Report*, April 2008, table 1.1. Sub-prime loans are typically made to borrowers with incomplete or weakened credit history, payment delinquencies and bankruptcies. Alternative-A mortgages are mortgages with lower credit quality than prime mortgages, but better than sub-prime. For statistical purposes a sub-prime loan has a credit scoring between 620 and 660 on the Fair Isaac & Co scale (minimum 300; maximum 900). For an analysis of the sub-prime market, see: J. Kiff and P. Mills, 'Money for Nothing and Checks for Free: Recent Developments in U.S. Sub-Prime Mortgage Markets', Working Paper, IMF, July 2007. On the subprime crisis, see also: IMF, *Global Financial Stability Report*, October 2007.
2. M. Draghi, *'Statement by Mario Draghi, Chairman of the Financial Stability Forum'*, International Monetary and Financial Committee Meeting, 14 April 2007, Washington, DC.
3. Bank of England, *Financial Stability Report*, April 2007, p. 7.
4. IMF, *Global Financial Stability Report*, October 2007, ch. 1, for these aspects and for an interesting description of the crisis.
5. S. Scholtes, 'Hedge Funds Hit at Sub-prime Aid for Homeowners', *Financial Times*, 1 June 2007.
6. UBS, *Unwind of the BSAM Funds Cause a Flight to Quality – and Opportunities*, 26 June 2007.
7. A.E. Khandani and A.W. Lo, 'What Happened to the Quants in August 2007?', Working Paper, Massachusetts Institute of Technology, forthcoming.
8. The most notorious bank run in the British history took place in May 1866 at the time of the collapse of Overend Gurney & Co. Bank.
9. House of Commons Treasury Committee, *The Run on the Rock*, Fifth Report of Session 2007–08, Vol. 1, pp. 13–14.
10. For an interesting description of the so-called structure master trust programmes in the UK, including Granite, see Fitch Rating, 'Master of House – A Review of UK RMBS Master Trust', *Structured Finance*, RMBS – UK, Special Report, 8 June 2008.
11. Ibid., p.35.
12. Ibid., p. 36.
13. Ibid., p. 39.
14. Ibid., p. 38.
15. See: Bank of England, *Financial Stability Report*, no. 22, October 2007, p. 11.
16. 'Recent Turbulence in Global Financial Markets and Northern Rock's Liquidity Crisis', Memorandum from the FSA to the Treasury Committee, 9 October 2007, p. 4.
17. M. King, *'Turmoil in financial markets: what can central banks do?'*, paper submitted to the Treasury Committee, 12 September, 2007, p. 7.
18. M. King, *'The Governor's Speech at the Northern Ireland Chamber of Commerce and Industry'*, Belfast, 9 October 2007, p. 5.
19. See: Bank of England, *Financial Stability Report*, no. 22, October 2007, p. 33.
20. M. King, *'The Governor's Speech'*, pp. 7–8.
21. Bank of England, *Financial Stability Report*, October 2007, p. 12.

22. Bank of England, H M Treasury, Financial Services Authority, *Financial Stability and Depositor Protection: Strengthening the Framework*, HM Treasury, January, 2008.

8 The New Regulatory Framework: The Financial Services Authority

1. A. Alcock, *The Financial Services*, p. 8.
2. J.R. Barth, *et al.*, *Rethinking Bank Regulation*, Cambridge University Press, 2006, pp. 85–92.
3. M. Taylor, 'The Policy Background', in M. Blair (ed.), *Financial Services & Markets Act 2000*, Blackstone Press, 2001, p. 1.
4. P. Ciocca, 'Vigilanza: una o più istituzioni', mimeo, Banca d'Italia, 2001.
5. C. McCarthy, 'Financial Stability Analysis in the UK', Macroprudential Supervision Conference, 8 November 2006.
6. P. Ciocca, 'Vigilanza'.
7. R. Abrams and M. Taylor, 'Issues in the Unification of Financial Sector Supervision', in C. Enoch, *et al.* (eds), *Building Strong Banks Through Surveillance and Resolution*, IMF, 2002, p. 147.
8. H. Davies, 'Reforming Financial Regulation: Progress and Priorities', in E. Ferran and C.A. Goodhart (eds), *Regulating Financial Services and Markets in the Twenty First Century*, Hart Publishing, p. 20.
9. The case of Finland is similar.
10. C. Briault, *Revisiting The Rationale for a Single National Financial Services Regulator*, FSA Occasional Paper Series, 16, 2002, p. 29.
11. Ibid., p. 16.
12. Ibid., p. 17.
13. P. Cottrell, 'The Financial System of the United Kingdom', p. 117.
14. D. Lascelles, *Waking up to the FSA: How the City Views its New Regulator*, Centre for the Study of Financial Innovation, 2001, p. 3.
15. The expression used by the Bank of England (see J. Townend, *The Euro, the UK and the City of London*, Bank Negara Malaysia, Kuala Lumpur, 2002).
16. E.P. Davis, *The Regulation of Funded Pensions*, FSA Occasional Paper Series, 15, 2001, p. 5.
17. See Chancellor Brown's statement, quoted in FSA, *The Transfer of the UK Listing Authority to the FSA*, Consultation Paper 37, 1999.
18. In several points the FSMA grants the Treasury law-making powers (secondary legislation). In the English legal system the government does not have autonomous lawmaking powers, so that each time it is necessary for a specific mandate to be granted by an Act of Parliament to the administrative authority involved, which exercises it by means of rules and orders that have to be published and controlled or authorized by Parliament, unless the enabling law itself recognizes that the regulatory provisions can enter directly into force without further intervention by Parliament. Legal writings thus consider parliamentary control to be 'very weak' insofar as it generally consists in no more than a simple notification of the outline of the orders with right of discussion but not of amendment. In reality there also exists the possibility of formulating a petition of annulment, but it is considered

a difficult procedure to implement; lastly, a request for explicit approval by Parliament is rare.

19. On the legal nature of the FSA, see above.
20. House of Lords Delegated Powers and Deregulation Committee – Joint Committee on Financial Services and Markets, *First Report*, Annex B, para 13, 1999.
21. E. Ferran and C.A. Goodhart, 'Regulating Financial Services and Markets in the Twenty First Century: an Overview', in E. Ferran and C.A. Goodhart, *Regulating Financial Services*, p. 1.
22. M. Taylor, 'Accountability and Objectives of the FSA', in M. Blair (ed.), *Financial Service and Markets Act*, p. 26.
23. Ibid., p. 28.
24. FSA, *A New Regulator for the New Millennium*, 2000, pp. 7–9.
25. A. Alcock, *The Financial Services*, pp. 118–22; M. Taylor, 'The Policy Background', p. 114.
26. This is how commentators have interpreted the legal wording: 'the Authority must have regard to . . . the responsibilities of those who manage the affairs of authorized persons' (Sec. 2 (3)(b)) (see M. Taylor, 'Accountability and Objectives of the FSA', p. 35).
27. D. Cruickshank, *Competition in UK Banking. A Report to the Chancellor of the Exchequer*, HMSO, 2000. The interim report can be found as an annex (annex F) to the final text.
28. P. Ciocca, op. cit.
29. On this point, see R. Abrams and M. Taylor, 'Issues in the Unification of Financial Sector Supervision', p. 174.
30. D. Cruickshank, *Competition in UK Banking*, pp. 319–32.
31. See also C. Briault, 'Revisiting the Rationale', p. 6.
32. On this point, see National Audit Office, Financial Services Authority, *A Review Under Section 12 of the FSMA 2000*, HMSO, 2007, pp. 21–4.
33. M. Taylor, 'Accountability', p. 17.
34. By contrast, the Bank of England is a public-law institution, even though its employees are not considered to be public employees.
35. M. Taylor, 'Accountability', p. 21.
36. In recent times (2006–2007), NAO has reviewed the efficiency and effectiveness with which the FSA has used its resources, when discharging its statutory functions, but this happened upon invitation of the Treasury, which acted under Sec. 12 of the FSMA (see above, under c.)
37. A. Alcock, *The Financial Services*, pp. 47–8.
38. FSMA 2000 (Regulated Activities) Order 2001 and its amendments.
39. Four categories of persons are exempt under the Treasury Order: those exempt with reference to every regulated activity (includes central banks and international organizations); those exempt with reference to the taking of deposits (includes local authorities and charities); those exempt with reference to certain activities (includes electronic exchanges); and those exempt with reference to a type of activity (includes gas companies). The inclusion of such different persons in the same classification system is evidence to the outside observer of the apparent bizarreness of English law-making, which can be explained by the attempt to unify a stratification of rules and practices in heterogeneous fields and of very different origin.

40. See Sch. 1.5.
41. As regards the exceptional circumstances, the Treasury has made express provision for the case of a serious risk to the entire financial system owing to a change in the regulating provisions. See M. Threipland, 'Rules and Guidance', in M. Blair (ed.), *Financial Services and Markets Act*, p. 151.
42. FSA, *The FSA's Risk Assessment Framework*, 2006.
43. C. McCarthy, 'Financial Stability Analysis', p. 5.
44. Ibid.
45. Clifford Chance, 'Principles-Based Regulation – Problems of Uncertainty', mimeo, 2007.
46. FSA, *Principles for Businesses* (PRIN 1.1.2). The principles are: integrity ; skill, care and diligence; risk management and control; financial prudence; proper market conduct; regard to customers' interests and treat them fairly; regard to communication with clients; fair management of conflicts of interest; suitability of firm's advice to its customers; protection of clients' assets; cooperative relation with regulators.
47. Clifford Chance, 'Principle-Based Regulation'.
48. At the time of writing (2007) a consultation on the new text is under way.
49. C. McCarthy, *'Principles-based regulation: what does it mean for the industry?'*, Financial Services Skills Council Conference, 2006; D. Waters, *NEWCOB and Principles-based Regulation*, NEWCOB briefings, 2007.
50. FSA, *Business Plan 2007–08*, 2007, p. 38.
51. L. Minghella, 'Insolvency', in M. Blair (ed.), *Financial Services and Markets Act*, pp. 255–59.
52. *A framework for Guarantee Schemes in the EU*, October 2005.
53. The publication of information on risk exposures, risk assessment procedures and levels of capital will make it possible to compare the risk of different institutions.
54. It is worth recalling that since the FSA and the FSCS are not able to generate income on their own (like a central bank), they must finance their activity with funds paid in by supervised persons (cost of compliance). They point to their non-reliance on public funds as a sign of independence.
55. The reference parameters are turnover (not more than £5.6m), total balance sheet (not more than £2.8m) and employees (not more than 50).
56. HM Treasury-FSA-Bank of England, 'Banking reform – Protecting Depositors: a Discussion Paper', October 2007.
57. Level of thresholds (in billion pounds, approximate):

– deposit taking	1.8
– life and pensions	0.8
– investments	0.4
– general insurance	0.9
– home finance	0.1
– total	4.0

Source: note 58 below.

58. FSA, FSCS *Funding Review*, Policy Statement 07/19, November 2007.
59. The Treasury asked the economist DeAnne Julius to investigate the potential impact of regulation in this field in November 2000 and announced the transfer of regulation to the FSA in December 2001.

60. For small firms there is a similar Business Banking Code.
61. DTI, *Fair, Clear and Competitive. The Consumer Credit Market in the 21st Century*, The Stationery Office, 2003.
62. This assignment of powers is consistent with the Government's broader policy of promoting alternative dispute resolution procedures on the grounds that they are less costly and faster than the courts.

9 The Combined Code of Corporate Governance

1. In particular: the Loreburn Committee (1906), the Wrenbury Committee (1918), the Greene Committee (1926), the Cohen Committee (1945) and the Jenkins Committee (1962). See: S.F. Copp, 'The Institutional Architecture of the UK Corporate Governance Reform: An evaluation', *Journal of Banking Regulation*, vol. 7, nos. 1–2, p. 41, 2006. See also: K. Alexander, 'Corporate Governance and Banking Regulation', Working Paper no. 17, CERF Research Programme in International Financial Regulation, June 2004.
2. For an overview, see: A. Cadbury, *Corporate Governance and Chairmanship: A Personal View*, Oxford University Press, 2002.
3. D. Higgs, *Review of The role and Effectiveness of Non-executive Directors*, January 2003.
4. R. Smith, *Audit Committees Combined Code Guidance*, January 2003.
5. See: Financial Reporting Council, *Guidance on Audit Committees (The Smith Guidance)*, October, 2005.
6. R. Smith, *Audit Committee*, paragraph 2.3, p. 48.
7. The Enron scandal, which began to break in the USA in December 2000, provided justification for some changes of the Code (as we will see thereafter) and other limited initiatives, such as the Coordinating Group on Audit and Accounting Issues (CGAA), created in 2002 and finalized in 2003.
8. R. Smith, *Audit Committee*, paragraph 2.2, p. 47.
9. In 2000 the role of the entity authorized to supervise the accounting sector, the Consultative Committee of Accountancy Bodies (CCAB), was redefined. Said role includes the verification of members' behavior, even through investigative and disciplinary procedures, as well as the through the definition of technical standards and ethics criteria. These powers were transferred to a different entity, the Accountancy Foundation (then absorbed into the FRC), which operates through four boards: the Review Board (which monitors the functioning of the regulation system, in the public interest); the Audit Practices Board (which establishes accounting standards); the Ethic Standard Board (which guarantees ethical standards of accountants) and the Investigation and Discipline Board (which handles disciplinary cases in the public interest).

10 The Competition Act (1998) and Related Regulatory Framework

1. R. Whish, *Competition Law*, Buttersworth, 1993, p. 20.
2. Ibid., p. 23.

3. 'Section 10(6) of the 1973 Act provides an inexhaustive list of alternative criteria which may be used [to calculate the percentage market share which a firm enjoys] and on some occasions the MMC uses more than one method of measurement where it is not obvious which is correct'. See T. Frazer, *Monopoly, Competition and the Law: the Regulation of Business Activity in Britain, Europe and America*, Harvester Wheatsheaf, 1988, p. 24.
4. R. Whish, *Competition Law*, pp. 82–5.
5. T. Frazer, *Monopoly*, p. 28.
6. Ibid., ch. 3.
7. M. Wise, 'Review of Competitive Law and Policy in the United Kingdom', *OECD Journal of Competitive Law and Policy*, vol. 5, no. 3.
8. M. Wise, Ibid., p. 63.
9. M. Wise, Ibid., p. 90.
10. Competition Commission, General Advice and Information Guidance, consultation document, 2002.
11. M. Wise, 'Review', pp. 70–88.
12. Or the appropriate body in the other parts of the UK.
13. The Defence and Information sectors are exceptions in this respect, with the Secretary of State still deciding.
14. Competition Commission, Merger References: Competition Commission Guidelines, June 2003.
15. At present the Defence sector.
16. P. Freeman, *Regulation and Competition – Chalk and Cheese?: The Role of the Competition Commission*, University of Bath, 7 September 2006; P. Geroski, *Market Inquiries and Market Studies: the View from the Clapham Omnibus*, Chatham House, 1st July 2005.
17. P. Freeman, 'UK Competition Law after Modernisation', Lord Fletcher Lecture, 15 March 2005.
18. See: Competition Commission, Mergers References: Competition Commission Guidelines, June 2003.
19. Competitiveness is defined by the CC as the process of rivalry between firms (or other economic entities) vying for long-term clients. Market power is defined as the ability to 'reduce competitiveness substantially'. Generally this means the ability to increase prices above competitive levels, for an extended time period and in a profitable manner.

References

Abrams, R. and Taylor, M., 'Issues in the Unification of Financial Sector Supervision', in C. Enoch, D. Marston and M. Taylor (eds), *Building Strong Banks Through Surveillance and Resolution*, IMF, 2002.

Alcock, A., *The Financial Services and Markets Act 2000: A Guide to the New Law*, Jordan, 2000.

Alexander, K., *Corporate Governance and Banking Regulation*, Working Paper no. 17, CERF Research Programme in International Financial Regulation, June 2004.

Alfon, I. and Andrews, P., *Cost–Benefit Analysis in Financial Regulation*, FSA, Occasional Paper Series 3, 1999.

APACS, *The Plastic Card Review*, 2001.

Artis, M.S. and Lewis, M.K., *Monetary Control in the United Kingdom*, Philip Allan, 1981.

Avesani, R., 'FIRST: A Market-Based Approach to Evaluate Financial Risk and Stability', Working Paper, International Monetary Fund, December 2005.

Baird, R., *Report to the FSA on the Review of the Regulation of the Equitable Life Assurance Society from 1 January 1999 to 8 December 2000*, The Stationery Office, 2001.

Bank for International Settlements, *A Glossary of Terms Used in Payment and Settlement Systems*, Committee on Payment and Settlement Systems, Basel, March 2003.

——, 'BIS Quarterly Review. International banking and financial market developments', various issues.

——, *Credit Risk Transfer*, Report submitted by a Working Group established by the Committee on the Global Financial System, January 2003.

——, *Credit Risk Transfer*, The Joint Forum, Basel Committee on Banking Supervision, October 2004.

——, *Credit Risk Transfer: Developments from 2005 to 2007*, The Joint Forum, Basel Committee on Banking Supervision, April 2008.

——, *New developments in Clearing Settlement Arrangements for OTC derivatives*, Committee on Payment and Settlement System, March 2007.

——, *OTC Derivatives: Settlements Procedures and Counterparty Risk Management*, Report by the Committee on the Payment and Settlement Systems and the Euro-Currency, Standing Committee of the Central Banks of the Group of Ten Countries, Basel, September 1998.

——, *Payment System in the United Kingdom*, Committee on Payment and Settlement Systems "Red Book", Basel, 2003.

——, *The Role of Ratings in Structured Finance: Issues and Implications*, Report submitted by the Working Group established by the Committee on the Global Financial System, January 2005.

——, 'Triennial Central Bank Survey: Foreign Exchange and Derivatives Market Activity', Basel, various years.

Bank of England, *Banking Act Report for 1994–95*.

——, 'Competition and Credit Control', in Bank of England, *Quarterly Bulletin*, Vol. 11, no. 2, 1971.

——, *Financial Stability Report*, various issues.
——, *Financial Stability Review*, various issues.
——, *Inflation Report*, February 2001.
——, *Measuring the Contribution of Financial Services to the Economy: a Report on a Meeting of the Financial Statistics Users' Group*, in Bank of England, 'Monetary and Financial Statistics', May 2001.
——, *Monetary & Financial Statistics*, October 2001.
——, *Payment System Oversight Report 2004*, January 2005.
——, *Quarterly Bulletin*, various years.
——, *Report and Accounts*, various years.
——, *Report of the Board of Banking Supervision Inquiry into the Circumstances of the Collapse of Barings*, HMSO, 1995.
——, *Statistical Abstract*, various years.
——, *The Bank of England's Operations in the Sterling Money Markets*, May 2002.
——, *The UK Foreign Exchange Market and Over-the-Counter Derivatives Markets, 2001*. September 2004.
Bank of England, H.M. Treasury, Financial Services Authority, *Financial Stability and Deposit Protection: Strengthening the Framework*, H.M. Treasury, January, 2008.
Banker (the), various issues.
Banks, J. and Smith S., *Households Portfolio*, the Institute for Fiscal Studies, W.P. 00/14, 2000.
Barth, J.R., Caprio, G. and Levine, R., *Rethinking Bank Regulation*, Cambridge University Press, 2006.
Baumol, W., 'Contestable Markets: An Uprising in the Theory of Industry Structure', *American Economic Review*, no. 72, 1982.
Becht, M. and Mayer, C., Introduction, in F. Barca e M. Becht (eds), *The Control of Corporate Europe*, Oxford University Press, 2001.
Blair, M. (ed), *Blackstone's Guide to the Financial Services and Markets Act 2000*, Blackstone's Press, 2001.
Bowen, A., Hoggart, G. and Pain, D., *The Recent Evolution of the UK Banking Industry and Some Implications for Financial Stability*, Bank for International Settlements, 1999.
Briault C., *Revisiting the Rationale for a Single National Financial Services Regulator*, FSA, Occasional Paper Series, 16, 2002.
British Bankers' Association, *Banking Business: The Annual Abstract of Banking Statistics*, various years.
——, *Credit Derivatives Report*, various years.
Bruyère, R., Cont, R., Copinot, R., Fery, L., Jaeck, C. and Spitz, T., *Credit derivatives and structured credit. A guide for investors*. John Wiley & Sons, Chichester, 2006.
Bunn, P., 'Stress testing as a tool for assessing systemic risks', *Financial Stability Review*, Bank of England, June 2005.
Bunn, P. and Young, G., 'Corporate capital structure in the United Kingdom: determinants and adjustment', Working Paper, no. 226, Bank of England, 2004.
Bunn, P., Cunningham, A. and Drehmann, M., 'Stress Testing as a Tool for Assessing Risks', *Financial Stability Review*, Bank of England, June 2005.
Burnett, M., 'Financial Stability and the United Kingdom's External Balance Sheet', *Quarterly Bulletin*, Bank of England, Winter 2003.

Cadbury, A., *Corporate Governance and Chairmanship: A Personal View*, Oxford University Press, 2002.
Capie, F. and Collins, M., *Have the Banks Failed the British Industry?*, The Institute of Economic Affairs, 1992.
Central Statistical Office, *Share Ownership: A Report on Ownership of Shares as at 31 December 1992*, 1993.
Chan-Lau, J.A. and Ong, L.L., 'The Credit Risk Transfer Market and Stability Implications for U.K. Financial Institutions', Working Paper, IMF, June 2007.
Chaplin, G., Emblow, A. and Michael I., 'Banking System Liquidity: Developments and Issues', *Financial Stability Review*, Bank of England, December 2000.
Čihák, M., 'Introduction to Applied Stress Testing', Working Paper, IMF, March, 2007.
Ciocca, P., The Italian Financial System Remodelled, Palgrave Macmillan, 2005.
——, 'Vigilanza: una o più istituzioni', mimeo, Banca d'Italia, 2001.
Clark, G.L., *Pension Fund Capitalism*, Oxford University Press, 2000.
Clarke, M., *Regulating the City. Competition, Scandal and Reform*, Open University Press, 1986.
Clifford Chance, 'Principle-Based Regulation – Problems of Uncertainty', mimeo, 2007.
Collins, M., *Banks and Industrial Finance in Britain, 1800–1939*, Cambridge University Press, 1991, p. 86.
——, *Money and Banking in the UK: A History*, Croom Helm, 1988.
Committee on the Working of the Monetary System, *Radcliffe Report*, H.M. Stationery Office, 1959.
Competition Commission, *General Advice and Information Guidance*, Consultation Document, September 2002.
—— *Mergers References: Competition Commission Guidelines*, June 2003.
—— *The Supply of Banking Services by Clearing Banks to Small and Medium-sized Enterprises. A Report to the Chancellor of the Exchequer*, The Stationery Office, London, 2002.
Cooper, J., *The Management and Regulation of Banks*, Macmillan, 1984.
Copp, S.F., 'The Institutional Architecture of the UK Corporate Governance Reform: An Evaluation', *Journal of Banking Regulation*, Vol. 7, nos 1–2, 2006.
Cottrell, P., 'The Financial System of the United Kingdom in the Twentieth Century', in L. De Rosa (ed), *International Banking and Financial Systems*, Ashgate, 2003.
Counterparty Risk Management Policy Group II, *Toward Greater Financial Stability: A Private Sector Perspective*, New York, 2005.
Cruickshank, D., *Competition in UK Banking: A Report to the Chancellor of the Exchequer ('Cruickshank Report')*, The Stationery Office, London, 2000.
——, 'How bank reform was sabotaged', *The Financial Times*, 22 February 2005.
Davey, M., 'Mortgage Equity Withdrawal and Consumption', in Bank of England, *Quarterly Bulletin*, Vol. 41, no. 1, 2001.
David, B. and Simon, S. 'Accounting Treatment: Where Are We?', *International Financial Law Review*, vol. 25, Supplement, July 2006.
Davis, E.P., *An Industrial Approach to Financial Instability*, in Bank of England, Discussion Paper, no. 50, 1990.
——, and Steil B., *Institutional Investors*, The MIT Press, 2001.

——, *The Regulation of Funded Pensions*, FSA, Occasional Paper Series 15, 2001.

Davies, H., 'Rational Expectations – What Should the Market, and Policyholders, Expect from Insurance Regulation?', AIRMIC Annual Lecture, 29 January 2002.

——, 'Reforming Financial Regulation: Progress and Priorities', in E. Ferran and C.A. Goodhart (eds), *Regulating Financial Services and Markets in the Twenty First Century*, Hart Publishing.

Deaton, A., *Understanding Consumption*, Oxford University Press, 1992.

De Nicolò, G., Corner, R. and Tieman, A., 'European Financial Integration, Stability and Supervision', in IMF, *Euro Area Policies: Selected Issues*, IMF, August, 2005.

Department for Works and Pensions, *Security in Retirement: Towards a New Pensions System*, TSO, 2006.

——, *Personal Accounts: A New Way To Save*, TSO, 2006.

Department of Trade and Industry, *Small and Medium-sized Enterprise Statistics for the UK*, 2000.

—— *Statistical Press Release*, various years.

—— *Fair, Clear and Competitive. The Consumer Credit Market in the 21st Century*, HMSO, 2003.

Di Cesare, A., 'Do Market-Based Indicators Anticipate Rating Agencies?: Evidence for International Banks', *Temi di Discussione del Servizio Studi*, no. 593, Banca d'Italia, May, 2006.

Disney, R., Emmerson, C. and Smith, S., *Pension Reform and Economic Performance in Britain in the 1980s and 1990s*, Institute for Fiscal Studies, London, mimeo, 2001.

Dodd, R., 'The Structure of OTC Derivatives Markets', *The Financier*, Vol. 9, nos 1–4, 2003.

Draghi, M., 'Hedge Funds and Financial Stability', *Financial Stability Review*, Special Issue on Hedge Funds, Banque de France, April 2007.

——, *Statement by Mario Draghi, Chairman of the Financial Stability Forum*, International Monetary and Financial Committee Meeting, 14 April 2007, Washington, DC.

European Central Bank, 'Developments in the EU Framework for Financial Regulation, Supervision and Stability', *Monthly Bulletin*, November 2004.

——, *EU Banking Sector Stability*, various issues.

——, *EU Banking Structures*, various issues.

European Commission, 'Green Paper on Financial Services Policy (2005–2010)', *COM*, 2005, no. 177.

Ferguson, R. and Laster, D., 'Hedge Funds and Systemic Risk', *Financial Stability Review, Special Issue on Hedge Funds*, Banque de France, April 2007.

Ferran, E. and Goodhart, C.A., 'Regulating Financial Services and Markets in the Twenty First Century: an Overview', in E. Ferran, C.A. Goodhart (eds), *Regulating Financial Services*.

Financial Reporting Council, *Good Practice Suggestions from the Higgs Report*, June 2006.

——, *Guidance on Audit Committees (The Smith Guidance)*, October 2005.

Financial Services Authority, *A New Regulator for the New Millennium*, 2000.

—— *Building the New Regulator*, Progress Report 1, 2000.

—— *Business Plan 2007–08*, 2007.

—— 'Cross-sector Risk Transfers', Discussion Paper, May 2002.
—— *Fairness of Terms in Consumer Contracts. Statement of Good Practice on Mortgage Exit Administration Fees*, January 2007.
—— 'Financial Risk Outlook', various issues.
—— *Funds of Alternative Investments Funds*, Consultation Paper 07/6, March 2007.
—— 'Recent Turbulence in Global Financial Markets and Northern Rock's Liquidity Crisis', *Memorandum from the FSA to the Treasury Committee*, 9 October 2007.
—— 'Hedge Funds: A Discussion of Risk and Regulatory Engagement', Discussion Paper, 05/4, June 2005.
—— 'Hedge Funds and the FSA', *Discussion Paper*, no. 16, August 2002.
—— 'Interim Prudential Sourcebook: Banks', *FSA Handbook*.
—— *Principles for Businesses* (PRIN 1.1.2).
—— 'Private Equity: A discussion of Risk and Regulatory Engagements', Discussion Paper, November 2006.
—— 'Review of the Liquidity Requirements for Banks and Building Societies', Discussion Paper, 07/7, December 2007.
—— 'Senior Management Arrangements, Systems and Controls', *FSA Handbook*, Chapter 11, July 2007.
—— 'Stress Testing', Discussion Paper, 05/2, May 2005.
—— 'Stress Testing Thematic Review', October, 2006.
—— *The FSA's Risk Assessment Framework*, 2006.
—— web site: International & EU, Capital Requirement Directives/Basel2/Statistical Data.
Financial Stability Forum, 'Report of the Financial Stability Forum on Enhancing Market and Institutional Resilience', April 2008.
Fitch Ratings, *Master of House – A Review of UK RMBS Master Trust*, Structured Finance, RMBS – UK Special Report, 8 June 2005.
FSMA 2000 (Regulated Activities) Order 2001 and its amendments.
Frazer, T., Monopoly, Competition and the Law: The Regulation of Business Activity in Britain, Europe and America, Harvester Wheatsheaf, 1988.
Freeman, P., UK Competition Law After Modernisation, Lord Fletcher Lecture, 15 March 2005.
Freeman, P., Regulation and Competition – Chalk or Cheese?: The Role of the Competition Commission, University of Bath, 7 September 2006.
Garofalo, P., Roselli, A., Ownership Structure and Firm Performance in Italy, London School of Economics – FMG Working Paper, forthcoming.
George, E., 'Are Banks Still Special?', Bank of England, Quarterly Bulletin, February 1997.
Geroski P., Market Inquiries and Market Studies: The View from the Clapham Omnibus, Chatham House, 1 July 2005.
Gibbard, P. and Stevens, I., 'Corporate Debt and Financial Balance Sheet Adjustment: A Comparison of the United States, the United Kingdom, France and Germany', Working Paper, no. 317, Bank of England, 2006.
Gieve, J., 'The City's Growth: The Crest of the Wave or Swimming with the Stream', Speech at the Bank of England to the London Society of Chartered Accountants, March 2007.
Goodhart, C.A.E. and Segoviano Basurto, M.A., 'Banking Stability Index', Working paper, International Monetary Fund, mimeo, 2007.

Goodhart, C.A.E. and Ferran E. (eds), Regulating Financial Services and Markets in the Twenty First Century, Hart Publishing, 2001.
Gower, L.C.B., Review of Investor Protection: Report, part 2, 1985.
Guidelines for Disclosure and Transparency in Private Equity. Final Report of the Working Group chaired by David Walker, November 2007.
Grady, J. and Weale, M., British Banking, 1960–85, Macmillan, 1986.
Gray, D., Merton, R. and Bodie, A. A New Framework for Analyzing and Managing Macrofinancial Risk of an Economy, NBER, Working Paper, no. 12637, October 2006.
Haldane, A., Hall, S. and Pezzini, S., 'A New Approach To Assessing Risks to Financial Stability', Financial Stability Paper, Bank of England, no. 2, April 2007.
Hall, M., 'Secondary Banking Crisis', in Newman, P., Milgate, M. and Eatwell, J. (eds), The New Palgrave Dictionary of Money and Finance, Macmillan Press, 1992.
Hedge Fund Standards, Consultation Paper of the Hedge Fund Working Group chaired by Andrew Large, October 2007.
Higgs, D., Review of the Role and Effectiveness of Non-executive Directors, January 2003.
Hill, I., 'Ownership of United Kingdom Quoted Companies at the End of 1997', Economic Trends, no. 543, Office of National Statistics, February 1999.
HM Treasury, Medium and Long-Term Retail Savings in the UK. A Review ('Sandler Report'), The Stationery Office, 2002.
—— Report to the Committee Set Up to Consider the System of Banking Supervision, HMSO, 1985.
HM Treasury – FSA – Bank of England, 'A framework for Guarantee Schemes in the EU', A Discussion Paper, October 2005.
—— 'Banking Reform – Protecting Depositors: a Discussion Report', October, 2007.
Hoggart, G. and Saporta, V., 'Cost of Banking System Instability', *Financial Stability Review*, Bank of England, 10, 2001.
Hoggarth, G. and Whitley, J., 'Assessing the Strength of UK Banks Through Macroeconomic Stress Tests', *Financial Stability Review*, Bank of England, June 2003.
House of Commons Treasury Committee, The Run on the Rock. Fifth Report of Session 2007–2008, Volume I, January 2008.
House of Lords, 'Delegated Powers and Deregulation Committee – Joint Committee on Financial Services and Markets', First Report, 1999.
Institute of International Finance, Principles of Liquidity Risk Management, March 2007.
International Financial Services London, 'Banking', City Business Series, various issues.
—— 'Derivatives', City Business Series, various issues.
—— 'Fund Management', City Business Series, August 2006.
—— 'Fund Management Brief', September 2001.
—— 'Hedge Funds', City Business Series, April 2007.
—— 'International Financial Markets in the UK', City Business Series, various issues
—— 'Securitisation', City Business Series, March 2007.
—— The City Table, various issues.

International Monetary Fund, 'Euro Area Policies: Selected Issues', Country Report, no. 05/266, August 2005.

—— Financial Soundness Indicators: Compilation Guide, 2006.

—— Financial System Stability Assessment – United Kingdom, February 2003.

—— Global Financial Stability Report, various issues.

—— United Kingdom – Staff Report for the 2006 Article IV Consultation, February 2007.

—— World Economic Outlook, Chapter IV, April 2006.

Jackson, P., 'Deposit Protection and Bank Failures in the United Kingdom', *Financial Stability Review*, Bank of England, Autumn, 1996.

Jenkinson, N., New markets and new demands: challenges for central banks in the wholesale market infrastructure, Bank of England, Central Bank Conference on Payment System and Monetary and Financial Stability, November, 2007.

Khandani, A.E. and Lo, A.W., 'What Happened to the Quants in August 2007?' 'Evidence from Factors and Transactions Data', NBER, Working Paper, forthcoming.

Kiff, J. and Mills, P., 'Money for Nothing and Checks for Free: Recent Developments in U.S. Sub-Prime Mortgage Markets', Working Paper, IMF, July 2007.

King, M., 'Turmoil in Financial Markets: What Can Central Banks Do?', Paper submitted to the Treasury Committee, 12 September 2007.

——, Public Policy and the Corporation, Cambridge University Press, 1977.

——, The Governor's Speech at the Northern Ireland Chamber of Commerce and Industry, Belfast, 9 October 2007, p. 5.

Kroszner, R.S., 'Central Counterparty Clearing: History, Innovation, and Regulation', Speech at the Conference on Issues Related to Central Counterparty Clearing, European Central Bank, Frankfurt, April 2006.

Krugman, P., Geography and Trade, The Massachusetts Institute of Technology Press, 1991.

Lane, P.R., and Milesi-Ferretti, G.M., 'A Global Perspective on External Positions', Working Paper, IMF, 2005.

Lascelles, D., Waking Up to the FSA. How the City Views Its New Regulator, Centre for the Study of Financial Innovation, 2001.

——, A Survey of the Risks Facing Banks, Centre for the Study of Financial Innovation, 2002.

Latter, T., 'Causes and Management of Banking Crises', in Bank of England, Handbook in Central Banking, no. 12, 1997.

Laurin, A. and Majnoni, G., 'Bank Loan Classification and Provisioning Practices in Selected Developed and Emerging Countries', Working Paper, no. 1, The World Bank, 2003.

Lavington, F., The English Capital Market, Augustus M. Kelley Publishers, New York, 1968, Reprint of Economic Classics, 1st edn, 1921.

Llewellyn, D.T., *The Evolution of the British Financial System*, The Institute of Bankers, 1985.

——, 'Competition and Structural Change in the British Financial System', in E. P. M. Gardener (ed), *The Future of Financial Systems and Services*, Macmillan, 1990.

——, 'Financial Regulation: a Perspective from the UK', *Journal of Financial Services Research*, 17, 1, 2000.

Löffler, G. and Posch, P.N., *Credit Risk Modeling Using Excel and VBA*, John Wiley, 2007.

Lombard Street Associates, 'The importance to the UK Economy of a Successful Financial Sector', *A report prepared for the British Bankers' Association*, 2006.
London Stock Exchange, The Stock Exchange Survey of Share Ownership, 1992.
London Stock Exchange and Oxea, *The Cost of Capital: an International Comparison*, City of London, 2006.
Mahajan, S., 'Concentration ratios for business by industry in 2004', *Economic Trends*, no. 634, Office for National Statistics, October 2006.
Marston D., Moore, M., Novoa, A., Tower, I. and Zanforlin, A., *The Conduit Phenomenon: Do Banks Achieve Lasting Risk Transfer?*, mimeo, IMF, September 2007.
Maw, N.G., Lord Lane of Horsell and Graig-Cooper, M., *Maw on Corporate Governance*, Dartmouth, 1994.
McCarthy, C., 'Transparency requirements and hedge funds', *Financial Stability Review*, Special Issue on Hedge Funds, Banque de France, April 2007.
——, 'Financial Stability Analysis in the UK', Macroprudential Supervision Conference, 8 November 2006.
——, 'Principles-based Regulation: What Does It Mean for the Industry?', Financial Services Skills Council Conference, 2006.
McGuire, P. and Tarashev, N., 'Tracking International Bank Flows', *Bank for International Settlements Quarterly Review*, December 2006.
Merton, R.C., 'On the Pricing of Corporate Debt: The Risk Structure of Interest Rates', *Journal of Finance*, no. 29, 1974.
Minghella, L., 'Insolvency', in Blair, M. (ed), *Blackstone's Guide to the Financial Services and Markets Act 2000*, Blackstone's Press, 2001.
Monks, A. and Stringa, M., 'Inter-industry Linkages Between UK Life Insurers and UK Banks: An Event Study', *Financial Stability Review*, Bank of England, 2005.
Morison, I., Tillett, P. and Welch, J., *Banking Act 1979*, Butterworth, 1979.
Muellbauer, J. and Murphy, A., 'Is the UK Balance of Payment Sustainable?', *Economic Policy*, October 1990.
Muellbauer, J., 'The Assessment: Consumption', *Oxford Review of Economic Policy*, vol. 10, no. 2, 1994.
Murfin, A., *Regulating the OTC Market in London*, The LBMA Indian Bullion Market Forum, New Delhi, January 2003.
National Audit Office, *Financial Services Authority: A Review Under Section 12 of the FSMA 2000*, HMSO, 2007.
National Statistics, 'Economic Trends', various issues.
——, 'Financial Statistics', various issues.
——, *Share Ownership: A Report on Ownership of Shares as at 31st December* 2004.
——, 'United Kingdom Balance of Payments (Pink Book), various years.
——, 'United Kingdom Economic Accounts', various issues.
——, 'United Kingdom National Accounts' (Blue Book), various years.
Nevin, E. and Davis, E.W., *The London Clearing Banks*, Elek Books, 1970.
Nickell, S., 'The UK Current Account Deficit and All That', Bank of England, 25 April 2006.
——, 'Two Current Monetary Policy Issues', Speech at a Market News International Seminar, Bank of England, September 2003.
Obstfeld, M., 'External Adjustment', *Review of World Economics*, Vol. 140 (4), 2004.

Office of Fair Trading, *Acquisitions and Mergers Involving UK Companies*, November 2001.
——, *Calculating Fair Default Charges in Credit Card Contracts: A Statement of the Office of Fair Trading position*, April 2006.
——, *Overview of the Enterprise Act*, 2002.
——, Press Release 130/06.
——, *The Banking Services to Small and Medium Enterprises*, London, 2002.
——, *The Major Provisions, New Guidelines*, OFT, no. 400, March 1999.
Organisation for Economic Co-Operation and Development, *Economic Outlook*, 2006.
——, *Bank Profitability: Financial Statements of Banks*, Paris, various issues.
Pagano, M., Panetta, F. and Zingales, L., 'Why Do Companies Go Public?: An Empirical Analysis', *Journal of Finance*, Vol. LIII, no. 1. February 1998.
Pemberton, H., 'Politics and Pensions in post-war Britain', in H. Pemberton, P. Thane and N. Whiteside (eds), *Britain's Pensions Crisis: History and Policy*, The British Academy – Oxford University Press, 2006.
Pensions Commission (The), *A New Pension Settlement for the Twenty-First Century*, HMSO, 2005.
——, *Implementing an Integrated Package of Pension Reforms: Final Report*, HMSO, 2006.
——, *Pensions: Challenges and Choices. The First Report*, HMSO, 2004.
Pyke, F., Becattini, G. and Sengenberger, W., *Industrial Districts and Inter-firm Co-operation in Italy*, International Institute for Labour Studies, Geneva, 1990.
Reid, J., *The Role of the Merchant Banks Today*, The Institute of Bankers, 1963.
Reid, M., *The Secondary Banking Crisis, 1973–75: Its Causes and Course*, Macmillan, 1982.
Revell, J., *The British Financial System*, Macmillan, 1973.
Roberts, R. and Kynaston, D., *City State*, Profile Books, 2002.
Rogers, D., *The Big Four British Banks: Organisation, Strategy and The Future*, Macmillan Business, 1999.
Ross, D., 'Bank advances and Industrial Production in the UK During the Inter-war Years: A Red Herring?', in Cottrell, P., Lindgren, H. and Teichova, A. (eds), *European Industry and Banking Between the Wars*, Leicester University Press, 1992.
Rule, D., 'Risk Transfer Between Banks, Insurance Companies and Capital Markets: An Overview', *Financial Stability Review*, Bank of England, December 2001.
Ryan, K., 'Building society conversions', *Financial Stability Review*, Bank of England, Autumn, 1996.
Sass, S., 'Anglo-Saxon Occupational Pensions in International Perspective', in H. Pemberton, P. Thane, and N. Whiteside (eds), *Britain's Pension Crisis*.
Sayers, R., *The Bank of England 1891–1944*, Cambridge University Press, Vol. 1, 1976.
——, *Modern Banking*, Oxford University Press, 1967.
Schinasi, G.J., *Safeguarding Financial Stability: Theory and Practice*, International Monetary Fund, 2006.
Schinasi, G.J., Craig, R.S., Drees, B. and Kramer, C., 'Modern Banking and OTC Derivatives Markets. The Transformation of Global Finance and Its Implications for Systemic Risk', IMF, Occasional Paper, no. 203, 2000.
Scholtes, S., 'Hedge Funds Hit at Sub-prime Aid for Homeowners', *Financial Times*, 1 June 2007.

Smith, R., *Audit Committees Combined Code Guidance*, January 2003.
Speight, G. and Parkinson, S., 'Large UK-Owned Banks' Funding Patterns: Recent Changes and Implications', *Financial Stability Review*, Bank of England, December, 2003.
Taylor, M., 'The Policy Background', in Blair, M. (ed), *Blackstone's Guide to the Financial Services and Markets Act 2001*, Blackstone's Press.
——, *Twin Peaks: A Regulatory Structure for the New Century*, Centre for the Study of Financial Innovation, 1995.
——, 'Accountability and Objectives of the FSA, 2001', in Blair, M. (ed), *Blackstone's Guide to the Financial Services and Markets Act 2000*, Blackstone's Press.
Threipland, M., 'Rules and Guidance, 2001', in Blair, M. (ed), *Blackstone's Guide to the Financial Services and Markets Act 2000*, Blackstone's Press.
Townend, J., *The Euro, the UK and the City of London*, Bank Negara Malaysia, Kuala Lumpur, 22 January 2002, mimeo.
Tucker, P.M.W., 'Managing the Central Bank's Balance Sheet: Where Monetary Policy Meets Financial Stability', Lecture to mark the fifteenth anniversary of Lombard Street Research, Bank of England, July, 2004.
Tudela, M. and Young, G., 'Predicting Default Among UK Companies: a Merton Approach', *Financial Stability Review*, Bank of England, June 2003.
UBS, 'Unwind of the BSAM Funds Cause a Flight to Quality – and Opportunities', *Mortgage Strategist*, 26 June 2007.
Vassalou, M. and Xing, Y., 'Default Risk in Equity Returns', *The Journal of Finance*, vol. LIX, no. 2, April 2004.
Waters, D., *NEWCOB and Principles-based Regulation*, keynote speech at NEWCOB briefings, January 2007.
Whish, R., *Competition Law*, Butterworths, 1993.
Wise, M., 'Review of Competition Law and Policy in the United Kingdom', *OECD Journal of Competitive Law and Policy*, Vol 5, no. 3, 2004.
Yarrow, A., 'The Challenges Facing Investment Banking in the UK', in *Big Bang 20 years on*, City of London, 2006.

Index